Palgrave Studies in Governance, Leadership and Responsibility

The fall-out from many high profile crises in governance and leadership in recent decades, from banking to healthcare, continues to be felt around the world. Major reports have questioned the values and behaviour, not just of individual organizations but of professionals, industries and political leadership. These reports raise questions about business corporations and also public service institutions. In response this new series aims to explore the broad principles of governance and leadership and how these are embodied in different contexts, opening up the possibility of developing new theories and approaches that are fuelled by interdisciplinary approaches. The purpose of the series is to highlight critical reflection and empirical research which can enable dialogue across sectors, focusing on theory, value and the practice of governance, leadership and responsibility.

Written from a global context, the series is unique in bringing leadership and governance together. The King III report connects these two fields by identifying leadership as one of the three principles of effective governance however most courses in business schools have traditionally treated these as separate subjects. Increasingly, and in particular with the case of executive education, business schools are recognizing the need to develop and produce responsible leaders. The series will therefore encourage critical exploration between these two areas and as such explore sociological and philosophical perspectives.

More information about this series at
http://www.palgrave.com/gp/series/15192

Francisca Farache
Georgiana Grigore • Alin Stancu
David McQueen
Editors

Values and Corporate Responsibility

CSR and Sustainable Development

palgrave
macmillan

Editors
Francisca Farache
Brighton Business School
University of Brighton
Brighton, UK

Georgiana Grigore
School of Business
University of Leicester
Leicester, UK

Alin Stancu
Bucharest University of Economic Studies
Bucharest, Romania

David McQueen
Bournemouth University
Bournemouth, UK

ISSN 2662-1304 ISSN 2662-1312 (electronic)
Palgrave Studies in Governance, Leadership and Responsibility
ISBN 978-3-030-52465-4 ISBN 978-3-030-52466-1 (eBook)
https://doi.org/10.1007/978-3-030-52466-1

This Palgrave Macmillan imprint is published by the registered company Springer Nature Switzerland AG.
The registered company address is: Gewerbestrasse 11, 6330 Cham, Switzerland

Contents

Notes on Contributors

Adrian A. Baumgartner is the Chief Operating Officer (COO) of LGT Bank, Hong Kong, and he is responsible for the whole operational infrastructure of the entity. In addition, he serves as Deputy Regional COO Asia and is part of various local management committees in Asia.
Prior to this, he was heading the Management Office of LGT in Asia where he was responsible for developing businesses and driving strategic initiatives in the region. Some of the key initiatives were co-leading one of the largest private banking acquisitions in Asia and establishing a new banking operation in Thailand. Based on his personal interests, Baumgartner is also in charge of the corporate social responsibility (CSR) strategy and its related activities of LGT in Asia. He is further deepening his knowledge in this area by pursuing a Doctorate in Business Administration with a focus on CSR topics. He holds a Master's degree in International Business from Grenoble École de Management, France, and a Bachelor's degree in Banking and Finance from the University of Zurich, Switzerland.

Candice C. Chow is Assistant Professor of Strategic Management at McMaster University, Canada, and is the Co-founder and Principal of Elevae—a values-based strategy advisory firm in Toronto, Canada. Chow possesses over 25 years of senior strategic management experience with multinational organisations, serves as a member of the board of directors for a technology start-up, and provides board-level advisory to both private and non-profit organisations. Chow received a Doctorate in Business Administration (DBA) from Henley Business School, UK; an MBA from the Ivey Business School, Canada; and a Bachelor's degree in Mechanical Engineering from Imperial College, London, and holds a Chartered Financial Analyst (CFA) designation. Her research interests include values, strategic leadership, CSR, sustainable futures, and corporate governance.

Francisca Farache is Principal Lecturer in Marketing and Subject Group Leader for Marketing, Events, and Tourism at Brighton Business School, UK. She holds an MA in Marketing and a PhD in Business, both of which are from the University of Brighton. She is involved in several research projects, mostly related to social responsibility. Her research interests include corporate social responsibility, CSR communication, and business ethics. Her work has been published in the following journals: *Journal of Business Ethics*, *Journal of Business Research*, *Corporate Communication: An International Journal*, *Journal of Consumer Marketing*, and *Latin American Business Review*.

Kerstin Fehre is Professor of Strategy at Vlerick Business School, Belgium. Her research focuses on the causes and consequences of strategic decisions with a special interest in sustainability. Previously, she was an assistant professor at the Strategic Management Institute of the Karlsruhe Institute of Management. Fehre holds a PhD in Economics from the RWTH (Rheinisch-Westfälische Technische Hochschule) Aachen University. She studied strategic management at Leipzig Graduate School of Management where she graduated as Diplom-Kauffrau and ESCP-EAP (European School of Management), Paris. Fehre was working for several years in corporate finance at Bankhaus Metzler, Goldman Sachs, Deutsche Bank, and Edmond de Rothschild.

Georgiana Grigore is Associate Professor of Marketing at the University of Leicester, School of Business, UK. She is also chair of an annual international conference in 'Social Responsibility, Ethics and Sustainable

Business', which she co-founded in 2012. Her major area of research is in marketing and corporate responsibility concepts and practices, including changes that result from digital media. In the last years, she has written several books, including *Corporate Responsibility and Digital Communities* and *Corporate Social Responsibility in the Digital Age* that explore a contemporary intersection of two fields: corporate responsibility and digital technology. Her publications also include applications of post-psychoanalytic theories to consumer-brand relationships and shopping in marketing theory. Her research received external funding, including from Arthur W. Page Center (2014/2015 and 2015/2016) and British Academy/Leverhulme (2017/2019). She completed an EU-funded Doctorate in Marketing from the Bucharest University of Economic Studies using relationship-marketing theory to examine the impact of corporate responsibility on stakeholders. Prior to her Doctorate, she received a Master's degree in Strategic Marketing and a Bachelor's degree in Marketing from the same university. Before her PhD, Grigore was a marketing specialist and consultant in the retail industry and a trainer for a series of practitioner workshops and marketing and corporate responsibility courses.

Mohammad Tazul Islam is an associate professor at the Dhaka School of Bank Management, Bangladesh Institute of Bank Management, Bangladesh.

Nada K. Kakabadse is Professor of Policy, Governance, and Ethics at Henley Business School, University of Reading, UK, and a visiting professor at the US, Australian, French, Israeli, Kazakhstani, and Chinese universities. She is an elected, active member of the European Academy of Science and Arts (EASA) and head of its EU Representation Office, Brussels. She has written over 210 scholarly articles, 23 books, and over 100 chapters in international volumes. Her current interests are boardroom effectiveness, governance, leadership, CSR and ethics, diversity, and the policy design of the state. She is also a consultant to major global corporations, third-sector organisations, and governments and sits on international boards.

Katsuhiko Kokubu is a professor at the Graduate School of Business Administration, Kobe University, Japan. He is also the Head of Sustainability Alliance Management, Strategic Entrepreneurship and Sustainability Alliance Management Initiatives (SESAMI) Program, Kobe University, Japan.

Gerhard Kosinowski is a researcher at the Chair of Strategic Management at WHU—Otto Beisheim School of Management, Vallendar, Germany. He also serves as a senior relationship manager for international clients at DZ PRIVATBANK Switzerland AG, a cooperative private bank in Zurich, Switzerland. The unique combination of academic and work experience allows him to conduct practically relevant research in the field of cooperative studies. His main research interest concerns the way cooperative banks create value for their stakeholders. In this context, he holds a Bachelor's and a Master's degree from the University of St. Gallen (HSG) and finalises his PhD at the WHU—Otto Beisheim School of Management.

Dušan Kučera works as Head of the Centre for Business Ethics at the University of Economics, Prague. After a two-year electro-technical practice in heavy industry, he studied Protestant Theology at Charles University in Prague, Germany, and the United States. He worked five years as a pastor, editor, and teacher of Philosophy. He decided to work in the commercial sphere as a coordinator of the foreign language department and HR manager and coordinator of executive education in SKODA AUTO (Volkswagen). In the last ten years his specialisation is in managerial personality issues with an impact on responsible and ethical management behaviour based on the concept of a value system. His challenge is focused on the potentials of spirituality in management and business. His last research is focusing on the ethical challenges of artificial intelligence and autonomous systems. He is Assistant Professor of Business Ethics in the international MBA programme and Master's programmes of the Faculty of Business Economics at the University of Economics and international programme of the Faculty of Finance and Accounting. He is publishing and lecturing in companies and different institutions at home and abroad.

David McQueen is a researcher, author, and lecturer in the Faculty of Media and Communication at Bournemouth University, UK. His research interests include broad questions of media, power, and politics; critical perspectives on PR and the media; lobbying; CSR, energy issues, and 'greenwashing'.

Atle Andreassen Raa is Lecturer in and National Coordinator of the course History of Economic Ideas at the Norwegian Business School, BI, Norway. He holds a PhD in Economics and Management from BI. His research is in the fields of corporate social responsibility and economic theory. He has researched on how public sector in Norway adopted private sector ideas and techniques in the late twentieth century and has written on this in the book *Næringsliv og Historie* (Business and History). His work has also been published in the SAGE *Journal of Management Learning*.

Anca-Teodora Şerban-Oprescu is an associate professor in the Department of Modern Languages and Business Communication, School of International Business and Economics at the Bucharest University of Economic Studies, Romania. She teaches business communication, intercultural communication, and research methodology. With a PhD in Cultural Studies and Postdoctoral Studies in Economics, Şerban-Oprescu is actively looking for ways to integrate social sciences and humanities in original pieces of research.

Alin Stancu is Professor of Corporate Social Responsibility and Public Relations in the Department of Marketing at the Bucharest University of Economic Studies, Romania. His main areas of research include customer care, consumer experience, corporate responsibility, and public relations. He is the co-founder of the International Conference on Social Responsibility, Ethics and Sustainable Business (www.csrconferences.org) and co-editor of the book series 'Palgrave Studies in Governance, Leadership and Responsibility'.

Omary Swallehe has more than 13 years of teaching in higher education in both Africa and Asia. He has taught a number of subjects in the area of marketing and business management. Swallehe started his career as a bank officer at CRDB BANK PLC, where he rose to the rank of In-charge of Marketing and Customer Service. His experience in the industry and academia makes him one of the highly distinguished individuals in the area of marketing. He has conducted a number of studies and attended international conferences and consultancies both within and outside the country. Swallehe is an alumnus of Bangalore University, India; Durham University, Bradford University, and CIM, UK; and Mzumbe University, Tanzania. In a nutshell Swallehe has obtained his higher education in three continents, namely Africa, Asia, and Europe. In terms of membership in professional bodies, Swallehe is a member of the Chartered Institute of Marketing, Tanzania Institute of Bankers, and Patron of Mzumbe University Marketing Association (MUMA).

Amelia Turner recently completed a BA (Hons) in Politics from Bournemouth University, UK, where she was a part-time research assistant for Prof. Darren Lilleker and Dr David McQueen. Her research interests include energy issues, environmental policy, and Green Party policy.

Florian Weber is a research fellow at the Strategic Management Institute of the Karlsruhe Institute of Management, Germany. He holds a PhD in Economics from the Karlsruhe Institute of Management and a Diploma in Business Administration from the University of Mannheim. His research expertise is in the fields of corporate social responsibility (CSR), family businesses, and corporate response to the European migration crisis. Weber has several years of working experience in a multinational family firm and is working as a strategy manager in a German utilities company.

List of Figures

List of Tables

1

Corporate Responsibility and the Value of Value(s)

Georgiana Grigore, Alin Stancu, Francisca Farache, and David McQueen

We live in a world of competing and sometimes, it seems, increasingly antagonistic values. These values are shaped by a bewildering multitude of experiences, as well as diverse political, religious, ethical and cultural assumptions of how to behave, how to treat others and how we understand what is 'right' and 'wrong' at the most fundamental level. So, what

G. Grigore (✉)
School of Business, University of Leicester, Leicester, UK

A. Stancu
Bucharest University of Economic Studies, Bucharest, Romania
e-mail: alin.stancu@mk.ase.ro

F. Farache
Brighton Business School, University of Brighton, Brighton, UK
e-mail: f.farache@brighton.ac.uk

D. McQueen
Bournemouth University, Bournemouth, UK
e-mail: dmcqueen@bournemouth.ac.uk

F. Farache et al. (eds.), *Values and Corporate Responsibility*, Palgrave Studies in Governance, Leadership and Responsibility,
https://doi.org/10.1007/978-3-030-52466-1_1

if anything could we hold on to as common values that might underpin corporate social responsibility (CSR) in an international context? The United Nations (UN) Sustainable Development Goals for 2030 reflect a worldwide common agenda for sustainable development, built around the painstakingly negotiated shared values of the UN Charter and subsequent efforts to build a peaceful world of mutually respectful coexistence and justice. Each of the UN's ambitious 17 Sustainable Development Goals (SDGs) includes a range of governmental, corporate and personal responsibilities as citizens and specifies a framework for collective action through a Global Partnership. The role of business and the private sector in this partnership is essential, but cannot be untangled or divorced from the actions of political leaders and bodies, the UN system and other international institutions, civil society, indigenous peoples, the scientific and academic community—'and all people' (UN 2015). It is in this spirit that we explore the importance of values in CSR.

In this book, we capture and explore different aspects of value in corporate social responsibility (CSR). This includes the historical development of value in CSR, how value is linked to a positive vision of the future and how it is communicated by a range of private and public organizations to various audiences. The book also contrasts corporate strategic value with cooperative value, and community value. Finally, it explains how leaders' values can drive responsible business practice and enhance social cohesion, solidarity and resilience in fractured and unequal communities. The book therefore asks the reader to consider what value means in CSR (for business and society, both by drawing from the past and by looking into the future), where it comes from and how it is enacted (organizational legacies or managers' values) and its purpose (communicative value, co-operation, community). The book also presents CSR as a global project by noting how values are cultural. Understanding value creation or co-creation, value delivery and value measurement in corporate responsibility, and connecting these with corporate and societal values, offers a chance to re-legitimize businesses in their attempts to meet sustainability goals, including those ambitious targets mapped out by the UN.

1.1 Defining Value: An Economic Perspective

Defining value in a way that prioritizes sustainability is both a business opportunity and a challenge. Markets aim to create all sorts of value: economic value, social value, brand value, lifetime value and so on. Some values sit uneasily alongside others.

From the economic reductionism perspective, value might be reduced to cost-benefit calculations (from the era of Fordism) where this means '*value for money*' and the emphasis is on 'more of something for less money' (or less labour). In business studies, especially in marketing, the concept of value is most commonly understood as a subjective measure of the perceived utility of a product or service (Grönroos and Ravald 2011). The economic value offered by firms to society is just one kind of value. Most obviously, value has a more everyday meaning relating to our beliefs about right and wrong, or as it relates to ethics. One of the Oxford Dictionaries' definitions presents value as 'principles or standards of behaviour; one's judgement of what is important in life'. We see a return to this definition in the consumer as citizen and in CSR. The legitimacy of economic value is that this was what 'the free market' promises to consumers and ironically economic value may be easier to justify morally than the market's expansion into, or claims around, other value domains.

In terms of who creates (economic) value, the cost-benefit approach invites the view that value is created by an organization, at first through production, and later through marketing and/or branding, that is, *brand value* or the recognition that value is not (just) in production, but in the symbolic meanings of brands. This is an 'internal' perspective of value that suggests it is created inside the organization by the actors who assemble it. However, this view has been challenged by the idea of a 'value system' and more recently by the idea of 'value in use' and 'shared value'.

For example, Porter's (1985) *value system* theorization recognizes that value is incrementally created through material and immaterial changes. This may be 'internal', capturing the different functions of an organization, but it also recognizes external actors or stakeholders. For example, as aluminium is extracted from the ground, then transformed into a statement of design and lifestyle 'cool' in the form of an iPhone. In other words, the Porter's approach adopts a macro (i.e., business system) level of analysis of value, as it shows all the activities or operations necessary to transform raw materials into goods/services that are consumed by people. The 'value system' allows an examination of where value is added, where more can be added (or costs reduced) and what sorts of value may be added, and some see it as an important planning tool to meet 'sustainable competitive advantage' (Priem et al. 1997).

Such macro arrangements also have ramifications for marketing practices where consumers are seen as a primary source of value. The turn to the consumer is best captured in 'relationship marketing' where marketers nurture, expand and exploit what they know about consumers and aim to extract value from 'long-term mutually beneficial relationships'. Alternatively, it can be found in the idea of '*customer lifetime value*'—a prediction of the net profit attributed to entire future relationships with customers—that recognizes consumers as more valuable than transactions. In recent years, especially in marketing, another target for value has been *consumer data*. Data is seen as value in itself and is inherently valued by business (e.g., consumer databases or insight, value exchange, integrated campaigns), but raises significant privacy issues about how and whether businesses respect consumers/individuals' boundaries (see, e.g., Shoshana Zuboff's 2019, *Surveillance Capitalism*, a chilling presentation of business models and algorithms underpinning the digital economies). In parallel to 'escalating market value and values', consumers and other stakeholders 'learn' to be savvy. They seek new values from their engagement with markets and these might be financial, but also result in other demands, that is, *ethical business practice*.

1.2 Ethical Business Practice, CSR and Value(s)

As ideas about value expand in business contexts, we are naturally drawn back to broader definitions of values. For example, several authors note that Western economies keep perpetuating several values such as *individualism*, with implications for care and responsibility (Bauman 2013), *materialism*, with a contested debate about implications for human relationships (Fromm 1976; Illouz 2007; Miller 2008; Molesworth and Grigore 2019) or *competitiveness*, with implications for identity (Marcuse 1964). The task of businesses might seem to be to persistently create new value, which risks a sort of imperialism where markets seek to capture more and more 'values' in their quest for new value with the implication that all aspects of life become marketized. Similar ideas are captured in Klein's (2009) '*No Logo*', Barber's (2008) '*Consumed: How markets corrupt children, infantilize adults, and swallow citizens whole*', Kuttner's (1999) '*Everything for Sale: The virtues and limits of markets*' or Sandel's (2012) '*What money can't buy: the moral limits of markets*' where the authors draw attention to the fact that markets erode moral values. Indeed, in an experiment about how people behave when they received financial incentives in a simulated marketplace conducted by researchers at the Universities of Bonn and Bamberg the main result was that: 'people decide very differently depending on whether they act in markets or outside of markets [...] individually, outside of markets, people have difficulties in killing these mice, they don't want the money. In markets most people actually find it easier to kill the mice even for very small amounts of money' (DW 2013).

Although business might be about the generation of value, ethical issues in business are therefore also tied to the moral values held by individuals and the contexts in which they are situated (Forsyth 1992). This brings us to an alternative way of seeing value: '*shared value*'. Porter and Kramer (2019) suggest that the purpose of organizations needs to be redefined so that there is a focus not just on profit and value for money, but on creating shared value, such that economic value can also create value for society. This view brings together a company's success and social progress, opening the possibility of new discourses around new sources of value that can be obtained by connecting business and society. In other words, organizations need to create economic value in a way that *also* creates value for society. The shared value perspective places CSR at the hearth of business, and Porter and Kramer (2019) see this as 'our best chance to legitimize business again'.

The origins of CSR can be tracked to at least the nineteenth century (religiously motivated) and in a more secular form from the 1920s when

Clark mentions that businesses have obligations to society. A decade later, Berle (1932: 1365) suggests that managers have to provide 'safety, security, or means of support for that part of the community which is unable to earn its living in the normal channels of work or trade'. One of the most referenced early definition of CSR is Bowen's (1953: 6) one, who states that it encompasses 'the obligations of businessmen to pursue those policies, to make those decisions, or to follow those lines of actions which are desirable in terms of the objectives and values of our society'. From these early conceptualizations, we note that there was a search for a deeper purpose of firms in society that extends beyond just making money or achieving financial value, to accomplishing contributions to or 'value' for the community and society.

CSR takes place within specific cultural contexts and therefore produces local or regional types of CSR theories/philosophy and practices. CSR has been developed in Western developed countries and is therefore underpinned by free market logic, conditions and values, but varies significantly in each country (Dahlsrud 2008; Gjølberg 2009; Jamali et al. 2017). Dahlsrud (2008) and Gjølberg (2009), for example, argue that CSR 'cannot be separated from the contextual factors of the nation in which it is practiced'.

As such, studies on 'CSR and values' attempt to understand the context, or culture, or 'local' philosophy to identify nuances in various CSR theories and practices. Culture is learned within a society and therefore shapes collective or individual values. Organizations operate in national or regional relations that create a distinctive environment for their practice; hence CSR is also dependent on the contexts or institutional dynamics in which it is assembled. For example, Wang and Juslin (2009) show how CSR can be interpreted through a moral philosophy—Confucianism—that reveals the ethical values in CSR work in Chinese culture. In their paper, the authors focus on a 'harmony approach' which draws on Confucian values to show how people can be motivated to assume individual responsibilities which in turn can lead to self-cultivation, self-control and a harmonious society (Wang and Juslin 2009). In such context, the motivation for conducting CSR becomes a cultivation of virtues, where people learn to live in harmony with nature, and hence they are able to assemble a 'harmonious society'. Other studies that focus on developing countries show how CSR has been introduced by multinationals, aiming to introduce a set of values that does not account for specific practices and contexts, which results in a gap between the public discourse of CSR and the actual practice (Jamali et al. 2017), that is, a '*selective decoupling*', where rather than transform an institution or a context, CSR remains a decoupled practice separate from the realities or conditions on the ground. Jamali et al. (2017) question whether CSR can actually improve the lives of beneficiaries they claim to help or the communities especially where such CSR practices remain divorced from the conditions in which they take place.

1.3 The Role of Value(s) in Corporate Responsibility Theories and Practices

In this book, we look at concepts and practices that might better explain and align both the 'value' and 'values' of corporate responsibility and offer solutions to individuals engaged in making corporate responsibility a reality, rather than a discredited marketing exercise. The edited collection brings together papers presented at the 7th International Conference on Social Responsibility Ethics and Sustainable Business, held at Norwegian Business School in Oslo on the 12th and 13th of October 2018. This conference invited submissions that explore the intersections between and ramifications of 'value(s)' and 'corporate social responsibility'. In this book we therefore (re)connect value(s) and corporate social responsibility. We present articles that include current thinking and developments by both academics and practitioners, combine theoretical foundations on value and CSR with practical insights and help managers in decision-making processes. Additionally, we present conceptualizations from various cultures including Japan, Tanzania, Bangladesh, United Kingdom, Norway, France, Germany, Belgium and Romania.

The first part of the book adopts a theoretical approach on value and values, and their role in shaping CSR frameworks, tools, conceptualizations, and then how practice is informed by such theories. For example, in Chap. 2, Candice Chow and Nada Kakabadse talk about the importance of executives' values in shaping enterprises' corporate responsibility practices. Making use of a 'values-theory' lens and drawing on stories from Canadian executives, this chapter shows how executives' values have come to the fore and shaped their views concerning corporate responsibility practice. Additionally, these stories highlight the link between executives' values and corporate responsibility adoption, that is, the more robust the values, the stronger the individual's belief in their ability to drive change without influence from external constraints. This chapter concludes by advocating for the need to emphazise and integrate management values into all levels of further and higher education. *Personal reflexivity* and *immersive experiential learning* should be championed to help strengthen and raise awareness of individuals' values and to acknowledge that the personal growth process is an essential driver for positive change.

Moving from the importance of executives' values in shaping organizational practices, then in Chap. 3, Atle Andreassen Raa problematizes philanthropy from the perspective of economic theory. The author concludes by relating the stakeholder-shareholder dichotomy in CSR discourses with a corresponding dichotomy in the interpretation of Adam Smith's 'invisible hand' with or without morality and ethics included. In this way, Chap. 3 deepens our understanding of how philanthropy and CSR can be reconciled from an economic and ethical perspective. Then, in Chap. 4, Dušan Kučera situates the desirable and declared value concept of CSR (corporate social responsibility) and Sustainable Development Goals (SDGs) with the present regression of moral values in Western society and Central and Eastern Europe (CEE). The author argues that from a philosophical perspective, the '*crisis of values*' and the '*moral recession*' of the Western societies are caused by a modern dualist conception of corporate goals. In Chap. 5, Gerhard Kosinowski introduces a strategic tool to create '*cooperative value*'. His theoretical approach shows how and why cooperative banks' activities exceed the creation of value for their members. Drawing on 24 in-depth interviews with practitioners from German cooperative banks, the author reveals that they have the aspiration to be a high-quality, long-term partner for all their clients and, as such, they act as orchestrators for their members and non-member clients.

The second part of the book provides case studies, or 'local' interpretations of, or empirical studies on how, by corporate responsibility into organizational strategies and practices, value for all stakeholders can be generated, which in turn may cultivate values. For example, in Chap. 6, David McQueen and Amelia Turner present a case study exploring the environmental and sustainable values of UK energy firm *Ecotricity* and its founding-director and owner, Dale Vince. The authors consider Ecotricity's expansion and diversification from a clean energy provider to offering a range of sustainable business initiatives including electric car charging stations, grid-scale battery storage, green mobile phone service and vegan school food supplies. It also explores marketing strategies and media coverage of the company and assesses the extent to which the director's single-minded and uncompromising values have helped secure a loyal, niche customer base and could provide a model for future business success in the face of the rapidly accelerating climate crisis. The chapter concludes with a critical discussion of CSR in light of this crisis and the need for sustainability to take centre stage at every level of business decision-making and strategic planning.

From a case study exploring the environmental and sustainable values of UK energy firm, we then move to Chap. 7, where Adrian Baumgartner proposes the concept of strategic corporate social responsibility (SCSR), defined as a corporation's clearly articulated and communicated policies and practices towards gaining a competitive advantage by addressing unmet social needs. His study shows that SCSR activities have a positive impact not only on corporate financial performance (CFP), or economic value (EV) but also on societal value (SV). The proposed framework aims to support future research on CSR and related concepts, as well as to provide practical guidance and recommendations to business leaders aiming to implement the principles of CSR in their business. In Chap. 8, Florian Weber and Kerstin Fehre examine how corporate social responsibility activity (CSRA) and corporate social responsibility communication (CSRC) impact legitimacy. The empirical results indicate that neither CSRA, nor CSRC have a standalone effect; nonetheless, CSR is important for organizational legitimacy. The authors suggest that a CSR strategy that combines high levels of CSRA with low levels of CSRC is the most effective way for (re)gaining legitimacy, while an opposite strategy that combines low levels of CSRA with high levels of CSRC emerges is the worst. In another empirical study, Anca-Teodora Şerban-Oprescu provides an analysis of the impact of cultural and educational values on the entrepreneurial mindset. Chapter 9 therefore focuses on three main aspects: the connection between education and entrepreneurship; the risk aversion in entrepreneurship, and related ethics, social responsibility and entrepreneurship. The author concludes that Romanians still need to have a more profound understanding of the core values that make for ethical and socially responsible behaviour in independent ventures.

In Chap. 10, Mohammad Tazul Islam and Katsuhiko Kokubu interrogate the use of legitimacy theory to infer managers' perceptions of corporate social reporting in a bank from a developing country, Bangladesh. Their study finds that CSR as a concept is not clear to practitioners and regulators, who mostly view it as corporate philanthropic activity. Moreover, the authors find that there is no structured format for CSR reporting; instead the reporting format is bank-centric. From a legitimacy theory perspective, the study therefore confirms that the legitimate reasons for CSR reporting in the banking industry of Bangladesh are mostly driven by external stakeholder influences (i.e., regulators, employees, local community, NGOs, political leader and civil society). In Chap. 11, Omary Swallehe evaluates activities of the corporate citizens in Tanzania to find the best way of aligning CSR initiatives to obtain mutual benefits for both the organizations and the general public. Drawing on a survey of both public and private organizations, the authors find that the majority of the organizations regard CSR as a source of competitive advantage through legitimization of companies' offerings to the customers and general public. When CSR is not seen to provide competitive advantage opportunities, then the organizations are unlikely to justify the 'value' of CSR for their organization.

1.4 Value(s) and Corporate Responsibility: Quo Vadis?

The complex and diverse 'context and culture' for understanding CSR and values touched on above changed worldwide in 2020. This was because, as we have all discovered, Covid-19 changed everything. It has been said that our lives will never be the same, but exactly how is hard to say as this book goes to press. Optimists believe that this pandemic will make us more compassionate and empathetic, others perhaps cling to the hope that everything will be as it was before. Pessimists think that these are the last days of humanity, or that at the very least we are on the brink of an economic downturn that will rival the Great Depression of the 1930s. As editors, we were caught in the midst of the pandemic in February and March 2020 and, we discussed by video conference from our homes, rather than our usual workplaces, the impact that this dramatic global lockdown could have on corporate responsibility and values while finalizing this book. Notions of values and responsibility have already changed, that is for sure. Many companies are suffering enormous losses, or bankruptcy, while others struggle on and show their solidarity and responsibility to customers, their staff and the wider community in empathetic and creative ways. Not all companies are making losses: Amazon, for instance, is making gains. However, not everything is about financial gains, as we are learning. We have lost our freedoms and we are locked in our homes. Keeping your distance is now, paradoxically, a sign that you love someone, better still, that you love and care for everyone, even people you have never met and never will. The need for empathy and care are at the heart of the final chapter of the book by David McQueen, Francisca Farache and Georgiana Grigore which explores how Nietzsche's troubling notions of the 'herd', 'masculine', warrior values and attitudes to empathy for the weakest members of society have been shown to resonate in disturbing ways in the response of several right-wing populist leaders to the Coronavirus pandemic sweeping the globe in 2020. What seemed, at worse, shocking unpreparedness and a casual disregard for the well-being of vulnerable groups, or the wider safety of the nation, indicated a lack of responsibility that was thrown into dramatic relief by the quick, decisive action of other leaders, organizations and businesses.

So, this book ends with initial reflections on what extent such a worldwide health crisis is shaping our understanding of both economic value and values? There are many more issues we have not touched on. What kind of responsibilities will companies undertake, and what will be the external stakeholders' expectations during such 'unprecedented' times? How will this pandemic shape our future? And how will companies demonstrate their responsibility and values to society? There are questions for future research. In this book, we join contemporary conversations on the intricate relationship between values and corporate responsibility, and we hope that it can be used for future theorizations on CSR and values, or applications within different national or organizational contexts.

References

Barber, B. R. (2008). *Consumed: How markets corrupt children, infantilize adults, and swallow citizens whole.* WW Norton & Company.

Bauman, Z. (2013). *The Individualized Society.* London: John Wiley & Sons.

Berle, A. A. Jr. (1932). 'For Whom Corporate Managers Are Trustees: A Note', *Harvard Law Review*, 45(8), 1365–1372.

Bowen, H. R. (1953). *Social responsibilities of the businessman.* University of Iowa Press.

Dahlsrud, A. (2008). 'How Corporate Social Responsibility Is Defined: An Analysis of 37 Definitions', *Corporate Social Responsibility and Environmental Management*, 15(1), 1–13.

DW. (2013). 'Markets erode moral values, researchers find', DW, Available at: https://www.dw.com/en/markets-erode-moral-values-researchers-find/a-16813795

Forsyth, D. R. (1992). 'Judging the morality of business practices: The influence of personal moral philosophies', *Journal of business Ethics*, 11(5–6), 461–470.

Fromm, E. (1976). *To Have or to Be?* London: Abacus.

Gjølberg, M. (2009). 'The Origin of Corporate Social Responsibility: Global Forces or National Legacies?', *Socio-Economic Review*, 7(4), 605–637.

Grönroos, C., & Ravald, A. (2011). 'Service as business logic: implications for value creation and marketing', *Journal of Service Management*, 22(1), 5–22.

Illouz E (2007). *Cold intimacies: The making of emotional capitalism*. Polity: Cambridge.

Jamali, D., Lund-Thomsen, P., & Khara, N. (2017). 'CSR institutionalized myths in developing countries: An imminent threat of selective decoupling'. *Business & Society*, 56(3), 454–486.

Kuttner, R. (1999). *Everything for sale: The virtues and limits of markets*. University of Chicago Press.

Klein, N. (2009). *No logo*. Vintage Books Canada.

Marcuse, H. (1964). *One-dimensional man: the ideology of advanced industrial society*. Croydon: Routledge & Kegan Paul.

Miller, D. (2008). *The comfort of things*. Polity.

Molesworth, M., & Grigore, G. (2019). Scripts people live in the marketplace: An application of Script Analysis to Confessions of a Shopaholic. *Marketing Theory*, 19(4), 467–488.

Porter, M. E. (1985). Value chain. *The Value Chain and Competitive advantage: creating and sustaining superior performance*. NY: Free Press.

Porter, M. E., & Kramer, M. R. (2019). 'Creating shared value', In *Managing sustainable business* (pp. 323–346). Springer, Dordrecht.

Priem, R. L., Rasheed, A. M., & Amirani, S. (1997). 'Alderson's transvection and Porter's value system: a comparison of two independently developed theories', *Journal of Management History*, 3(2), 145–165.

Sandel, M. J. (2012). *What money can't buy: the moral limits of markets*. Macmillan.

UN. (2015). Transforming our world: the 2030 Agenda for Sustainable Development. The United Nations. Accessed at: https://sustainabledevelopment.un.org/post2015/transformingourworld

Wang, L., & Juslin, H. (2009). 'The impact of Chinese culture on corporate social responsibility: The harmony approach', *Journal of Business Ethics*, 88(3), 433–451.

Zuboff, S. (2019). *Surveillance capitalism and the challenge of collective action*. Sage CA: Los Angeles, CA: SAGE Publications.

Part I

Theoretical Perspectives on Values

2

Personal Values and Corporate Responsibility Adoption

Candice C. Chow and Nada K. Kakabadse

2.1 Introduction

Our daily environment is rife with complex and global challenges. Climate change, social inequality, political unrest, the depletion of our resources, mass immigration, and business instability are all taking a toll upon our own and others' lives.

For example, environmental issues have developed into grand challenges that are creating immense disruptions to society and its systems that extend way beyond the interests of individual firms. Businesses, as economic engines of society, draw upon environmental and social

---

All vignettes are adopted from Chow, "The Influence of Executives' Values on Corporate Responsibility Adoption" (DBA thesis, Henley Business School, 2018).

C. C. Chow (✉)
McMaster University, Hamilton, ON, Canada

N. K. Kakabadse
Henley Business School, University of Reading, Reading, UK
e-mail: n.kakabadse@reading.ac.uk

F. Farache et al. (eds.), *Values and Corporate Responsibility*, Palgrave Studies in Governance, Leadership and Responsibility,
https://doi.org/10.1007/978-3-030-52466-1_2

resources that have implications on the sustainability and wellbeing of our planet.

As globalisation inevitably marches forward organisations grow in scale and economic power, while at the same time sovereign governments become increasingly ineffective at protecting resources and maintaining environmental and social balance across national boundaries.

In 2018 82% of the wealth created worldwide went to the top 1%, whilst the poorest half of population saw no increase in their wealth (The Global Wealth Report 2019). The question is—what role and responsibility does business have in society?

Addressing these challenges and building towards a responsible and sustainable future in our current environment necessitates new ways of thinking and acting. We need to call upon our virtues and employ a systems-thinking approach, which embraces the complex, paradoxical framing and management of issues, as well as forward-looking consciousness.

These values recognise humanity's centrality and moral compass within the business context. The upper hierarchy of organisations—executives—are responsible for shaping their businesses' strategic direction. This means that executives' value systems have a significant influence on their perception of businesses' role and responsibilities in society.

Corporate responsibility (CR) or related concepts, such as Sustainability and Sustainable Development, require firms to understand actions that "further some social [or environment] good beyond the interests of the firm and that which is required by law" (McWilliams and Siegel 2001: 117:1). As a result CR inherently represents social, ecological, moral, and ethical values.

Amoral rationality (Ghoshal 2005) is taught in business schools that have created a generation of students who ignore the moral responsibilities of real-world management, but in fact ethical, social, and ecological values need to be considered as part of the construct of a global rationality (Melé and Parra 2006) in every managerial decision. The divergence of management values, split across an industrial-organisation-economic approach, needs to be replaced by a stakeholder-oriented CR approach (Swanson 1999).

In this chapter, we contribute to the theme of this book—Values and Corporate Responsibility—CSR and the Sustainable Development Goals by sharing our perspectives on why values matter when it comes to driving sustainable and responsible practices. Making use of a 'values-theory' lens, we further consider how values can influence management decisions and behaviours. Much of this is illustrated using stories told by Canadian executives about how their personal values have come to the fore and shaped their views on CR practice. These stories are part of a case study research approach designed to explore how leaders' values influence CR adoption (Chow 2018).

This material additionally highlights the danger of treating strategy and values as contentious and bi-polar concepts, while showing how the values division of managers and leaders as both citizens and business actors is leading to the deterioration of our society and planet's sustainability. As an alternative, we propose a balanced business management approach to social and environmental sustainability and economic prosperity. This is values-driven and expands beyond a hierarchical and linear approach to profit maximisation.

2.2 How Values Influence Behaviour

Values help determine social attitudes and ideologies on the one hand and social behaviour on the other (Rokeach 1973). They also formulate the core aspects of self (Hitlin 2003) and drive motivational forces and actions (Schwartz 2012) while remaining relatively stable. However, values do change through the course of our lives (Meglino and Ravlin 1998), although this change does not occur in isolation.

Instead, our values vary as a result of the different stages of life we experience. There are three elements that guide the organising principles of our values. Cognitive—related to a person's assessment of what is good and bad. Affective—related to the emotional response triggered when our values are threatened or affirmed. And Directive—related to the motivation to pursue desirable goals (Kluckhohn and Strodtbeck 1961).

Highly central values have a stronger influence upon our actions and are more resistant to change (Abelson 1988). Because values also encompass motivational dimensions that influence action, motivational characteristics are often exhibited as goals (Locke 1991), which in turn act as links between values and behaviour (Schwartz 1994).

However, many people's values remain largely hidden and are rarely well articulated (Posner 2010), until situations occur in which values conflict takes place. Behaviours are often conducted in a spontaneous manner, unless one's values are contemplated consciously beforehand (Gorlin and Schuur 2019). Taking time to consciously reflect on our values allows us to consider and seek out our true purpose, and this can have an immense influence on setting out meaningful, responsible, and positively impactful goals.

When values become conscious, the values–behaviour link is also stronger (Schwartz et al. 2017). The ability to consciously apply values to goal-setting and alignment with actions requires four key attributes: (1) values centrality, (2) values as a motivational construct, (3) values awareness, and (4) values as cognitive and affective aspects of reasoning.

2.2.1 Values Centrality

An individual's values are the basis of their self-identity and so we try to behave and act in a way that fits this identity concept (Hitlin 2003). While values hierarchy is important in influencing behaviour, it is the centrality of values to self that proves to be the most influential. The more central our values are, the stronger their influence is on our behaviour (Steg et al. 2014; Woodward and Shaffakat, 2016). Highly central values also generate stronger affective reactions, have a stronger influence on actions, and are most resistance to change (Abelson 1988; Bardi and Schwartz 2003).

2.2.2 Values Motivate Through Goals and Outcome Valence

Different values are distinguished by the type of motivation or goals that are expressed, which in turn contain the directive attribute that influences actions (Schwartz and Bilsky 1987). Goals help to set intentions that generate engagement through a series of smaller actions, which potentially lead to a desired outcome.

From this perspective, individual actions are not so much aligned with one's values, but are the results of goals set which reflect one's value(s). This being the case values have a temporal effect, and the motivational forces of these values direct goal-setting based on the individual's time horizon.

The direct effect of values on singular actions and short-term goals is less pronounced, as influence is masked by situational dynamics and the main objectives of the task at hand (Locke 1991).

The following example highlights how one executive's values, formed over time, initially directed their professional goals and purpose, before turning into a very personal conviction.

Vignette 1: Personal Conviction to Fight Climate Change

> *I want my kids to look back and say, wow dad did something that had a really positive impact on helping us solve one of the Earth's biggest challenges .... Ryan—executive*

Ryan grew up in a family where work ethics were highly valued. He recalled his grandmother would rise before dawn to tend her garden, and how meticulous she was in keeping it weed-free.

Ryan excels in sports and through hard work and persistence became an elite athlete who competed at an international level. During his travels as a young man, he noticed the damage being done to the oceans and environment as a result of people mindlessly discarding trash. These made an impression that planted the seed for his strong ecological beliefs.

After graduating from business school, Ryan made a successful career for himself in the telecommunication business. But the issue of ocean pollution continued to haunt him, as he developed his knowledge further and researched the challenges posed to the planet by climate change.

He recognised that his life purpose was to combat climate change and eventually left a successful career in the telecommunication sector to settle back in his hometown and build a hub for clean tech innovation. Funding did not come easily but through hard work and persistence his business grew and flourished.

Ryan's determination to address climate change is not only evident from the stated legacy he wants to leave behind for his children, but from also from what he described as "a lot of blood, sweat and tears" to grow a start-up business to a scale that has become impactful and transformative.

2.2.3 Values Awareness

Work context incentives, constraints, recognition, and sanctions can often be overwhelming, suppressing the influence of values on behaviour (Grojean et al. 2004). These situational factors interrupt decision-making processes and can influence behaviour and immediate decision-making, unless an individual is consciously contemplating their values (Giddens 1984).

The perils of unconscious decision-making are widely recognised and can often lead to unethical behaviour, often while the perpetrator is completely unaware that they are acting inappropriately (Fassin 2005; Sturm 2017). When values have been primed (e.g. Verplanken and Holland 2002), one's ability to scan for information relevant to the values improves, meaning values awareness is a factor in indirectly influencing actions.

The following example shows how one executive's deliberate act to bring certain corporate values into the boardroom helped resolve an ethical dilemma.

Vignette 2: Bringing Values Awareness to Ethical Decision-Making

> *Fortunately, because of a values-based system … [the] eventual dilemma was solved very quickly, which is the right thing [to do] ….*
> *Peter—executive.*

Peter understood the importance of living by the values of an organisation. When he found out his company had overcharged a customer for millions of dollars over a period of several years, he was faced with an ethical dilemma. Should he tell the customer or not?

His customer was unaware of the overcharging and their accounting books on the matter had been closed. Peter sat down with his executives in the board room to discuss whether they should tell the customer and refund the amount, or keep quiet about the situation.

If the company did not inform the customer, they would never know. The transaction had been completed and all of the financial statements produced, audited and published. As CEO, refunding the customer could lead to the reinstatement of financial statements, lowering of reported earnings and unhappy shareholders.

After deliberating with his executive team, Peter made the decision to live by their corporate values, 'customer-first and transparency.' They decided to refund the customers for the full amount owed and adjusted their financial statements accordingly.

Peter's deliberate act to raise and remind the organisation of its shared corporate values reflects his belief in doing the right thing, and that the conscious application of values ensures corporate decisions are undertaken with consistency and thoughtfulness.

2.2.4 Values as Cognitive Process and Affective Aspects of Reasoning

The process of turning values into action requires both cognitive and affective aspects of reasoning (Tenbrunsel and Smith-Crowe 2008). When values are supported by persuasive arguments or moral reasoning, they are less prone to change.

Reason is a driver for pro-values behaviour (Maio et al. 2001).The affective component of values, on the other hand, energises or initiates actions (Schwartz et al. 2017). The strength of values increase when individuals use reasoning to support certain values (Steg et al. 2014), and these individuals are better able to ignore situational incentives and exhibit pro-values behaviour.

In today's dynamic and fast-paced business environment, increased competition, lack of time and resources (Trevino 1986) affect individuals' capacity to support their reasoning (Hambrick et al. 2005). This, in turn, weakens the impact of values on behaviour and undermines one's ability to comprehensively scan the environment and assess alternative options for rational decisions.

An addiction to fast decision-making leads to managers failing to reflect and consciously apply their values. Instead, they often fall back on reflexive experience and what has worked for them in the past, or imitate other firms' solutions (Hambrick et al. 2005).

Previous studies have found that people tend to rationalise their behaviours, even when misaligned from their values. This weakens the influence of their personal, championed values when it comes to action. Over time, their reasoning process reprioritises certain values over others.

Reflecting on one's values and actions strengthens wisdom-embedded mindfulness, which can foster various positive outcomes, since wisdom "is the ability to perceive and evaluate the long-run consequences of behaviour" (Ackoff 1999: 14).

The idea of using wisdom in mindfulness practice can, if applied appropriately, facilitate moral, emotional, and cognitive developments for ethical and CR behaviours. This could include developing a relationship with stakeholders to benefit the environment (Waddock 2001).

2.3 Values Are Fundamental to Progress in Humanity

The deepest resources for the transformation of business, as for society as a whole, lie within the human heart.—Cardinal Vincent Nicholas (Hollensbe et al. 2014)

'Liquid' organisations are characterised as featuring a high pace of innovation, uncertainty and complexity (Bauman 2007), resulting in their leadership becoming a determinate factor as to whether the institution will ultimately succeed or fail.

Leaders' personal values operate as a perceptual filter that shapes corporate decisions and behaviour, and acts as a motivator for creating business value (Hambrick and Mason 1984). Without normative values that direct the purpose of businesses and corporate strategies, short-term progress in technological advancement and economic optimisation is likely to compromise long-term sustainable progress for humanity.

This suggests that organisations' overarching goals and business objectives should reflect normative and idealistic beliefs (Swanson 1999). Indeed organisations should link purpose with a set of broader human values (Hollensbe et al. 2014).

While general trust in business has declined, there are both large and small organisations which have found purpose by grounding their businesses through a set of values. For example, orphan drug development (designed to treat rare diseases through a highly risky and potentially unprofitable research and development process) is motivated by founders' values towards humanity (Bruyaka et al. 2013).

The intensively-analysed Merck's river blindness business case (Bollier et al. 1991) highlights the complexity and multitude of value motivations at play, which go far beyond a simple binary values view that prioritises either economic optimisation or social impact as the dominant business objective.

Social enterprises also prioritise social over economic values, while ensuring economic viability for the sake of their own continuity and to attract capital (Hlady-Rispal and Servantie 2018). Many (e.g. Swanson 1999; Waldman and Siegel 2008; Hartman et al. 2017) argue that social issues should not be separated from economic impact, and that the integration of normative and instrumental aspects of CR are both necessary and desirable.

2.4 The Challenge of Values Bifurcation in Management

The idea that corporations have moral and social obligations is not a new one. In the eighteenth century, before the industrial era, privileges were bestowed on businesses that were deemed to be socially beneficial.

The academic debate over the legality of sacrificing profits for the public interest (i.e. corporate responsibility) began in 1932 when opposing articles by Dodd (1931) versus Berle (1932) appeared in the Harvard Law Review symposium on "For Whom are Corporate Managers Trustees?" The proposition of a 'shareholder value doctrine' position ultimately won.

Merrick Dodd of Harvard Law School disagreed vehemently with Adolf Berle (1932) of Harvard Business School's shareholder primacy thesis. Dodd 1931: 1148:1) argued for "a view of the business corporation as an economic institution which has a social service as well as a profit-making function." In return Dodd (1931) stated that the proper goal of corporate managers was not just to make money for shareholders, but also to secure jobs for employees, provide better quality products for consumers and generate contributions to the community's welfare as a whole.

The concept of maximising shareholder value creation has become an often-used management doctrine and was promoted during the 1950s and 1960s by two scholars, Franco Modigliani and Merton Miller. They showed that a firm's value is independent of its capital structure and dividend policy.

This idea was further promoted in the 1980s by consultants including McKinsey & Co, as well as academics such as Alfred Rappaport. One of the most influential figures in this debate was Nobel Prize-winning economist, Milton Friedman (1970: 1:3). He promoted the shareholder primacy argument, which suggested companies had a responsibility to "conduct the business in accordance with their desires, which generally, will be to make as much money as possible while conforming to the basic rules of the society."

The purpose of using CR to maximise profits while remaining focused on moral standards continues to divide academic thinking to this day (c.f. Waldman and Siegel 2008).

Incidents of corporate irresponsibility regularly highlight the dark side of a single-minded focus on maximising shareholder value. A plethora of corporate failure examples include Enron, which pledged to "create significant value for shareholders"; Lehman Brothers, "maximising shareholder value," and MCI WorldCom, "a proven record of shareholder value creation." More recent disasters include Volkswagen and other auto manufacturers' emissions cheating, and Mylan's epi-pen pricing scandal, all of which represent just the tip of a sizeable corporate irresponsibility iceberg.

Businesses have a duty and obligation to other stakeholder groups in relation to their licence to operate. This purpose should extend beyond acting as a simple vehicle for economic return. From a legal perspective, shareholders do not own the corporation. Rather they own corporate securities, commonly called "shares." As share owners, shareholder rights are relatively limited.

For example, shareholders do not have the right to exercise control over the corporation's assets, something which in reality sits within the domain of the corporation's board of directors. As such corporate directors must also possess moral values.

Many scholars and practitioners believe that corporations do not possess moral values in the same way people do (e.g. Donaldson 1982; Goodpaster and Matthews 1982; Ewin 1991). However, although only humans can have "mens rea," corporate values are collective value projections. Without morals as a guiding compass for corporate decisions, CR is a competitive strategy that will lose its appeal when something more promising comes along (Besio and Pronzini 2014).

It should be noted that ethics is a component of CR (Carroll 1979), without which the ethical rationality behind CR investments would ebb and flow with the economy.

Sadly, corporate scandals show little sign of abatement, despite changes to accounting regulations, the financial accountability framework, and the promotion of sustainable reporting and corporate transparency. Instead there is an increased perception of corporate "greenwashing" and general scepticism about businesses' CR authenticity.

Many such actions are viewed as invalid public relations exercises, designed to repair or build tarnished brand images and reputations (Kakabadse et al. 2006) as a screen for unpublicised unethical practices (Basu and Palazzo 2008). Trust between countries, sectors, senior executives and government has been steadily declining for many years now (Hollensbe et al. 2014). Building trust and goodwill means a corporation's CR value-orientation is an important consideration for a company that desires legitimacy.

The different values-orientations of CR—social, ethical, moral, ecological, economic—give rise to different organisational approaches: (1) an unconcerned or non-issue approach; (2) the damage control approach; (3) a compliance approach; (4) a profit-driven approach; and (5) a values-oriented approach, grounded in holistic, ethical thinking (Colbert et al. 2003; van Marrewijk and Werre 2003).

2.5 The Influence of Organisational Values on Personal Values

Every organisation has a story or myth about how it was founded and the most important aspect of this tale is how the organisation views itself, and how it wants to be viewed by outsiders.

Although 'master story' beliefs are not economically driven, they can result in financial gain or loss (Simon 2009). A master story is supported by core values, otherwise known as the organisation's mission. Individuals who have core values that differ from the organisation often face dilemmas which impact how they operate.

Organisational values are manifested by processes, policies, procedures, and reward systems. If the consequence of one's actions is deemed to be undesirable and the behaviour is discouraged, the individual's values are expected to change (Meglino and Ravlin 1998). Through the process of socialisation and by observing what works and what does not, individuals begin to adopt the dominant values of their organisation (England 1967).

As members succeed by abiding and manifesting the organisation's values, these values are further reinforced (Elizur and Sagie 1999). As a result organisational values influence individuals' ethical behaviour as well their attitudes towards CR engagement (Singhapakdi and Vitell 1993; Grojean et al. 2004). Corporate culture that embraces a set of well-defined ethical values positively influences ethical behaviour and attitudes towards CR (Alteer et al. 2013).

The influence of organisational values was studied by George England (1967). He found values that directly influence actions are "operative," and are the direct result of stated organisational priorities. Conversely personal values that are not aligned with organisational objectives are "intended," and have no direct influence on managers' actions at work. Despite this, they may influence how one perceives and interprets information.

External variables include work pressures and demanding conditions, which over time can impinge upon an individual's values system and create a shift (Kluckhohn 1958). As a result, organisational values are more striking than those of individuals in respect of adopting CR (Dickson et al. 2001). Personal values also tend to remain latent and passive (Bansal 2003).

Middle managers are more likely to succumb to pressure to conform to organisational standards (Posner and Schmidt 1984), and the longer a member stays in an organisation, the more their values will resemble those preferred by the organisation (Wiener 1982).

A reluctance to incorporate values in a CR context is prevalent across business practice. Ethics and moral principles as CR motivators are subservient to branding and maximising value (Ditlev-Simonsen and Midttun 2011). Business managers also tend to push their personal values to one side, including morals and ethics, in order to satisfice the "expected" values-free approach to management decision-making (Crane 2000).

However, how companies justify their CR actions influence management motivation, reinforce corporate values' (Steg et al. 2014) future CR positions, and influence the type of actions which are undertaken (Basu and Palazzo 2008). This is important in cross-cultural contexts, where a divide between different institutions, philosophies, and cultural values is often present (Barkema et al. 2015).

This disconnect between expectations and behaviour indicates that leaders understand the importance of moral principles, but in reality pragmatic CR remains a norm that is dominated by neo-classical economic thinking, influenced in turn by the pressures of short-term organisational priorities.

The following example shows an executive's perspective on CR as an institutional norm. After significant self-reflection, this executive found himself working in a different kind of business with a model that encourages the advancement of CR adoption.

Vignette 3: Advocating for a Different Kind of Business Model

> *For existing businesses to change their stripes, I think it's kind of hard .... we need to educate them (the next generation) about different kinds of business forms .... Nolan—executive*

Nolan had a very successful international career trajectory early in his career. He enjoys travelling and outdoor activities and has held various executive positions in companies with different CR orientations. After taking the helm of a multi-national organisation, he decided to make a drastic change to lead a much smaller regional co-operative.

The co-operative model has a business mandate that reaches far beyond profit maximisation. Co-ops are owned by customers and/or employees, who are invested in the firm's products and services. Community engagement and wellbeing are a key imperative for co-ops.

As Nolan reflected on his past corporate experience as an international business executive, he realised that he needed to shift careers into a different kind of company. He sought a role that focused on people and embraced sustainability and responsible practice, while still appreciating economic value. His belief was that business models which put shareholders first impede action on social and environmental challenges.

Nolan's passion for nature, coupled with the self-reflection on his life journey led him to find his true professional vocation—making a positive difference to climate change. His challenges with institutional barriers to CR propelled him to join firms which hold multiple business objectives: social, environmental and economic.

Nolan explained: "I feel strongly aligned with this organisation's purpose. It fits with me personally. I believe strongly in climate change and the influence of man on climate, it's never been a doubt for me."

Since joining his new co-op organisation, Nolan has taken an active role to build cross-industry collaborative platforms and encourage environmental stewardship innovation as he continues to lobby for regulatory reforms.

2.6 The Importance of Leaders' Values

Strategic Leadership Theory (SLT) explains how top managers' values, perceptions, and personalities affect their views and selective perception of information, and their interpretation of information (Cannella et al. 2009). Corporate strategy development, including its CR approach, is a deliberate and explicit process designed and executed by executives (Olie et al. 2012).

Executives structure their decision situations to fit their view of the world (Finkelstein and Hambrick 1990). Strategy and organisational outcomes are highly influenced by executives' values (Hemingway and MacLagan 2004) and, with businesses becoming more complex, strategic leaders' values hierarchy is increasing in salience (Carter and Greer 2013).

While senior leaders do influence the collective corporate value-orientation, organisations also exert influence effect on individual executives. Executives experience social influence from others on the top management team, creating a circle of reinforcement of personal, work, and organisational values (Chattopadhyay et al. 1999). Depending on the executives' value strength, they can either shape their organisational culture or be influenced by their organisational culture.

The following case study highlights how one executive's past corporate experience shaped his beliefs as a leader, leading to his view that positive culture is shaped by senior executives.

Vignette 4: Tone from the Top

> *We started at the top and making [our values] a priority ... we made it happen throughout the organisation. Not just by declaring this is the way of the world, [but acting] on it by hiring and firing .... Alex—executive*

Alex was brought up in organisations where positive culture and strong set of values were important in creating engagement and a sense of community. He attributed much of his personal growth to responsible leadership and his mentor-CEO when he was a young manager. Alex recalled with admiration how his mentor-CEO was the perfect example of an astute businessman who had integrity and also cared deeply for the community he operated in.

(continued)

Vignette 4: (continued)

These values are central to the mentor-CEO's value system. They were lived by in the organisation, and exemplified by its leader. Alex views CR as an important means to engage and contribute back to the communities in which his business operates. As he observed other competitors' misbehaviour through their poor treatment of customers and employees, Alex concluded that organisational culture is key to enabling ethical employee conduct and building lasting customer loyalty.

When he took the helm of a mid-sized firm, he decided to take his executives off-site and engage in conversations about personal values and what this meant in their work setting. He commented:

> *We had a very tough, three or four weeks of off-site, personal conversations about what we were trying to get out of it, what our personal lives are like, and a very strong commitment at the end, that we were in this together, that we were to make this place, the best place to work that any of us have ever been. And make sure our employees are part of that. ... that was the best thing I ever did.*

Alex built his management practice around a set of aligned values and made a deliberate effort to ensure the people they hired and retained shared the same set of values. He believes that good values start at the top and then proliferate throughout the organisation.

2.7 The Case Studies on How Values Influence Different Personal CR Adoption Practices

This qualitative and completed study is based on 20 executive cases located in Canada (Chow 2018), and it revealed three distinctive outcomes of the executives' values-to-action process: (1) Personal CR adoption, (2) Strategic and personal CR adoption, and (3) Transformational CR adoption.

2.7.1 Personal CR

Executives fitting the Personal CR adoption profile primarily channel CR where they have the most control of it—through their own behaviours. Yin (2017) found that leaders' influence on CR adoption is more significant when employee responsibility is at stake. Examples of Personal CR effort emerging from the interview data included support for employees' personal development through corporate education sponsorship, fair promotions, concern for employee wellbeing, and upholding ethical principles. These executives focus on their own personal behaviour that reflects their values of relationship, compassion, care, and ethics.

The following example shares an executive's early stage career CR experiences, formative values and how his experiences prompted him to develop empathy and provide support for his employees.

Vignette 5: The Value of Relationship

> *I've come to the belief that a lot of manager issues, performance issues, workplace issues are often rooted in the people, in the person, not necessarily a reflection of the organisation. … I try to be more sympathetic. … I try to be more open. I try to listen more. Riu—executive*

Riu recalled his upbringing as a child in Asia where some parents of high standing refuse to let their children take risks, and instead encourage them to follow traditional career paths, such as becoming a lawyer, doctor or engaging in other 'respectable' professions.

Jobs with such stability were widely viewed as a sign of success. Riu's work experience however was not so positive. He joined the finance industry after graduation and soon after encountered a toxic management relationship, where employees were not listened to and opinions went unvalued.

Riu was deeply unhappy and so decided to leave for a better company. Shortly after having spent some time with the new firm, he was laid off and became unemployed. This set-back was traumatic for someone in a society where status and stability are endearing social values.

His next career attempt to start-up his own business did not work out the way he wanted either, as he found himself constantly disagreeing with his business partners. As he reflected on his decision to leave the first firm, Riu lamented that perhaps, if he could manage his emotions more maturely, he could have avoided the job loss. Riu reflected on his journey and found that he needed to work on finding his purpose.

While he was still examining his professional goals, he reflected on a value that had become endearing to him—relationships. Because of his past negative manager-employee experiences, he recognised that developing positive relationships between managers and employees is of vital importance. To align his behaviour with his values, Riu explained that he now takes time to listen to his employees, and advocates for their career development.

(*continued*)

Vignette 5: (continued)

With regards other enterprise-level CR practices, Riu said: "I dug my heels in on people. I haven't dug my heels in on business. It's not worth it." Institutional norms and perceived business mandates appear to restrict what Riu could undertake.

Ultimately Riu did make a shift to work in a co-op business, where community engagement is valued and a longer-term approach is taken to building community-client relationships. For Riu, his goal is about finding happiness after years of career instability. The co-op business allows him to make a contribution to the greater good as part of a deliberate business mandate.

2.7.2 Strategic and Personal CR

Strategically-oriented CR executives carefully weigh the needs of different stakeholders, including shareholders within the business environment they lead. They seek to optimise and create a balanced outcome without compromising their ethical principles or financial outcomes.

By harbouring a long-term business horizon mindset, Strategic CR executives engage in Personal CR, such as employee development and relationship building. Because Strategic CR executives are still partly limited in their actions by a set of institutional CR adoption norms, in other words they still have to achieve long-term financial success, they align personal values with behaviours in the corporate context. This equates to complementing strategic CR efforts with their own Personal CR position. This observation is in line with studies which suggest that individuals will undertake compensatory actions for unsatisfied needs (Vogel et al. 2016), such as the need for purpose and for values congruence (Baumeister and Vohs 2001).

The following example offers a snapshot of an executive's formative years, and how he adopted a personal practice of care towards his employees. However, when it came to demonstrating environmental responsibility at an organisational level, he ensured that a business case approach was utilised.

Vignette 6: Strategic Rationality Required in Determining CR Investments

> *All of the initiatives that we have fall under one of three pillars ... people, customer and profit. we started a new leadership development program ... in learning. ... [For environmental investments it] isn't a choice of what you're going to do. It's a choice of when you're going to do it. I need to have more than just a benefit for the environment. As long as the business case is there [and] that the project pays for itself. Sign me up. Chung—executive*

Chung grew up in a rural part of Canada and came from a working-class family. Not being endowed with privileged access to a broader range of employment opportunities that many urban children tend to possess, Chung learned early in life that he had to work hard.

He undertook many different jobs in order to pay for his education. Because of Chung's humble background, he was unaware of hierarchy in organisations. Trained as an engineer, he made an extra effort to build employee relationship by walking the factory floor and learning about his people's lives.

When Chung became company President, he took pride in nurturing employee development. He worked hard to match talent with job roles, and invested in education and learning. He did not treat individuals as mere resources to be disposed when they no longer performed, but instead saw people with potential that needed to be nurtured.

However, when faced with environmental initiatives, Chung believes that a business case approach should be prioritised. Profits remain an important factor in sustainability and to him, CR investments should be strategic and yield a return. At the same time Chung agreed that profits, in an environmental sense, are not for the enrichment of shareholders and should be reinvested in the future.

While Chung's environmental CR orientation reflects strategic rationality, when it comes to people, his caring values appear to be influenced by his past experiences and upbringing.

2.7.3 Transformative CR

The final CR adoption profile is Transformative CR, reflecting what Dunphy et al. (2003) describe as "the sustaining corporation," where leaders see their corporations as a "self-renewing element of the society and its ecological context" (p. 17). CR reflects both the means and the end. For Transformative CR executives, profits are of equal importance to their social and environmental objectives. These executives choose a business context where they can align personal values with their organisational objectives and outcomes.

The following example highlights how one defining encounter prompted an executive to take actions that transformed his business, while continuing to make significant contributions to the environment and society.

Vignette 7: CR Becomes a Personal Conviction

> *I think that was really was my experience, you know in ... having the realisation that you can make a difference, and you can change ... otherwise [nothing] would be changed, had you not got involved and taken a stand. Sasha—executive*

Sasha retold the story when he noticed a pesticide placard on a lawn near his children's school as he was dropping them off at school. He thought to himself how terrible it was to have pesticide on lawns where children would be playing. The encounter prompted him to take action.

Sasha lobbied the municipal government to ban pesticide use in areas where children were playing. He created a green solution for his clients and urged them to take a leadership role by adopting pesticide-free products. It was an uneasy beginning as his clients were rather reluctant to switch, and there was no compelling business case to do so. But Sasha believes in the importance of environmental stewardship and his conviction was contagious.

Over time, clients were convinced to adopt environmentally-friendly products. Sasha's CR did not stop at green lawn care products. He further expanded his CR efforts into the community and employee engagement work. He believes that engaged employees are critically important for improved customer service and long-term performance.

As he expanded his community programs, he saw significant benefits in employee and customer satisfaction scores. Sasha also supports a number of philanthropic causes outside of work and believes that his involvement with the community stems from his past experiences.

He says: "I think I've developed a lot of empathy over the years as I had some challenging experiences." He lost his middle son in a car accident and he witnessed his father battling cancer. To him, it was through these trials that he built his values. And it is through empathy that he realised the importance of CR and how leaders have the responsibility to drive change.

Sasha adds: "I do think that it's senior executives in an organisation that need to be engaged and motivated to drive this type of activity." He believes CEOs' commitment and dedication is the foremost factor in driving CR activities and transforming businesses.

The participating executives in this study have all shared very different life stories. These include defining moments and reflections on their personal journeys, which have helped them arrive at different meanings and value systems.

While many of these executives share common value principles, such as integrity, transparency, care and empathy, their own personal values differ. The Transformative CR executive example demonstrated his personal conviction to environmental sustainability, making social contributions through employee engagement, and the importance of leadership in driving change. All of these factors were powerful motivators for both his business and personal transformation.

Conversely, for the Strategic CR executive, strategic rationality still governed the formulation of business goals and objectives. While he understands the importance of environmental stewardship, the benefits of such investments have to be justified. To align their personal values with actions, Strategic CR executives tend to engage in CR actions that are more employee-responsibility oriented.

Personal CR executives share many of these same value principles. However, perception of their role in leading change appears to be restricted by institutional norms and prescribed business mandates. Strong convictions held by Transformative CR executives are triggered by impressionable past events that raise their awareness of values conflict. Their values strength increases as a result.

The participating executives' defining moments and past experiences appear to strongly influence the type and strength of their values. This affects their world view and attitudes towards CR (Papagiannakis and Lioukas 2012). Some of these values turn into convictions that are articulated as personal missions, which in turn encourage a more Transformative CR effort.

2.8 Conclusion: Values-Based CR Is the Way Forward

Our individual values are by-products of unique personal experience, educational background (Mazutis 2013), socio-economic environment (Hofstede 1980), and upbringing (Huang 2013).

In the same way societal culture shapes individual values, organisational culture has been observed to influence individuals' values systems. Business objectives, priorities, structure, decision-making processes, policies, procedures, and incentive systems all play a part in this process (Pant and Lachman 1998; Grojean et al. 2004).

In a predominantly economically driven institutional culture, social and moral values are found to be downplayed or decoupled (Swanson 1999) as they translate from a societal context to an institutional one. Executives believe that personal values need to be set aside in order for them to advance their career (Lincoln et al. 1982).

This values "decoupling" puts a wedge between an organisation's formal structures and its practical needs and objectives. While an organisation may show concern about certain social challenges, and even have mission statements and procedures to back this up, unspoken rules and informal practice can hinder the manifestation of such values.

The prevalence of using a 'business case' to rationalise CR investments has become prevalent over the past two decades, highlighted by research which closely links CR and corporate financial performance (Orlitzky et al. 2003; Schreck 2011). This type of management rationale is a classic example of values decoupling. It limits opportunities for radical change, devalues the importance of these initiatives, and reduces CR responses to complex challenges into measurable management tasks that conform to current business practices yielding. In other words it yields little more than incremental and superficial change (Hahn et al. 2018).

If CR standards are to prove more than cosmetic, boards of directors and top executives must work diligently to examine every facet of the organisation's relationship with stakeholders and the environment. They should also adopt a values-based, forward-looking view of its impact and contribution.

The following questions must be considered by senior executives when a new or existing strategic initiative is under review:

1. Is what we are proposing to do fully compliant with our code of CR/ethical conduct?
2. Is there anything here that could be considered ethically objectionable?
3. Is this proposed action in harmony with our core values?
4. Are any conflicts or concerns evident?

The final litmus test for responsible strategy is 'can you confidently look into your children's eyes and share with them the implications of your strategy, vision and actions?'

The case studies highlighted in this chapter recognise different CR adoption practices, which are likely to be the result of different executives' upbringings and past experiences. Their formative values have been strengthened and brought into their consciousness through personal growth and reflexivity. These values also influence their attitudes towards CR, as well as their perceived business mandate.

The objective of this inquiry is not to judge the nobility of the individuals' stated value principles, or criticise the types of CR adoptions they have embraced. Rather, these findings reveal aspects of values that could yield enormous motivational power in driving transformative practice.

Convictions—values with strength—are formed as the result of personal challenges or traumatic events we encounter, as well as significant personal reflection over time. The stronger the values, the stronger the individual's belief in their ability to drive change without influence by external constraints.

Many of the participating executives recognise the importance of leadership values in influencing CR adoption, and the particular significance of ethical and moral value dimensions.

Executives' values set the tone for their organisations (Posner and Schmidt 1984), influence strategic decision-making (Cannella et al. 2009) and exert organisational influence on their employees' personal values (Finegan 1994). The vital link between executives' values and CR adoption should not be overlooked. Management values need to be integrated into all levels of further and higher education. Personal reflexivity and immersive experiential learning should be championed to help strengthen and raise awareness of individuals' values. This personal growth process is an important driver for positive change.

References

Abelson, Robert. "Conviction." *American Psychologist* 43, no. 4 (1988): 267–275.

Ackoff, Russell. "On Learning and the Systems that Facilitate It." *Reflections: The SoL Journal* 1, no. 1 (1999): 14–24.

Alteer, Ahmed M., Sofri B. Yahya, and Md H. Haron. "Auditors' Personal Values and Ethical Judgement at Different Levels of Ethical Climate: A Conceptual Link." *Journal of Asian Scientific Research* 3, no. 8 (2013): 862–875.

Bansal, Pratima. "From Issues to Actions: The Importance of Individual Concerns and Organizational Values in Responding to Natural Environmental Issues." *Organization Science* 14, no. 5 (2003): 510–527.

Bardi, Anat, and Shalom Schwartz. "Values and Behaviour: Strengths and Structure of Relations." *Society for Personality and Social Psychology* 29, no. 1 (2003): 1207–1220.

Barkema, Harry, Xiao-Ping Chen, G. Gerard George, Y. Yadong Luo, and Anne Tsui. "West Meets East: New Concepts and Theories." *Academy of Management Journal* 58, no. 2 (2015): 460–479.

Basu, Kunal, and Guido Palazzo. "Corporate Social Responsibility: A Process Model of Sensemaking." *The Academy of Management Review* 33, no. 1(2008): 122–136.

Bauman, Zygmunt. *Times, Liquid. "Living in an Age of Uncertainty".* (Cambridge: Polity, 2007).

Baumeister, Roy F., and Kathleen D. Vohs. "The Pursuit of Meaningfulness in Life," in *Handbook of Positive Psychology*, eds. Charles R. Snyder and Shane J. Lopez. (Oxford University Press, 2001), 608–618.

Berle, Adolf A. "For Whom Corporate Managers are Trustees: A Note." *Harvard Law Review* 45, no. 8 (1932): 1365–1372.

Besio, Cristina, and Andrea Pronzini. "Morality, Ethics, and Values Outside and Inside Organizations: An Example of the Discourse on Climate Change." *Journal of Business Ethics* 119, no. 3 (2014): 287–300.

Bollier, David, Stephanie Weiss, and Kirk O. Hanson. "Merck & Co., Inc.(A)." *Business Enterprise Trust* (1991).

Bruyaka, Olga, Hanko K. Zeitzmann, Isabelle Chalamon, Richard E. Wokutch, and Pooja Thakur. "Strategic Corporate Social Responsibility and Orphan Drug Development: Insights from the US and the EU Biopharmaceutical Industry." *Journal of Business Ethics* 117, no. 1 (2013): 45–65.

Cannella, Bert, Sydney Finkelstein, and Donald C. Hambrick. *Strategic leadership: Theory and research on executives, top management teams, and boards.* New York: Oxford University, 2009.

Carroll, Archie B. "A Three-Dimensional Conceptual Model of Corporate Performance". *Academy of Management Review* 4, no. 4 (1979): 497–505.

Carter, Suzanne M., and Charles R. Greer. "Strategic Leadership: Values, Styles, and Organizational Performance." *Journal of Leadership & Organizational Studies* 20, no. 4 (2013): 375–393.

Chattopadhyay, Prithviraj, William H. Glick, C. Chet Miller, and George P. Huber. "Determinants of Executive Beliefs: Comparing Functional Conditioning and Social Influence." *Strategic Management Journal* 20, no. 8 (1999): 763–790.

Chow, Candice. "The Influence of Executives' Values on Corporate Responsibility Adoption" (DBA thesis, Henley Business School, 2018).

Colbert, B., D. Wheeler, and R. E. Freeman. "Focusing on Value: Reconciling Corporate Social Responsibility, Stakeholder Theory and Sustainability in a Network World." *Journal of General Management* 28, no. 3 (2003): 1–28.

Crane, Andrew. "Corporate Greening as Amoralization." *Organization Studies (Walter de Gruyter GmbH & Co. KG.)* 21 no. 4 (2000): 673.

Dickson, Marcus W., D. Brent Smith, Michael W. Grojean, and Mark Ehrhart. "An Organizational Climate Regarding Ethics: The Outcome of Leader Values and the Practices that Reflect Them." *The Leadership Quarterly* 12, no. 2 (2001): 197–217.

Ditlev-Simonsen, Caroline D., and Atle Midttun. "What Motivates Managers to Pursue Corporate Responsibility? A Survey Among Key Stakeholders." *Corporate Social Responsibility and Environmental Management* 18, no. 1 (2011): 25–38.

Dodd Jr., E. Merrick. "For Whom are Corporate Managers Trustees." *Harvard Law Review* 45 (1931): 1145.

Donaldson, Thomas. *Corporations and Morality*. Englewood Cliffs, NJ: Prentice-Hall, 1982.

Dunphy, Dexter, Suzanne Benn, and Andrew Griffiths. "Setting the Agenda for Corporate Sustainability," in *Organizational change for corporate sustainability*, eds. Suzanne Benn, Melissa Edwards, and Tim Williams. (London: Routledge, 2003).

Elizur, Dov, and Abraham Sagie. "Facets of Personal Values: A Structural Analysis of Life and Work Values." *Applied Psychology* 48, no. 1 (1999): 73–87.

England, George W. "Personal Value Systems of American Managers." *Academy of Management Journal* 10, no. 1 (1967): 53–68.

Ewin, Robert E. "The Moral Status of the Corporation." *Journal of Business Ethics* 10, no. 10 (1991): 749–756.

Fassin, Yves. "The Reasons Behind Non-ethical Behaviour in Business and Entrepreneurship." *Journal of Business Ethics* 60, no. 3 (2005): 265–279.

Finkelstein, Sydney, and Donald C. Hambrick. "Top-Management-Team Tenure and Organizational Outcomes: The Moderating Role of Managerial Discretion." *Administrative Science Quarterly* 35 (1990): 484–503.

Finegan, Joan. "The Impact of Personal Values on Judgments of Ethical Behaviour in the Workplace." *Journal of Business Ethics* 13, no. 9 (1994): 747–755.

Friedman, Milton. "The Social Responsibility of Business is to Increase Its Profits." *The New York Times*, September 13, 1970.

Ghoshal, Sumantra. "Bad Management Theories are Destroying Good Management Practices." *Academy of Management Learning & Education* 4, no. 1 (2005): 75–91.

Giddens, Anthony. *The Constitution of Theory*. (Los Angeles: University of California Press, 1984).

Goodpaster, Kenneth E., and John B. Matthews. "Can a Corporation have a Conscience." *Harvard Business Review* 60, no. 1 (1982): 132–141.

Gorlin, Euginia I., and Reinier Schuur. "Nurturing Our Better Nature: A Proposal for Cognitive Integrity as a Foundation for Autonomous Living." *Behavior Genetics* 49 no. 2 (2019): 154–169.

Grojean, Michael W., Christian J. Resick, Marcus W. Dickson, and D. Brent Smith. "Leaders, Values, and Organizational Climate: Examining Leadership Strategies for Establishing an Organizational Climate Regarding Ethics." *Journal of Business Ethics* 55, no. 3 (2004): 223–241.

Hahn, Tobias, Frank Figge, Jonatan Pinkse, and Lutz Preuss. "A Paradox Perspective on Corporate Sustainability: Descriptive, Instrumental, and Normative Aspects." *Journal of Business Ethics* 148, no. 2 (2018): 235–248.

Hambrick, Donald C., and Phyllis A. Mason. "Upper Echelons: The Organization as a Reflection of Its Top Managers." *Academy of Management Review* 9, no. 2 (1984): 193–206.

Hambrick, Donald C., Sydney Finkelstein, and Ann C. Mooney. "Executive Job Demands: New Insights for Explaining Strategic Decisions and Leader Behaviors." *Academy of Management Review* 30, no. 3 (2005): 472–491.

Hartman, Laura P., Patricia H. Werhane, Cynthia E. Clark, Craig V. Vansandt, and Mukesh Sud. "Strategic Global Strategy: The Intersection of General Principles, Corporate Responsibility and Economic Value-Added." *Business and Society Review* 122, no. 1 (2017): 71–91.

Hemingway, Christine A., and Patrick W. Maclagan. "Managers' Personal Values as Drivers of Corporate Social Responsibility." *Journal of Business Ethics* 50, no. 1 (2004): 33–44.

Hitlin, Steven. "Values as the Core of Personal Identity: Drawing Links between Two Theories of Self." *Social Psychology Quarterly* (2003): 118–137.

Hlady-Rispal, Martine, and Vinciane Servantie. "Deconstructing the Way in Which Value is Created in the Context of Social Entrepreneurship." *International Journal of Management Reviews* 20, no. 1 (2018): 62–80.
Hofstede, Geert. "Culture and Organizations." *International Studies of Management & Organization* 10, no. 4 (1980): 15–41.
Hollensbe, Elaine, Charles Wookey, Loughlin Hickey, Gerard George, and Cardinal Vincent Nichols. "Organizations with Purpose." *Academy of Management Journal* 57, no. 5 (2014): 1227–1234.
Huang, Shihping Kevin. "The Impact of CEO Characteristics on Corporate Sustainable Development." *Corporate Social Responsibility and Environmental Management* 20, no. 4 (2013): 234–244.
Kakabadse, Nada K., Cécile Rozuel, and Andrew Kakabadse. "Environment: Who is Responsible and How to Govern It?" in *Corporate Social Responsibility Reconciling Aspiration with Application*, eds. Andrew Kakabadse and Mette Morsing. (New York: Palgrave Macmillan, 2006).
Kluckhohn, Clyde. "The Scientific Study of Values," in *University of Toronto Installation Lectures: 3 lectures*, eds. Kluckhohn Frye and Wigglesworth. (Toronto: University of Toronto Press, 1958).
Kluckhohn, Florence R., and Fred L. Strodtbeck. *Variations in Value Orientations.* (Row, Peterson & Co, 1961).
Lincoln, Douglas J., Milton M. Pressley, and Taylor Little. "Ethical Beliefs and Personal Values of Top Level Executives." *Journal of Business Research* 10, no. 4 (1982): 475–487.
Locke, Edwin A. "Goal Theory vs. Control theory: Contrasting Approaches to Understanding Work Motivation." *Motivation and Emotion* 15, no. 1 (1991): 9–28.
Maio, Gregory, Lindsay Allen, and Mark M. Bernard. "Addressing Discrepancies between Values and Behavior: The Motivating Effect of Reasons." *Journal of Experimental Social Psychology* 37, no. 2 (2001): 104–117
Mazutis, Daina D. "The CEO Effect: A Longitudinal, Multilevel Analysis of the Relationship between Executive Orientation and Corporate Social Strategy." *Business & Society* 52, no. 4 (2013): 631–648.
McWilliams, Abagail, and Donald Siegel. "Corporate Social Responsibility: A Theory of the Firm Perspective." *Academy of Management Review* 26, no. 1 (2001): 117–127.
Meglino, Bruce M., and Elizabeth C. Ravlin. "Individual Values in Organizations: Concepts, Controversies, and Research." *Journal of Management* 24, no. 3 (1998): 351–389.

Melé, Domènec, and Manuel Guillén Parra. "Intellectual Evolution of Strategic Management and Its Relationship with Ethics and Social Responsibility." Working Paper, IESE Business School, 2006.

Olie, René, Ad van Iterson, and Zeki Simsek. "When do CEOs versus Top Management Teams Matter in Explaining Strategic Decision-Making Processes? Toward an Institutional View of Strategic Leadership Effects." *International Studies of Management & Organization* 42, no. 4 (2012): 86–105.

Orlitzky, Marc, Frank L. Schmidt, and Sara L. Rynes. "Corporate Social and Financial Performance: A Meta-Analysis." *Organization Studies* 24, no. 3 (2003): 403–441.

Pant, P. Narayan, and Ran Lachman. "Value Incongruity and Strategic Choice." *Journal of Management Studies* 35, no. 2 (1998): 195–212.

Papagiannakis, Giorgos, and Spyros Lioukas. "Values, Attitudes and Perceptions of Managers as Predictors of Corporate Environmental Responsiveness." *Journal of Environmental Management* 100 (2012): 41–51.

Posner, Barry Z. "Another Look at the Impact of Personal and Organizational Values Congruency." *Journal of Business Ethics* 97, no. 4 (2010): 535–541.

Posner, Barry Z., and Warren H. Schmidt. "Values and the American Manager: An Update." *California Management Review* 26, no. 3 (1984): 202–216.

Rokeach, Milton. *The Nature of Human Values.* (New York: The Free Press and Collier Macmillan, 1973).

Schreck, Philipp. "Reviewing the Business Case for Corporate Social Responsibility: New Evidence and Analysis." *Journal of Business Ethics* 103, no. 2 (2011): 167.

Schwartz, Shalom H., and Wolfgang Bilsky. "Toward a Universal Psychological Structure of Human Values." *Journal of Personality and Social Psychology* 53, no. 3 (1987): 550.

Schwartz, Shalom H. "An Overview of the Schwartz Theory of Basic Values." *Online Readings in Psychology and Culture* 2, no. 1 (2012): 1–20. https://doi.org/10.9707/2307-0919.1116.

Schwartz, Shalom H. "Are There Universal Aspects in the Structure and Contents of Human Values?." *Journal of Social Issues* 50, no. 4 (1994): 19–45.

Schwartz, Shalom H., Jan Cieciuch, Michele Vecchione, Claudio Torres, Ozlem Dirilen-Gumus, and Tania Butenko. "Value Tradeoffs Propel and Inhibit Behavior: Validating the 19 Refined Values in Four Countries." *European Journal of Social Psychology* 47, no. 3 (2017): 241–258.

Simon, Charles. *Building a Successful Voluntary Culture.* (Vermont: J.L. Publishing, 2009).

Singhapakdi, Anusorn, and Scott J. Vitell. "Personal and Professional Values Underlying the Ethical Judgments of Marketers." *Journal of Business Ethics* 12, no. 7 (1993): 525–533.

Steg, Linda, Jan Willem Bolderdijk, Kees Keizer, and Goda Perlaviciute. "An Integrated Framework for Encouraging Pro-environmental Behaviour: The Role of Values, Situational Factors and Goals." *Journal of Environmental psychology* 38 (2014): 104–115.

Sturm, Rachel E. "Decreasing Unethical Decisions: The Role of Morality-Based Individual Differences." *Journal of Business Ethics* 142, no. 1 (2017): 37–57.

Swanson, Diane L. "Toward an Integrative Theory of Business and Society: A Research Strategy for Corporate Social Performance." *Academy of Management Review* 24, no. 3 (1999): 506–521.

Tenbrunsel, Ann E., and Kristin Smith-Crowe. "13 Ethical Decision Making: Where We've Been and Where We're Going." *The Academy of Management Annals* 2, no. 1 (2008): 545–607.

"The Global Wealth Report 2019". Credit SUISSE. Accessed October 30, 2019, https://www.credit-suisse.com/about-us/en/reports-research/global-wealth-report.html.

Trevino, Linda Klebe. "Ethical Decision Making in Organizations: A Person-Situation Interactionist Model." *Academy of Management Review* 11, no. 3 (1986): 601–617.

Van Marrewijk, Marcel, and Marco Werre. "Multiple Levels of Corporate Sustainability." *Journal of Business Ethics* 44, no. 2–3 (2003): 107–119.

Verplanken, Bas, and Rob W. Holland. "Motivated Decision Making: Effects of Activation and Self-Centrality of Values on Choices and Behavior." *Journal of Personality and Social Psychology* 82, no. 3 (2002): 434.

Vogel, Ryan M., Jessica B. Rodell, and John W. Lynch. "Engaged and Productive Misfits: How Job Crafting and Leisure Activity Mitigate the Negative Effects of Value Incongruence." *Academy of Management Journal* 59, no. 5 (2016): 1561–1584.

Waddock, Sandra. "Integrity and Mindfulness: Foundations of Corporate Citizenship." *Journal of Corporate Citizenship* 1 (2001): 25–37.

Waldman, David A., and Donald Siegel. "Defining the Socially Responsible Leader." *The Leadership Quarterly* 19, no. 1 (2008): 117–131.

Wiener, Yoash. "Commitment in Organizations: A Normative View." *Academy of Management Review* 7, no. 3 (1982): 418–428.

Woodward, Ian, and Samah Shaffakat. "Understanding Values for Insightfully Aware Leadership." *INSEAD Working Papers Collection, no. 2016/05/OBH*, 2016, pp. 1–58.

Yin, Juelin. "Institutional Drivers for Corporate Social Responsibility in an Emerging Economy: A Mixed-Method Study of Chinese Business Executives." *Business & Society* 56, no. 5 (2017): 672–704.

3

The Value of Philanthropy: Some Economic and Ethical Perspectives from Adam Smith to the Post-World War II Era

Atle Andreassen Raa

3.1 Introduction

Corporate Social Responsibility (CSR) is regarded as an important business practice that assists in obtaining the Sustainable Development Goals. This chapter contributes to a discussion of the value of philanthropy as a part of CSR (Carroll 2008). Philanthropy, however, is not always regarded as the best way of practicing CSR (Levy 2002). It has been said to be paternalistic, which results in recipients becoming dependent on the donors, and therefore more helpless in controlling their own lives. Archie B. Carroll called it "the icing of the cake" in his metaphorical CSR pyramid (Carroll 1991). To do good came as an extra dimension on top of being profitable, obeying the law and following ethical obligations with regard to what is right and fair. Later the four categories were reduced to three, because philanthropy was collapsed into ethics (Carroll 2008).

A. A. Raa (✉)
Norwegian Business School, BI, Oslo, Norway

F. Farache et al. (eds.), *Values and Corporate Responsibility*, Palgrave Studies in Governance, Leadership and Responsibility,
https://doi.org/10.1007/978-3-030-52466-1_3

Still philanthropy need not only be charity or giving money and smaller gifts to others who are in acute need. It can be strategic, giving the company a better reputation and therefore a valuable tool for the companies. When someone gets a donation to help start up a firm, or a fishing-boat to give them the opportunity to feed themselves, this can be a great way to contribute to getting a better life. A capitalist society, with philanthropic instead of greedy companies, can make the whole market system more acceptable to people.

The relation between corporate philanthropy, CSR and sustainable development has changed over time and varies among countries as well. CSR has played a far less prominent role in the European welfare states than in the USA. There, the main part of CSR rested on the shoulders of corporations, because governments preferred less intervention in the private sector. But private philanthropy has been important in many countries. In fact, it can be difficult to draw up a line of demarcation between corporate and private philanthropy. Very often a businessman, who has become rich through his company, later in his life decides to share some of his money with others.

Not all studies see philanthropy as an inferior part of CSR. An interesting perspective on the value of corporate philanthropy can be found in von Schnurbein et al. 2016. They argue that corporate philanthropy has a special role to play outside of the classical CSR concept. Based on the economic, motivational, creative and moral characteristics of corporate philanthropy, the authors establish a clear distinction between the two concepts.

3.2 How to Define the Value of Philanthropy in Economic Theory?

Value is a multidimensional concept (Mooya 2016). We can speak of market or economic values, but also of spiritual and moral values. Many things are valuable to us without having a price. The classical economists in the nineteenth century meant that value was created by, and could be measured in, man-hours of work. Value was not identical with market price. The neoclassicals from the late nineteenth century explained value as subjective utility of the individual and regarded prices in competitive markets as a measure of these values. In our days, Amartya Sen, an outstanding economist who also refers to Adam Smith, emphasizes ethics as a part of economic theory (Sen 1977). The value of philanthropy has been said to increase because it develops mutual trust in the community (McKean 1975).

3.2.1 Overview of Economic and Ethical Perspectives on the Value of Philanthropy over the Last 250 Years

Philanthropy has been practiced for a long time throughout history. To what degree certain economic actions are valuable to individuals and the society is an important part of what economists study. Textbooks in main stream economics do not often take up CSR. The discourse of philanthropy is a bit different in CSR literature and economic theory. In the first, whether philanthropy is strategic enough for the company is often discussed. Theoretical economists look at this in a broader perspective. They see philanthropy as one way in which transactions that have consequences for resource allocation, macroeconomic activity levels, income distribution, and utility and happiness for the single member of the society can be achieved. Investigating how economists have defined and discussed philanthropy can give us a better understanding of its value, also in a CSR perspective. Table 3.1 gives an overview of different economic approaches to the value of philanthropy in economic theory.

3.3 Eighteenth Century–1870: Classical Political Economy

3.3.1 Adam Smith

In the early phases of the industrial revolution and capitalism one saw increasing poverty among many people in England. As a consequence of

Table 3.1 Economic and ethical perspectives on the value of philanthropy—overview of the three periods

Period	Central economists	Keywords	Value
Classical political economy—eighteenth and nineteenth century	Adam Smith Robert Malthus David Ricardo Jeremy Bentham John Stuart Mill	Self-interest The invisible hand Beneficence, sympathy, The impartial observer The law of population The iron law of wages Utilitarianism	Use and exchange value isolated Does income redistribution have value?
Neoclassical economics late nineteenth century to 1950	Henry Stanley Jevons Carl Menger Leon Walras Lionel Robbins	Economics as physics Subjective utility approach Homo economicus Pareto optimality Ordinal utility	Marginal utility as value Value in models of self-interest Value-free economics
Neoclassical and ethical economics 1950–1980	Kenneth Arrow Gary Becker Kenneth Boulding Edmund Phelps William Vickrey Amartya Sen	Interactive utility functions	The value of unselfish behavior Value in interactive utility functions

this, philanthropy became widely debated among economists and others in eighteenth-century England (Wootton 2018).

Landreth and Colander 1994, 68, stated that "*Adam Smith has often been called the father of economics*" and his *Wealth of Nations (WON)*, published in 1776 has been looked upon as the first modern economic textbook (Mooya 2016; Landreth and Colander 1994). In his book, Smith proposed that self-regulating markets (*the invisible hand*) would bring about the maximum good for society. Since then, Smith's view has had relevance for how economists have interpreted philanthropy. He argued that when each person follows his or her private interests, this will also unintentionally realize the public good. Smith writes:

> It is not from the benevolence of the butcher, the brewer, or the baker, that we expect our dinner, but from regard to their own interest. We address

> ourselves, not to their humanity but to their self-love, and never talk to them of our own necessities but of their advantages. Nobody but a beggar chooses to depend chiefly upon the benevolence of his fellow citizens. (Smith 2004/1776, 12)

But 17 years before WON, he gave out his other famous book, *The Theory of Moral Sentiments (TMS)* (Smith 1976/1759). There he claimed that man has many motives, not only self-interestedness. He writes:

> *How selfish soever man may be supposed, there are evidently some principles in his nature, which interest him in the fortune of others, and render their happiness necessary to him, though he derives nothing from it except the pleasure of seeing it.* (Smith 1976/1759, 9)

It has been claimed that there is an apparent incongruity between TMS—which appears to recommend and endorse sympathy—and WON, which appears to recommend and endorse selfishness (McLean 2006). In TMS, we see that Smith believed that people would often naturally offer a helping hand to those who needed it (Otteson 2013).

We can easily be a bit confused about to what degree Adam Smith valued philanthropic acts. A closer study of the relation between economics, self-interest and morality in his works can help us in explaining how he valued philanthropy. Smith's principle of sympathy seems to imply that he values altruistic acts very much. The use of the phrasing 'the pleasure' implies that Smith presents a moral and psychological explanation for why we act ethically and that philanthropy also has value for the donor.

How did Smith explain our non-egoistic motives? According to him, our faculty of sympathy was not in itself strategic, and he distanced himself from the egocentric explanation of his time, inspired by Thomas Hobbes' writings (Khalil 2001). Smith meant that self-interest (*virtue of prudence*) and interest in others (*virtues of beneficence*) came from the same source but differed in degree. Sympathy for oneself is very high, and for others its relative intensity is proportional with proximity-related factors.

This social proximity is analogous to genetic proximity, the inclusive fitness hypothesis that we will address below. The value of philanthropy is higher for the donor if the recipient of the donation is socially closer to the donor. And Smith did not view beneficence as rooted in any moral dictum, maxim or canon of duty. This is not what will give value to the donor, according to Smith. It always has to be voluntary and never forced upon one (Smith 1976/1759).

The core of his argument is that we are impartial and reflective spectators who are acting from another (what he calls) 'station' in a role that examines and judges our own acts. Sympathy is stronger when others are close to us. Then the value to the donor will be higher. We do not see things only from the other person's 'station' either, because that would mean that we fully adopt the needs of others, while at the same time dismissing our own needs and wants as illegitimate, immoral and selfish (Smith 1976/1759, III.3).

3.3.2 Thomas Robert Malthus

More critical to philanthropy was the economist and clergyman, Thomas Robert Malthus (1766–1834). He argued that an increase in relief for the poor would fail to have any benefits (Backhouse 2004). The relatively young Malthus got into a dispute with his father about improving the conditions of average families in England. From the son's famous *Essay on population from 1798*, man had to live on a subsistence level, procreating during good times and starving during the bad. An improvement of their income level would result in more children and as a result of that people would fall again to the subsistence level of income. Human betterment therefore was impossible; poverty and misery were inevitable for the majority of people in every society. So, from this economist's view, it seems that philanthropy has little value for the recipient and the society.

3.3.3 David Ricardo, Jeremy Bentham and John Stuart Mill

The classical period lasted till around 1870. Malthus' view on subsistence wage as the highest possible for workers was dealt by his colleague and friend, David Ricardo, because of the harsh competition for jobs among workers (*iron law of wages*—Ricardo 2004/1817).

But as classical economy became influenced by the utilitarian philosophy of Jeremy Bentham (1748–1832) and John Stuart Mill (1806–1873), views changed. Bentham believed that a society should maximize happiness for all of its members, also by redistributing income. Mill took in many matters a middle course between Smith and Malthus and went far towards social capitalism, where income distribution was a political matter that could not uniquely be decided by the market forces. He put more emphasis on the value of equality, also for women (Pressman 2014). He became a spokesman for an ethically informed economy and objected strongly to the relative powerlessness of the workers (Galbraith 1987).

The value of philanthropy in the period of classical economy from Adam Smith till about 1870 is attached to the naturalist political idea of a free and rational individual against the medieval religious governed men and the economic ideas of the unregulated markets against mercantilism. Ideas and beliefs (Zeitgeist) in this period reflected this. People to a large extent had to master their own faith, and not to any large degree rely on support from the authorities and their fellow men.

3.4 1870–1950: Utilitarianism and Neoclassical Economics

3.4.1 Background

In the end of the nineteenth century, we had come to the age of the Second Industrial Revolution, when national income in many countries grew, technology became more advanced and workers' organizations and people's movements grew stronger. From about 1870, mainstream economic theory changed from classical to a neoclassical tradition. We saw more rivalry between political and economic ideas, especially between conservatives and socialists. The labour and cost-based value theory of the classical political economists was replaced by a subjectivist utility and preference-based value thinking. A good service had its value decided by a subjective feeling of utility from the individual who consumed it. Marginal utility of consuming was falling when people consumed more of a product, and marginal utility of income for people was also falling. Value was linked to the utility of, and demand for, the marginal or last unit of a good.

3.4.2 Henry Stanley Jevons (1835–1882), Carl Menger (1840–1921) and Leon Walras (1834–1910)

The marginalist revolution was a discovery made independently by these three persons from England, Austria and France (Pressman 2014). Neoclassical economics had its roots in Adam Smith's invisible hand and was based on laissez-faire, but his idea regarding sympathy from TMS in 1759 was not included. Neoclassical economics was based on methodological individualism, formal reasoning by mathematics and the utilitarian philosophy of nineteenth-century philosophers mentioned above. Jevons was inspired by physics in his analysis of the economy (Pressman 2014). With the help of mathematics, based on profit maximization and individual utility maximization, Leon Walras tried to prove that Adam Smith's metaphor of the invisible hand or market forces could lead to an equilibrium with the optimal economic situation for the society. The consequences were that the neoclassicals strongly supported the idea of a *homo economicus,* acting on self-interest, and tended to assume away many of the social and moral aspects of economic life. The economic policy recommendations were still Adam Smith's invisible hand, but without his reflections on ethics.

3.4.3 Lionel Robbins (1898–1984) Dissociation of Economics and Ethics

Jevons and some other early marginalists believed in *cardinal utility*, which implied that utility could be measured by a number, and therefore one could still make interpersonal utility comparisons. Later this approach was replaced by an *ordinal utility* approach (Pressman 2014). The influence of Pareto-optimality and ordinal utility coincided with the view that interpersonal comparison of utility was not feasible. This also crowded out evaluations on the value of philanthropy in the neoclassical models. According to the influential British neoclassical economist, Lionel Robbins, it was necessary to dissociate economics and ethics (Fontaine 2007). Welfare in neoclassical economy was based on the isolated individual's utility maximization and on Pareto-optimality, where income distribution became defined away from the models. Economic analysis was now supposed to be neutral and value free.

3.5 After World War II: Incorporating Unselfish Behavior into Economic Theory

3.5.1 Growing Interest in Philanthropy in the USA in the 1950s

After World War II, politicians in the USA started to be interested in philanthropy due to tax questions (Madrakhimova 2013). The tax status of private foundations had come under attack for misuse of money. In the early 1960s, an inquiry into grantmaking of those foundations was launched, and this led economists to engage themselves in the issue (Fontaine 2007). This political and institutional process led to new perspectives among theoretical economists. Philanthropy was attached to how income distribution could influence the economic system, and the assumption of the self-interested '*homo economicus*' found itself challenged. It was also studied as a part of public finance questions (Vickrey 1975). Economists started to construct mathematical formalized utility functions, which included the attributes of other people (Schwartz 1970; Becker 1974). In the early 1960s, a handful of economists articulated views on philanthropy (Fontaine 2007). They played a pioneering role in overcoming the limitations imposed by economists' earlier concentration on selfish motives when analyzing human behavior.

Utility functions that also include the utility of others had not been completely ignored by neoclassical economists like A. C Pigou (1877–1959) and Irving Fisher (1867–1947), but previously nothing had been done with it (Becker 1974). Emphasis on utility interactions, however, had been common at a far earlier point in the work of Thorstein Veblen (1857–1929), a more heterodox and sociologically oriented economist (Sandmo 2011). Veblen rejected the idea of the rational man early on and strongly criticized neoclassical economy in his time (Pressman 2014).

3.5.2 Kenneth Boulding (1910-93), Gary Becker (1930-2014) and Edmund Phelps (1933-)

Three works played a central role in the new interest among economist in unselfishness after World War II (Fontaine 2007). They were Kenneth Boulding's *The Economy of Love and Fear (*Boulding 1973*)*, Gary S. Becker's *A Theory of Social Interactions (*Becker 1974*)* and Edmund S. Phelps' *Altruism, Morality, and Economic Theory* (Phelps 1975). To some extent, this could be seen as a view that brought one back to ethics in economics, but the neoclassical approach to the value on philanthropy in this period was different from the earlier moral approach of Adam Smith.

Becker's view on interactive consumer functions was more egocentric than Smith's. He assumed that giving away money gives the donor negative utility but is offset against his pleasure (value) of seeing the other getting more utility. Boulding studied the economics of grants and public choice and saw philanthropy in light of empathetic identification (Boulding 1973). Edmund Phelps's Altruism, Morality, and Economic theory (Phelps 1975) has often been greeted as instrumental in the upswing of interest in unselfishness. Phelps regarded the "economics of altruism" as another effort in the extension of the domain of economics. He was one of many economists that (from observing the economic development at that time) had been become more critical to classical liberalism and the neoclassical invisible hand theory. About ten years before, Mancur Olson argued that the invisible hand had severe limits (Mancur

Olson 1965). Some economists argued that the invisible hand theory without Smith's moral ideas in TMS was wrong (Stovall et al. 2004).

3.6 The Theories Behind Interactive Utility Functions in the 1960s and 1970s

The rest of this chapter shows how some of the economists have explained the individual's interest in other persons' welfare, instead of only self-interest. Table 3.2 above gives an overview of the different explanations.

3.6.1 Kenneth Arrow (1921–2017): Implicit Social Contracts

The neoclassical Nobel Prize laureate in economics, Kenneth Arrow, proposed a positive relation, one of altruism rather than envy among people. He thought that the welfare of each individual depends not only on the utilities of himself and others, but also on his contributions to the utility of others (Arrow 1975, 17). Each individual is in some ultimate case motivated by pure egoistic satisfaction derived for the good accruing to him, such that each performs duties for the other in a way calculated to

Table 3.2 Theories of why utility function are interactive

Theory	Central economists	What determines utility from philanthropy
Implicit social contracts	Kenneth Arrow	Altruism rather than envy
Game theoretical approach	Robert Axelrod	Tit-for-tat dynamics
Behavior theory	Bruce Bolnick	Social psychology. Avoid mental discomfort
Social and biological relations	Adam Smith (1759) Daniel Friedman David Wilson	Increasing utility with social or biological proximity
Ethical perspectives Commitment	Amartya Sen	Second-order preferences take precedence over first-order preferences (desired self-identity)

enhance satisfaction for all. The value or satisfaction is what the donor gets from seeing that others increase their welfare, but also from the fact that s/he donates to an anonymous recipient, for instance as in the case of blood donations.

Arrow remarks that the third hypothesis is in the spirit of the philosopher Immanuel Kant's *categorical imperative* or the philosopher John Rawls view in his theory of justice. Arrow adds that, in real life, emphasis must be put on the *implicit nature of the social contract. H*e writes:

> *One gives good things, such as blood in exchange from a generalized obligation on the part of fellow men to help in other circumstances if needed.* (Arrow 1975, 18)

3.6.2 Robert M. Axelrod (1943–): Game Theoretical Approach

A game theoretical approach claims that altruism is not always behind philanthropy and explains the value of altruism in a game theoretical perspective with 'greedy actors'. In a repetitive game, tit for tat is usual. Many economists quote the political scientist work about cooperation here (Axelrod 1981). Altruism is seen as a kind of equivalent retribution. We learn to act with generosity because this can give us value later. People often act in ways that would be consonant with altruistic motivations, and businesses do engage in philanthropy, but this may equally well arise rather from fairly specific trends that evolve from enlightened self-interest or public demand (Phelps 1975; Hammond 1975).

3.6.3 Bruce Bolnick: A Behavior Theory of Philanthropy

Economists have also explained the value of philanthropy for donors through social psychology (Bolnick 1975). Individuals donate in order to avoid the 'social costs' of noncompliance with the shared norms of their in-groups. It is the magnitude of the 'social costs' in question which determines the *implicit value* of donating. The higher the social cost of dereliction, the greater the value that will be ascribed to the potential philanthropic action in question. The opportunities for application of social pressure are better and the implicit value of philanthropy is higher for the donor (McKean 1975). If the contribution to helping the recipient is remarkable, the expectation from society can also be higher. If each individual's contribution is small, free riders are more common. To be philanthropic thus has lower implicit value.

Value is higher if donating comes under the heading of widespread acceptance of rules or traditions (McKean 1975). These rules can vary between cultures and arise from different variables, for instance religion. Very often they are backed in perceived gains to most persons, opportunity application and social pressure, for instance in small communities, where violating good traditions will be more noticed.

3.6.4 David Sloan Wilson (1949–): Social and Biological Relations

Biologists speak about inclusive fitness, individual selection and kin selection in order to explain philanthropy (Friedman 2008). David Wilson, an evolutionary biologist, argues that altruism exists, and that the biological mechanism of group selection is responsible. He attaches this to evolutionary thinking (Wilson 2015). He writes: *"Selfishness beats altruism within groups. Altruistic groups beat selfish groups"* (ibid., 71).

It has, on the other hand, been argued that Wilson promotes a strong form of pervasive altruism, which seems to be inconsistent with many economic phenomena (Robson 2017). Other economists, however, have pointed to social and psychological relationships in groups (Bolnick 1975). They argue that group mechanisms that lead to philanthropy exist to a larger degree in smaller groups, where the members more often seek satisfaction, gratification, self-identification, and pleasure from the others. It is strongest in primary groups, with face-to-face personal contact between the members. It can also be strong among colleagues, neighbors, affect-oriented groups, in which the relationship between members is the major object of group activity. Not all economists agreed with these group explanations in the 1970s (Bolnick 1975, 200).

3.6.5 Amartya Sen (1933–): Ethical and Moral Perspectives

Ethics among economists is usually described as stimulating fair play, common courtesy and lawfulness (Phelps 1975). Traditions and rules of etiquette arise in order to reduce external costs that we would otherwise inflict on each other. People tell their children that "honesty is the best policy" (McKean 1975, 31). According to Sandel (2013), market reasoning is incomplete without moral reasoning.

An early ethical approach to the understanding of the value of philanthropy after World War II came from the economist and Nobel Prize laureate, Amartya Sen. He criticized the behavioral foundations of neoclassical economics (Sen 1997). Sen also claims that Smith's famous "butcher and baker" passage of self-interest in WON is over-quoted. According to Sen, Adam Smith did not see the invisible hand:

> *as a microcosm of all economic activities, but just an example of a case of pure exchange of commodities for which the pursuit of self-interest entirely suffices as a motivation. But there are many other economic situations, where a broader motivation comes in.* (Sen 1997, 7–8)

Sen introduces the concept of *commitment*, which he defines as a situation where people in practice do things that are not in their true self-interest. He notes that people for instance wish to be environmentally friendly and will sort their trash even if they could have been lazy free riders. This is what we called second-order preferences. We may prefer lamb instead of vegetables at the restaurant, but still we choose a vegetarian menu, because we feel morally uneasy with the consumption of animals. Sen writes:

> *Commitment is of course closely connected with one's moral in a broad sense ... covering a variety of influences from religious to political, from the ill-understood to the well-argued.* (Sen 1977, 329)

According to Sen, commitment drives a wedge between personal choice and personal welfare, and much of the traditional economic theory relies on the identity of the two (ibid, 329). He characterizes people who always act in their own interest and from their one-side preferences as rational fools (ibid., Sen 1977, 336). Sen writes:

> *A person thus described may be 'rational' in the limited sense of revealing no inconsistences in his choice behavior, but if he has no use for this distinction between quite different concepts, he must be a bit of a fool. The purely economic man is indeed close to being a social moron.* (Ibid., 336)

Altruism is without doubt a significant factor in our lives, but it is impossible to distinguish between wisely needed concern for others, and enlightened self-interest, which recognizes that one collects rewards if one helps others (McKean 1975). We have to conclude that the value of philanthropy for the donor, the interactivity of the utility models, depends on many interrelated factors.

3.7 Summary and Conclusions

Philanthropy has been seen as a part of CSR but not always as the best way of practicing it. It has also been regarded as a unique strategy with high value for the companies. This chapter has discussed the value of philanthropy from a perspective of economic theory. This includes values of philanthropy for the donor, the recipients and for the society as a whole.

The father of modern economics, Adam Smith, in his *Wealth of Nations*, argued that following one's self-interest in business would create economic growth. In *The Theory of Moral Sentiments*, he also claimed that we are impartial and reflected spectators in the community, and therefore can feel sympathy with our fellow men. Smith saw beneficence as a virtue that contributes to a more sustainable market economy.

In the nineteenth century, there were different views on the redistribution of income from rich to poor among the classical political economists. According to Thomas Malthus and David Ricardo, the majority of the people of necessity had to live at a subsistence income level. Jeremy Bentham and John Stuart Mill were more positive to redistribution policy.

After the classical political economists, two main interpretations of Adam Smith's approach to market economy have influenced the economic theory of the value of philanthropy. One is his theory of the self-interested market actor (*homo economicus*), an assumption of the neoclassical models of utility, especially in the period from 1870 to around 1950. The ambition of the neoclassicals was to develop a value-free economy, as a superstructure of unregulated competitive markets and with self-interested actors. There was no room for ethics, and therefore valuing of philanthropy was missing in this approach.

After World War II, a critique of the assumptions of the self-interested or selfish actor in economic models led to the development of interactive utility functions in which the individuals also got utility or value from giving to others. Enlightened self-interest, game theory and social behavior were the explanations for this philanthropic orientation. Amartya Sen, in an Adam Smith tradition, saw economics and philanthropy in an ethical perspective.

We can understand the rise of CSR as a movement against global neoliberalism (Levy and Kaplan 2008). Neoliberalism coexisted with a shareholder approach in business with more weight on profits for the owners. The proposal of my chapter is that this represents a narrow interpretation of Adam Smith's invisible hand, one that lacks reference to his moral values. Adam Smith should, as a consequence, not be used as a defense for this type of capitalism.

The emphasis on profits for the owners led to a loss of legitimacy in the society for business, and the stakeholder approach, which purported that companies must take care of the interests of all parties affected by them, was strengthened. CSR has been defined as: *"rather broadly to include topics such as business ethics, community investments, environment, governance and accountability, human rights, marketplace, and workplace"* (Carroll

2008, 38). The proposal here is that this must to a greater extent be identified with the moral approach of Adam Smith to capitalism. Therefore, the conclusion of the chapter is that capitalism with CSR is more in harmony with him.

One of the reasons for writing this chapter is also my conviction that interaction between CSR analysis and economics will not only bring more plurality to economic theory, but also improve CSR analysis of the values of corporate and individual philanthropy. In that way it can also be useful for those who work practically in governments, businesses and idealistic organizations while benefitting donors, recipients and, in accordance with Adam Smith, the market economy and society in the short and long run.

References

Arrow, Kenneth J. 1975. 'Gifts and Exchanges'. In *Altruism, Morality, and Economic Theory*, ed. Edmund S. Phelps, 13–28. New York: Russell Sage Foundation.

Axelrod, Robert. 1981. 'The Emergence of Cooperation among Egoists'. *American Political Science Review* 75 (2): 306–18.

Backhouse, Roger. 2004. *The Penguin History of Economics*. London: Penguin Books.

Becker, Gary S. 1974. 'A Theory of Socal Interactions'. *Journal of Political Economy* 82 (6): 1063–93.

Bolnick, Bruce R. 1975. 'Toward a Behavioral Theory of Philanthropic Activity'. In *Altruism, Morality, and Economic Theory*, ed. Edmund S. Phelps, 197–223. New York: Russell Sage Foundation.

Boulding, Kenneth E. 1973. *The Economy of Love and Fear: A Preface to Grants Economics*. Belmont, CA: Wadsworth Publ. Co.

Carroll, Archie B. 1991. 'The Pyramid of Corporate Social Responsibility: Toward the Moral Management of Organizational Stakeholders'. *Business Horizons* 34 (4): 39–48.

Carroll, Archie B. 2008. 'A History of Corporate Social Responsibility. Concepts and Practices'. In *The Oxford Handbook of Corporate Social Responsibility*, ed. Andrew Crane, Dirk Matten, Abagail McWilliams, Jeremy Moon, and Donald S. Siegel, 19–46. Oxford: Oxford University Press.

Fontaine, Philippe. 2007. 'From Philanthropy to Altruism: Incorporating Unselfish Behavior into Economics, 1961–1975'. *History of Political Economy* 39 (1): 1–46.

Friedman, Daniel. 2008. *Morals and Markets*. New York: Palgrave Macmillan US.

Galbraith, John Kenneth. 1987. *A History of Economics: The Past as the Present*. London: H. Hamilton.

Hammond, Peter. 1975. 'Charity: Altruism or Cooperative Egoism?' In *Altruism, Morality, and Economic Theory*, ed. Edmund S. Phelps, 115–31. New York: Russell Sage Foundation.

Khalil, Elias L. 2001. 'Adam Smith and Three Theories of Altruism'. *Recherches économiques de Louvain* 67 (4): 421-435.

Landreth, Harry, and David C. Colander. 1994. *History of Economic Thought*. 3rd ed. Boston, MA: Houghton Mifflin.

Levy, David, and Rami Kaplan. 2008.'Corporate Social Responsibility and Theories of Global Governance: Strategic Contestation in Global Issue Arenas' In *The Oxford Handbook of Corporate Social Responsibility*, ed. Andrew Crane, Dirk Matten, Abagail McWilliams, Jeremy Moon, and Donald S. Siegel, 432–451. Oxford: Oxford University Press.

Levy, Neil. 2002. 'Against Philanthropy, Individual and Corporate'. *Business & Professional Ethics Journal* 21 (3/4): 95–108.

Madrakhimova, Firuza. 2013. 'History of Development of Corporate Social Responsibility'. *Journal of Business and Economics* 4 (6): 509–20.

McKean, Roland N. 1975. 'Economics of Trust, Altruism, and Corporate Social Responsibility.' In *Altruism, Morality, and Economic Theory*, ed. Edmund S. Phelps, 29–44. New York: Russell Sage Foundation.

McLean, Iain. 2006. *Adam Smith, Radical and Egalitarian: An Interpretation for the 21st Century*. Edinburgh: Edinburgh University Press.

Mooya, Manya M. 2016. 'Aristotle to Marshall: The Evolution of Economic Value Theory'. In *Real Estate Valuation Theory: A Critical Appraisal*, ed. Manya M. Mooya, 23–41. Berlin: Springer.

Olson, Mancur. 1965. *The Logic of Collective Action: Public Goods and the Theory of Groups*. Vol. 124. Harvard Economic Studies. Cambridge, MA: Harvard University Press.

Otteson, James R. 2013. *Adam Smith*. London: Bloomsbury Academic.

Phelps, Edmund S. 1975. 'Introduction'. In *Altruism, Morality, and Economic Theory*, ed. Edmund S. Phelps, 1–9. New York: Russell Sage Foundation.

Pressman, Steven. 2014. *Fifty Major Economists*. 3rd ed. Abingdon: Routledge.

Ricardo, David. 2004. *The Principles of Political Economy and Taxation*. Mineola, NY: Dover Publications. First published 1817.
Robson, Arthur J. 2017. 'Group Selection: A Review Essay on Does Altruism Exist? By David Sloan Wilson'. *Journal of Economic Literature* 55 (4): 1570–82.
Sandel, Michael J. 2013. *What Money Can't Buy: The Moral Limits of Markets*. New York: Farrar, Straus and Giroux.
Sandmo, Agnar. 2011. *Economics Evolving: A History of Economic Thought*. Princeton, NJ: Princeton University Press.
Schnurbein, Georg von, Peter Seele, and Irina Lock. 2016. 'Exclusive Corporate Philanthropy: Rethinking the Nexus of CSR and Corporate Philanthropy'. *Social Responsibility Journal* 12 (2): 280–94.
Schwartz, Robert A. 1970. 'Personal Philanthropic Contributions'. *Journal of Political Economy* 78 (6): 1264–91.
Sen, Amartya. 1997. 'Economics, Business Principles and Moral Sentiments'. *Business Ethics Quarterly* 7 (3): 5–15.
Sen, Amartya K. 1977. 'Rational Fools: A Critique of the Behavioral Foundations of Economic Theory'. *Philosophy & Public Affairs* 6 (4): 317–44.
Smith, Adam. 1976. *The Theory of Moral Sentiments*. Vol. 1. The Glasgow Edition of the Works and Correspondence of Adam Smith. Oxford: Clarendon Press. First published 1759.
Smith, Adam. 2004. *The Wealth of Nations*. New York: Barnes & Noble. First published 1776.
Stovall, O.S., Neill, J.D., and Perkins, D. 2004. 'Corporate Governance, Internal Decision Making, and the Invisible Hand'. *Journal of Business Ethics* 51: 221–27.
Vickrey, William. 1975. 'Private Philanthropy and Public Finance'. In *Altruism, Morality, and Economic Theory*, ed. Edmund S. Phelps, 149–69. New York: Russell Sage Foundation.
Wilson, David S. 2015. Does Altruism Exist?: Culture, Genes, and the Welfare of Others. New Haven: Yale University Press.
Wootton, David. 2018. Power, Pleasure, and Profit: Insatiable Appetites from Machiavelli to Madison. Cambridge, MA: Harvard University Press.

4

A Historical Approach to Understanding Values and Its Importance for Corporate Responsibility

Dušan Kučera

4.1 Introduction

Addressing the multi-layered issues of values in a neoliberal business environment must be set against the narrow focus on financial indicators and market position which many companies remain fixated on. In connection with business and capitalism, modern history has been characterized by the mistreatment of people across the globe, including industrial-scale slavery, the period of violent colonization, post-colonial injustices and the cruel and highly destructive exploitation of natural resources. Naturally, the concept of corporate values (Carroll 2009) has far-reaching implications. However, the phenomenon of values depends on relationships between people and business partners to promote long-term sustainability and success. The current post-financial crisis situation after 2008,

D. Kučera (✉)
Centre for Business Ethics at the University of Economics,
Prague, Czech Republic
e-mail: dusan.kucera@vse.cz

F. Farache et al. (eds.), *Values and Corporate Responsibility*, Palgrave Studies in Governance, Leadership and Responsibility,
https://doi.org/10.1007/978-3-030-52466-1_4

described by sociologists as 'the Great Regression' (Geiselberger 2017) is characterized by many social contradictions and consequences of the climate crises (Wackernagel and Kitzes 2019, Page 2006). In the corporate context, studies also talk about the 'crisis of capitalism' (Harvey 1996; Sarkar 2012) and associated dislocation, alienation and personal 'feeling of emptiness' (Petříček 1997). The challenges of CSR and sustainable business, therefore, is focused on several negative consequences of this capitalist crisis. Meeting those challenges has become integral to the UN's Sustainable Developments Goals which address the social impacts of poverty, hunger, wars, gender inequality, misuse of human recourses, corporate scandals, and the ecological footprint of the self-centred managerial decision-making processes (Sustainable Development Goals 2015). For a more in-depth analysis of this crisis, readers are encouraged to consult any critique of the development of neoliberal economic orthodoxy (see Crouzet 2001).

Although in recent decades, despite the fact that many firms have attempted to find an approach to CSR philosophy and sustainability that can be implemented in the organizational structures, managers operate within relentless competitive markets and shareholder pressure to make a financial profit is a central business priority (Calhoun 2015). The original ruthlessness of capitalism has not disappeared. In fact, daily examples from the East and West show how upholding empathetic and sustainable values against relentless neoliberal headwinds remains extremely problematic. For example, the US President, Donal Trump, uses crude and militant rhetoric when speaking about the economy. The wording of the American President today is similar to wording that generals used in times of war. We hear him talk about the 'weaponization of economic tools' (The Economist 2019), and he also uses expressions like 'national emergency', the 'threat to our nation', or 'economic arsenal'. Trump talks about how to 'compete', 'fight', 'press', 'beat and defeat American enemies'. Such language, I argue, undermines any serious or sustained attempt to assert moral values in business worlds or societies. We follow daily news reporting of America's trade wars with China and the European Union, we hear arguments for economic sanctions, and witness daily demonstrations and protests in European cities and growing numbers of victims of the unfolding crisis in capitalism from countless homeless to climate refugees to low paid, insecure 'gig economy' workers. On the South American continent, we note the economic collapse of Venezuela and its political consequences, the issues of deforestation and political divisions in Brazil, economic and political crises in Argentina, Chile, Cuba, and so on. We can add to this string of crises, the endless war in the Middle East, now spreading to African countries which are already struggling with poverty and climate change, and as a consequence we see a growing migrant crisis. The latest blow to the world economy is the consequence of the coronavirus (OECD 2020), which is likely to have emerged from depleted natural habitats and the numerous biohazards associated with wildlife trade, poaching and associated 'wet markets'. In the contexts of such global political and economic developments, we cannot ignore all the negative impacts and short- to long-term consequences of the international trade.

The question then is, how can 'values' be defined, understood and applied to a business context, given the magnitude and scope of the various crises of capitalism touched on here? Almost every year, fresh evidence of the irresponsible behaviour of companies following individual managerial scandals emerges. A few examples include the 2008 financial crises, pipeline, oil tanker and oil rig spills, such as Deep Horizon 2010, the nuclear disaster in Fukushima (IAEA 2015), and now the Coronavirus pandemic. I argue that disasters are often caused by indifference, and a disregard of principles, values and societal responsibilities. The same was true of the reported bank scandals and fraud in the automobile industry, which are always paid for by the consumer or citizen. As business ethics academics, we keep a yearly list of corporate scandals behind which there is conscious managerial irresponsibility (Akdeniz 2015). Thanks to the Czech origin of the author, this chapter examines dangerous recent trends and developments of capitalism within the CEE countries. This area belongs to the regions where there is an increased relativization of democratic values and state institutions, which are nonetheless retreating under various accusations of injustice, unfairness and immorality.

The above issues and crises relate to the intricate relationship between the business sphere and the principle value framework. These issues provide an impetus to explore the often-overlooked relationship between economics and philosophy, or the field of social sciences concerned with ethical and moral questions. In economics, it is well understood that there is often a tense relationship between stakeholders and shareholders. This tension depends on the extent to which managers' understanding of CSR is rooted in a moral values framework; that would be more likely to support and benefit society. Each geographic area has its unique economic history and particular understanding of value which must inform managerial decisions made. The fundamental law of cause and effect suggests that someone will ultimately pay for all the damage caused by irresponsible businesses. However, such consequences will not be ascribed to corporations alone, but to the broader society, and especially, to the poorer, vulnerable or disadvantages groups, who may suffer for many years to come. Whilst the profit is private, the cost is public (Bell 1996). Related damages to society also include as yet uncosted externalities of 'corporate values', seen in the destabilization of democratic structures (Levitsky and Ziblatt 2018), the phenomenal growth of private and public debt and the growth of societal risk (Habermas 1973; Beck 1992; Schreck 2017).

So, what is the role of an academic who teaches and researches business ethics? How can academics alert managers to their more significant social and natural responsibility, such that they are made aware of the consequences of their actions on generations?

4.2 Underestimating the Value Orientation

In this part, I will start by introducing the origins of CSR, by presenting the characteristics of the 'spirit of capitalism' as formulated by Max Weber (2003), and actualized for the current situation (Fleck 2012). According to Weber, the Western philosophy of capitalism was built on the value system of Protestant ethics. He illustrated that Christian society internally corresponds with Jewish, or other eastern philosophies of values we inherited. The spiritual background and its newly discovered competencies become the content of current analyses, and the search for solutions of managerial failures (Kučera 2015). Many problems link to the current 'relativization of values', which was accelerated by a modern and postmodern approach of thought. Many researchers critically analyse the so-called post-truth society to point to the negative consequences in the social area and business (Asghar 2012; D'Ancona 2017; Salmon 2018).

The claims for value orientation are related to the demands of management and shareholder value. If we want to understand our responsibility for maintaining the value system, we should grasp our position in a historical and social context. Especially for engineers, economists and technicians or students of such focused schools on CSR, we need to approach some critical milestones and challenges and thus complement current narrow professional educational programs (Thomas et al. 2014; Norman 2017).

4.2.1 Challenges of Renaissance

Here, I talk about the 'value orientation' because there were several fundamental shifts in the meaning of values in the first centuries after the onset of the Renaissance. At the time of the Renaissance (fourteenth–sixteenth century), the causes of the later division of economics from universal and societal values were born. During this period, Western thinking placed economic considerations as an integral part of human society and the church policy. In the Middle Ages, people believed that all that man did should serve the highest goals and ideals of Christianity, a contrast to the later division of economics from societal and spiritual values. We know that even in the Middle Ages there were 'contradictions' between ideals and realities. Let us remember the philosophy of cheating and manipulating written by Machiavelli (2010). However, such behaviour was identified as a sin by Christian confession, a misdeed or compromise with evil (Mansfield 1998).

The modern era, however, begins at the time of the ultimate loss of clerical credibility and the dismounting of the Church monopoly. Many thinkers began to look for a new conception of the world and the role of man in society. So, which are the main elements that undermined the philosophy of any social responsibility and sustainability? Typical features of the Renaissance include a concentration on man, human reason and earthly life (anthropocentrism). The Renaissance is related to the expansion of individualism and speculative thinking, which remains in direct tension with an emphasis on collectively understood social responsibility. The Renaissance development of realism and national identity also developed in tension with the borderless Christian conception of Europe under the authority of Rome and the Catholic Church.

4.2.2 Challenges of Reformation and Modern Philosophy

In German Reformation, Martin Luther freed man from the monopoly of the Roman Catholic Church and raised individual living and making decisions in society. However, in Protestantism (which Max Weber sees as the foundation of the spirit of capitalism) the thinking and behaviour of man was inspired by faith in universal values. In contrast to the Renaissance focus on people's individual needs (the mechanistic and horizontal dimension of decision-making), the Reformation adhered to a vertical dimension of values that distinguishes divisions between 'good' and 'evil', regardless our individual (subjective) opinions or even the opinions of priests. Reformation thinking helped spur private entrepreneurship and the development of modern capitalism through faith in absolute values for everybody, and everywhere. The roots of Protestant ethics support a personal calling for an ordinary life, based on diligent daily work and trade, for which each individual bore a personal responsibility to the 'Almighty' and to whom he would be the subject of ultimate judgment (Troeltsch 1997). I argue that this kind of individual freedom and responsibility provides a foundation for the later development of private philanthropy and CSR. Protestant ethics tried to solve the changes brought about by the end of the Catholic, feudal order of the Middle Ages and the fact that suddenly absolute kings, or emperors no longer reigned. The responsibility now was to support every citizen and worker in society.

In order to understand the current social responsibilities to the future, we need to remind ourselves of other challenges. The lost security of the Middle Ages led philosophers to find new certainties. The question was: What new certainty did the modern era offer that has gradually become secular? The Modern era was characterized by and driven by rationalism, best expressed by René Descartes and his promise to arrive at a clear and distinct truth by critical thinking (Descartes 1998). The apparent result of this rationalism was new and transformative scientific discoveries.

Nevertheless, we have to remember the so-called Cartesian dualism, the division between rational thinking and nature. The endeavour for new knowledge was driven primarily by nations seeking new territory, wealth and power. Consequences were that efforts for political and economic supremacy also led to modern colonization and slavery—an unthinkable moral crime within the CSR framework today. However, the economic spoils of imperialism and slavery funded many discoveries in mechanics, physics, chemistry, and scientific enquiry more generally. Slavery may have brought 'positive' economic benefits, but bore many profound and intractable long-term negative consequences in terms of embedding racist ideology, producing unequal and divided societies and neo-colonial violence that plague the world. The Western powers also grew through the cheap labour of slaves and plundering of natural riches (Perry 2013). The general emphasis on natural science and technological progress helped the development of crafts and industrial cities. In order to rebuild the concept of social responsibility, we have first to overcome strict rational and speculative thought, or just mechanical functionality and effectivity.

The next challenge of this era is a positivistic confirmation of modern industrial development by the Church. We realize the strong influence of the first English economists, politicians, and entrepreneurs in the United States. The economic success of Western (colonial) powers was often attributed to God's blessing. Since then, we meet an optimistic spiritual motto 'God Save The Queen' in Britain, 'God Bless America' in the United States, or '*Gott mit uns*' in Germany at the beginning of World War II. This religious discourse reflected a supporting spiritual and religious dimension to capitalism with a lack of empathy or recognizable sense of social responsibility by twenty-first century standards. I argue this happened as the religious pillars of colonial capitalism were demanded and accepted as attempts to bring sense, order and a new security frame into a volatile modern world (Kučera 2015). Nevertheless, these are also signs that capitalism itself became a part of religion, and money became a new God (Tillich 2010). Moreover, this materialist turn overestimated capitalism's moral value and foundation, and under-estimated its destructive potential for those who were its victims. It was also dangerous for and corrosive of the development of any ethical responsibility in social affairs.

4.2.3 The Crisis of Modern Thinking

I have introduced historical developments that show us some of the fundamental thinking that supported and nurtured the roots of an emerging CSR concept, or fundamentally disrupted it. If we want to understand CSR's philosophical foundations well, rather than simply as a late twentieth-century academic phenomenon, corporate fashion or social demand, we must briefly orientate the debate in relation to some critical foundations of modern thinking. At the turn of the eighteenth and nineteenth centuries, the flowering of the industrial revolution throughout the West with all the asocial consequences of modern philosophy based on pure rationalism, utilitarianism and speculative thinking began (Allen 2017). Empiricism allowed corporations to ignore the universal value system from the past[1] and to create new values for the modern era according to new experiences and secular norms. The philosophical and social fundaments offered by John Locke's 'theory of human tabula rasa' taught that we get all necessary concepts and moral principles only with our life experiences (Anzenbacher 2002). The belief in technological progress (positivism) was born, and is again sanctified by financial results. In the past centuries it was justified by the amount of gold, silver, rubber, coffee, tea, wood and slaves. Naturally, this 'modern' concept of constant progress is quite antithetical to respecting diverse cultures, managerial ethics or environmental sustainability. Ecology, as a separate discipline, did not exist yet. Resources—both human and natural were seen as inexhaustible. There was not much space left for other values because that space was filled with a profit theory accompanied by selfishness (Acquaviva 2000).

Immanuel Kant attempted to prove the limits of such rationalism and empiricism through his criticism of pure and practical reason (Kant 1997, 1998b). To find the essential pillars of social responsibility, he

[1] In ways the philosopher Friedrich Nietzsche laid bare.

revealed the necessary transcendental differentiation of human thinking, the so-called 'categorical imperative' and thereby radically renewed the framework of social responsibility. He described it in the following words: 'Act only according to that maxim whereby you can at the same time will that it should become a universal law' (Kant 1998a). We see that this is a necessary philosophical root for any frame of social responsibility because Kant's goal is to act well. For Kant, to act well is an absolute value because universal human dignity is the highest value. In our context, this means that the last goal of social decision-making is the wellbeing and dignity of people. Thus, in order to understand the philosophical framework of the CSR, one can never become a mere means of achieving economic and corporate goals (Jones 1980).

In contrast to Kant's universal law is economic utilitarianism, which is well-known for depending more on the effect than on the quality of the responsible behaviour. For the understanding of a more profound context, in every useful publication about the history of philosophy or ethics, a comprehensive overview of modern developments from asocial to social responsibility involving corporations can be found (Maclntyre 1998).

The Industrial Revolution took place gradually in the eighteenth and nineteenth centuries. During this period, agriculture, production, raw materials mining, transport and other economic sectors were fundamentally transformed. In the midst of this transformation, one can understand why humane, cultural and social values were pushed into the background. Instead of caring for systematic long-term work, mass production, manufacturing, emphasis on strength and quantity prevailed. In companies, the position of man was reduced to the level of slave (for black) or to cheap worker (for white). In England and the United States, racism and the social status of the lower classes were subordinated to the development of agriculture, construction, engineering, energy and the military. Usage of machines includes a steam engine, electrification, assembly lines, mass production and the pursuit of efficient logistics did not allow for discussion about social responsibility in our sense today. We know the terrible consequences of asocial governments and management: social revolts, revolutions and their bloody repression. The gap between wealthy industrial magnates and their workers, the social, educational and health disparities which opened up, provided challenges which have yet to be met (Solomon 2016).

4.3 Searching for a Value Orientation in the Central and Eastern Europe

Any qualitatively new and higher level of social responsibility was needed to seek and develop on assumptions other than the ideals of the industrial and technological revolution.

4.3.1 Searching for Values in CEE

The author knows it from his own experience when his whole life was subjected to an official Marxist ideology based on materialism. Moreover, real socialism was enhanced by a self-proliferating interpretation of Leninism and Stalinism. Historical documents mercilessly confront us with millions of dead victims in Siberian labour camps. Naturally, this does not forget the European experience enhanced by Nazi concentration camps and German labour camps. I ask, what philosophy did the leaders of these practices have?

Marxism is in direct contrast to the global philosophy of free social responsibility and sustainability. The pre-establishment of cohesion and human rights is in contrast to the socialist reality of the Soviet camp (not to mention now communist regimes in Latin America). In CEE countries, Marxism interpreted society according to a model based on Base (Grundlage) and Superstructure (Űberbau, see Fig. 4.1). For my context, it is essential to remember that the base contains economy, economic and manufacturing relationships. The social sphere (also culture, law, religion) was not part of the base, but a part of the superstructure which has to grow from that base. It means that manufacturing relationships and production tools are supposed to influence all levels of human thinking and behaviour (Marx 2009).

Under communism, the cultural, legal and social environment in the USSR and satellite states was subordinated to the revolutionary Marxist

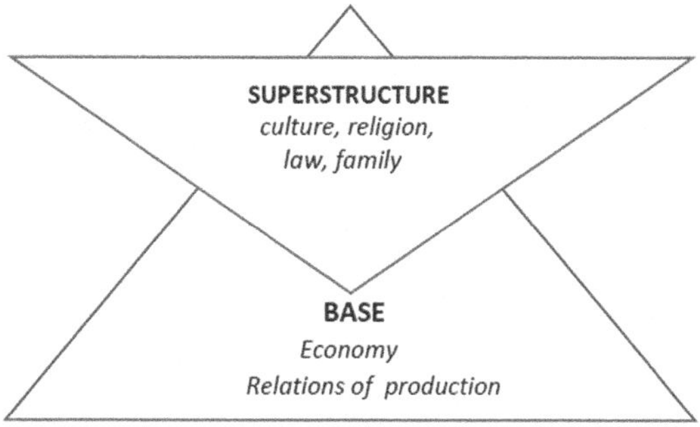

Fig. 4.1 Marxist structure of society. (Source: Own design)

vision supported with the power of state control. Any 'human', social or cultural considerations proceeded from universal moral (democratic) values were persecuted as bourgeois, and hence an old anti-communist ideology. The primary strategy of the socialist economy was oriented on the base—production, energy, economy, coal mining, gas, industry and military. Of course, economics also needed experts from different fields. They were described as 'working intelligence', which was involved in the construction of socialism focused on the Marxist base.

We recall this chapter of CEE because we have to deal with the intellectual legacy as well as the practical impact of the introduction of capitalism that happened in the 1990s. Social responsibility grows upon private property and personal freedom and democracy (Schumpeter 2008). However, under communism, with private companies, nationalized the state supervised everything that happened in society and in state-controlled companies in the spirit of Hobbes's *Leviathan (Hobbes* 2017*)*. Any personal initiative and responsibility were met with repression when someone became actively interested in strengthening individual freedom, education and criticism of the asocial and un-environmental practices of communists' regimes. Social responsibility for the overall well-being of individuals requires motivation for personal courage, which extends beyond that base and, on the contrary, comes out of the superstructure, which aims to change economic relations and existential conditions.

After 40 years of 'actually existing socialism' under the communist ideology of the USSR and Eastern bloc states came the revolution, when the 'iron curtain' was pulled down, and a new stage of history started—politically and economically. Many culturally and intellectually oriented people have followed the Western European tradition of thinking and social responsibility. A specific example was in German model of "Sozialwirtschaft" (social economy). However, people in CEE were educated and 'persuaded' as Marxist. The sociology and anthropology were defined by materialism, positivist rationalism, Freud's psychology, natural Darwinism and social Darwinism (Gregory 2000). The view of man has focused on his physical, economic or biological needs like the "selfish gene" (Dawkins 2016). For social responsibility, the influence of social Darwinism is crippling because it allows thought patterns based on class struggle, the welcome of the more energetic and the defeat (destruction) of the economically weaker. Although this principle is a part of the market economy, many ways of behaviour by management and entrepreneurs proved to be asocial and also scandalous. Critically, we must stand up to the logic of capitalism, where only the fittest survive (Dickens 2000). In CEE countries, we hear the governments speaking about the growth of GDP as the most important factor of state development (Martinez 2019). According to Marxisms we understood that family, marriage, the upbringing of children, moral values, cultural life, free journalism, the education, or the function of conscience, have been ridiculed as a utopia, and not a priority or part of primary economic strategy in CEE countries (Tabery 2017). Academic studies have sought lessons for social transformation from the failure of the communist economic system (Pullman 2011; Rusmisch and Sachs 2003), and the negative consequences of socialist ideology are evident in CEE countries until today (Hardy 2014).

4.3.2 Search for Values in Western Society for the Global Economy

Western relations between economy and social responsibility have also demonstrated their conflicts with neoliberal economic philosophy. We remember the discussion led by Milton Friedman (1970), saying that the social responsibility of Business is to increase its profit. Management education has undergone many stages—from the 'age of commerce' through the 'age of Enlightenment', 'scientific management' to management concerning human relations and explicit social responsibility (Witzel 2012; Crouset 2001). Today we live in the era of 'management gurus', who help us find the value of management by focusing on cultivating human needs. Authors such as P. F. Drucker, C. K. Prahalad, M. Porter, G. Hammel, focus on the development of 'man', but there is still a gap when it comes to understanding how 'man' can cultivate moral values within organizational contexts that are contained or delimitated by management, financial performances and profits. Henry Mintzberg and his concept of the rebalancing society between private, public, and plural shifted the managerial outlook further (Mintzberg 2015). Likewise, in individual European, American, or Asian states, there is a rigid debate and a struggle to understand the value in today's market and a globalized world to which we could agree (Yang 2011).

We see that Western social policy has also undergone several twists—post-war successes, attempts by French Keynesianism using the role of the state, but also a very cold social policy of Margaret Thatcher in Britain. However, people working hard in state-owned factories in the eastern bloc could only envy the growing living standards of their neighbours in the West. Western development was also radically slowed down by the financial crisis of 2008. The growing contradictions between the low incomes of workers with excessive pay of top managers gambling with the means of others, have fuelled new resentment, frustration and disappointments. The last years of the twenty-first century have caused new social unrest, new demonstration (i.e., Paris yellow vests), and new challenges to European issues of social responsibility and cohesion.

To restore the philosophical background of social responsibility, we can use the forgotten value concepts and remnants of cultural values, traditions, and values of human life in the development of the Western society both in the East and the West. We have indicated them in previous articles and summarize it at the end of this chapter. For educators in business schools, however, this means to think seriously about incorporating a value philosophy into teaching young managers and entrepreneurs or financiers and economists (Schüz 2018). In recent years, we have come to a very sophisticated concept of CSR, challenges of Business

Ethics, the rules of the Organization for Economic Cooperation and Development (OECD), the United Nations Global Compact, Principles for Responsible Management Education (UN GC PRME), and the Agenda 2030 with an application methodology (Arruda and Norman 2017). Also, the European Union regulations have undoubtedly contributed to value orientation in business and management, which encompasses the full scope and depth of corporate, social, and political responsibility that are closely intertwined.

4.4 Conclusion

In this chapter, I tried to open up one central theme—in what historical environments were social values born, and what does this mean for contemporary organizations. The development of human society, which is so strongly influenced by the management of local and international corporations is very dynamic and dramatic. Market 'progress' continues under the optimistic 'mechanisms of the market', and the emphasis on 'effective functions' of capitalism carries on (Sőderbaum 2008). Maybe some still rely on the 'invisible hand of the market', but also this narrow-minded perspective is critically discussed (Kaushik 2011). What we must not forget, however, in the social perspective, first of all, is about man, human society and future generations. Individuals live under the conditions of current policy and economic competition. In addition to the company's big social themes, we need to see the growing personal and psychological crises of managers (Lane 2000; Easterlin 2001).

Therefore, the question is again whether we want to help people in companies in any way, or to follow the interests of the owners and top managers only at the expense of the multitude of dependent workers and administrative assistants who are paid only to the extent that they can ensure their livelihoods for themselves and their families. A fundamental value in business would be a fair deal, a partnership agreement, a good position of both parties, and the possibility of confidence based on positive experience, otherwise known as a 'win-win' situation. It means that trade agreements need a value framework (Schiller 2003).

A positive signal in this development is that some passages of business and civil law are beginning to realize this. The legal basis of a business partnership and business as a whole uses values that transcend both speculative rationalism and practical experience (empiricism), in addition to romantic dreams of happiness and wealth at the expense of others. Therefore, many European laws have included managerial responsibility, maximum transparency, compliance, quality, nature-friendliness and respect for future generations (Andreisová and Kučera 2017).

If we summarize the uncovering of the roots of capitalistic thought, we see how much work is still waiting for us. Topics related to 'values' are always a big challenge in the current capitalist society. Rationalists still repeat the practical advantages of trade. Empiricists refer to the past or majority practice as an apology to current practices and the statistically reduced realities of business. We continue to follow these approaches in our own countries in discussions with entrepreneurs, managers and students of economics. In the West, but also in the CEE countries, concrete steps are being taken towards more responsible entrepreneurial and managerial practices (Kučera and Müllerová 2017; Gasparski 2017). First the transformation economies have to learn from the moral failures of the communist experiment (Pavlík 1999), second, Western society also needs to learn 'how to succeed without selling our soul', and third how to solve the ethical dilemmas in a competitive environment today (Frank 2010). If we introduced the mechanical model of Karl Marx (Fig. 4.2, where the *Base* (economy and production relations) determined the limits of

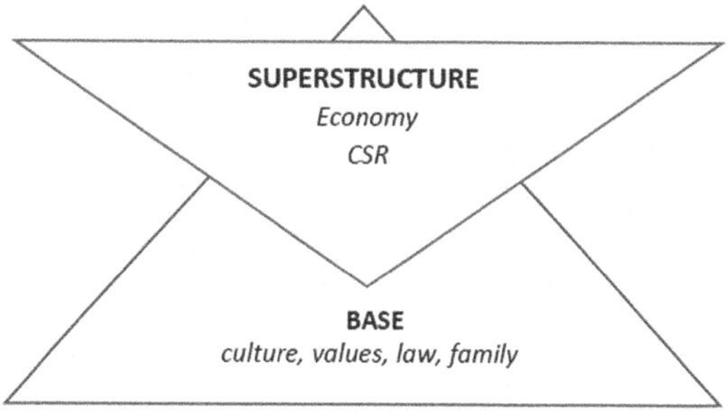

Fig. 4.2 CSR concept. (Source: Own)

Superstructure (culture, values, law, family), then we should create an analogous image based on CSR values:

What value scales will we be able to take into account in such an environment? Will a simple CSR concept that has its known limits suffice? (Vogel 2005). The crisis of Western capitalism is far deeper and the challenges for managerial responsibility are great, not only for the present but also for the future (Jonas 1984). There are still many basic prerequisites for managerial accountability and compliance in the game, such as trust between managers, businesses and peoples, reliability of business partners, adherence to contracts, threats to nature and constructive, rational intentions and a value dimension of thought and action. Without them, capitalist society will find itself in a deeper crisis (Žížek 2009; Harvey 2010; Sarkar 2012).

References

Alasdair C. MacIntyre, *Short History of Ethics: A History of Moral Philosophy from the Homeric Age to the Twentieth Century.* Routledge, 1998.

Archie Carroll, A *History of Corporate Social Responsibility: Concepts and Practices, Chapter.* In *The Oxford Handbook of Corporate Social Responsibility*, Chapter 2, 19–46. Oxford University Press, 2009.

Arno Anzenbacher, *Einführung in die Philosophie,* Verlag Herder, 2002.

Basu Kaushik, *Beyond the Invisible Hand: Groundwork for a New Economics*, Princeton University Press, 2011.

Can Akdeniz, *Corporate Scandals: Crime in the Age of Big Business.* Bad Bodendorf: First Publishing, 2015.

Clayes Gregory, The "Survival of the Fittest" and the Origins of Social Darwinism. *Journal of the History of Ideas*, 61 no. 2 (2000), 223–40.

Daniel Bell, *The Cultural Contradictions of Capitalism.* Basic Books, 1996.

David Harvey, *The Enigma of Capital: and the Crises of Capitalism.* Oxford University Press, 2010.

David Vogel, *The Market for Virtue: The Potential and Limits of Corporate Social Responsibility.* The Brookings Institution, 2005.

De Paula Arruda and Filho Norman, The agenda 2030 for responsible management education: An applied methodology. *The International Journal of Management Education*, 15, no. 2 (Part B 2017), 183–191.

Dušan Kučera, *Weberova teze „ducha kapitalismu" jako východisko pro hledání spirituálních potenciálů v podnikatelském a manažerském prostředí.* PhD diss., University of Economics, Prague, 2015.

Dušan Kučera, and Jana Müllerová, *The value orientation of the Czech companies in the frame of sustainable corporate responsibility.* In Innovation Management, Entrepreneurship and Sustainability, Oeconomica (IMES 2017), 496–504.

Elspeth Yang, *The Third World Where Is It?: Forgotten Corners of the World but We Have Life and Space!* Author House, 2011.

Ernst Troeltsch, *Die Bedeutung des Protestantismus für die Entstehung der modernen Welt.* Schutterwald, 1997.

Edward Page, *Climate Change, Justice and Future Generations.* Edward Elgar Publishing, 2006.

Erik Tabery, *Opuštěna společnost,* Paseka, 2017.

Henry Minzberg, *Rebalancing Society: Radical Renewal Beyond Left, Right, and Center.* Berrett-Koehler Publishers, 2015.

Jan Pavlík, On Market Consequences of post-Communist Immorality. *E-Logos, Electronical Journal for Philosophy,* University of Economics, Prague, 1999, http://e-logos.vse.cz/index.php?article=97

Gary Acquaviva, *Values, Violence, and Our Future.* Amsterdam: Rodopi, 2000.

Hans Jonas, *The Imperative of Responsibility: In Search of an Ethics for the Technological Age.* University of Chicago Press, 1984.

Harvey C. Mansfield, *Machiavelli's Virtue.* University of Chicago Press, 1996.

Heinrich Geiselberger, *Die grosse Regression. Eine internationelle Debatte über die geistige Situation der Zeit.* Berlin: Suhrkamp Verlag, 2017.

Christian Fleck, *Max Webers Protestantismus—These, Kritik und Antikritik.* Österreichische Zeitschrift für Geschichtswissenschaften, StudienVerlag, 2012.

IAEA (2015). *The Fukushima daiichi accident.* International atomic energy agency, https://www-pub.iaea.org/MTCD/Publications/PDF/AdditionalVolumes/P1710/ Pub1710-TV3-web.pdf

Immanuel Kant, *Kant's Methaphysics of Morals.* University of Memphis, Department of Philosophy, 1998a.

Immanuel Kant, *Critique of Pure Reason.* Cambridge University Press, 1998b.

Immanuel Kant, *Critique of Practical Reason.* Cambridge University Press, 1997.

Jamil Asghar, The Postmodernist Relativization of Truth: A Critique. *Islamic Studies,* 51, no. 3 (Autumn 2012), 295–312.

Jane Hardy, Transformations and crisis in Central and Eastern Europe: A combined and uneven development perspective, *Capital and Class,* 38, no. 1 (February 2014), 143–155.

Jürgen Habermas, *Legitimationsprobleme im Spätkapitalismus*, Suhrkamp, 1973.
Karl Marx, *Das Kapital*, Anaconda, 2009.
Lee E. Preston, and James E. Post, *Private Management and Public Policy: The Principle of Public Responsibility*. Stanford University Press, 2012.
Levitsky, S. & Ziblatt, D. (2018): *How Democracies Die*. Phoenix: Crown.
Lucie Andreisová, and Dušan Kučera, *Philosophical Assumptions for Understanding Selected Aspects of Civil-Law Liability of Czech Top Management*. Scientia et Societas VIII, no. 4 (December 2017): 23–39.
Luis R. Martinez, *How Much Should We Trust the Dictator's GDP Growth Estimates?* SSRN, 2019. https://ssrn.com/abstract=3093296 or https://doi.org/10.2139/ssrn.3093296.
Michal Pullman, *Konec experimentu. Přestavba a pád komunismu v Československu*. Scriptorium, 2011.
Ladislav Rusmish, and Stephen Sachs, *Lessons from the Failure of the Communist Economic System*. New York: Lexington Books, 2003.
Marvin Perry, *Western Civilization: A Brief History*, Volume II: From the 1400's. Wadsworth, Changing Learning, 2013.
Mathias Schüz, *Applied Business Ethics: Foundations For Study And Daily Practice*. World Scientific, 2018.
Mathis Wackernagel, and Justin Kitzes, *Ecological Footprint*, In Encyclopedia of Ecology, 2019.
Max Weber, *The Protestant Ethic and the Spirit of Capitalism*. Charles Scribner's Sons, 2003.
Miroslav Petříček, *Úvod do současné filosofie*, Herrmann & synové, 1997.
Morgen Witzel, *A History of Management Thought*. Routledge, 2012.
François Crouzet, *A History of the European Economy, 1000–2000*. University of Virginia Press, 2001.
Matthew D'Ancona *Post Truth: The New War on Truth and How to Fight Back*, London: Ebury Press, 2017.
Mikelle Calhoun, *Profits before People: Perversion of the Friedman Doctrine*. Academy of Management Proceedings, no. 1 (January 2015): 18560–18560.
Mildred Solomon, *The 4 big ethical questions of the Fourth Industrial Revolution*. World Economic Forum, 2016. https://www.weforum.org/agenda/2016/10/how-can-we-enjoy-the-benefits-of-the-fourth-industrial-revolution-while-minimizing-its-risks/
Milton Friedman, The Social Responsibility of Business is to Increase its Profits. *The New York Times Magazine* (September 13, 1970).
Niccolò Machiavelli, *The Prince*. University of Chicago Press, 2010.

OECD *Economic Outlook*, Interim Report, March 2020.
Paul Tillich, *Capitalism as Religion? A Study of Paul Tillich's Interpretation of Modernity.* Harvard University Press, 2010.
Peter Dickens, *Social Darwinism: Linking Evolutionary Thought to Social Theory.* Open University Press, 2000.
Peter Salmon, *The Moment of Truth*, New Humanist, Spring, 2018.
Peter Sőderbaum, *Understanding Sustainability Economics: Towards Pluralism in Economics*, Earthscan, 2008.
Rene Descartes, *Discourse on Method.* Hackett Publishing Co., 1998.
Peter Schumpeter, *Capitalism, Socialism, and Democracy,* 2008.
Richard Dawkins, *The Selfish Gene*. Oxford University Press, 2016.
Richard Easterlin, Income and Happiness: Towards a Unified Theory. *Economic Journal* 111, no. 473 (July 2001), 465–84.
Robert B. Schiller, *The Economics of Poverty and Discrimination.* Prentice Hall, 2003.
Robert Allen, *The Industrial Revolution: A Very Short Introduction.* Oxford University Press, 2017.
Robert Frank, *What Price the Moral High Ground? How to Succeed without Selling Your Soul. Ethical dilemmas in competitive environment.* Princeton University Press, 2010.
Robert Lane, *The Loss of Happiness in Market Democracies.* New Haven. Yale University Press, 2000.
Saral Sarkar, *The Crises of Capitalism: A Different Study of Political Economy.* Counterpoint, 2012.
Sustainable development *Transforming our world: The 2030 Agenda for Sustainable development.* 2015. http//:www.sustainabledevelopment.org.
Slavoj Žížek, *First As Tragedy, Then As Farce*. Brooklyn: Verso, 2009.
Thomas, H.; Lee, M.; Thomas, L.; Wilson, A. (2014) *Securing the Future of Management Education: Competitive Destruction or Constructive innovation.* Emerald Group Publishing, UK.
The Economist, June 8, 2019: *Weapons of mass disruption: America is deploying a new economic arsenal to assert its power.*
Thomas Hobbes, *Leviathan*, Oxford University Press, 2017.
Thomas Jones, Corporate Social Responsibility Revisited, Redefined. *California Management Review*, 22, no. 3 (Spring 1980): 59–67.
Ulrich Beck, *Risk Society. Towards a New Modernity.* Sage Publications, 1992.
Wojciech Gasparski, *Ethics and the Future of Capitalism,* Routledge, 2017.
Wolfgang Schreck, *How will capitalism end?* Verso, 2017.

5

Members, Clients and the Society: A Grounded Theory of Cooperative Banks' Value Creation

Gerhard Kosinowski

5.1 Introduction

Cooperative enterprises make a significant contribution to the global value chain. According to Henry (2018) cooperatives count for roughly 250 million jobs worldwide. Nonetheless, they are still underrepresented in academic research. Suter and Gmür (2013) argue that they are not even analyzed in the right manner as most of the research work tends to focus on economic aspects of the cooperative value creation. This is consistent with the findings of Levi and Davis (2008) who call cooperatives the enfants terribles of economics. Their special governance system and historical roots illustrate that cooperative organizations go far beyond the creation of sole economic value to their members. Therefore, they could serve as role models in times where corporate social responsibility is more needed than ever before.

G. Kosinowski (✉)
WHU—Otto Beisheim School of Management, Vallendar, Germany
e-mail: Gerhard.Kosinowski@whu.edu

F. Farache et al. (eds.), *Values and Corporate Responsibility*, Palgrave Studies in Governance, Leadership and Responsibility,
https://doi.org/10.1007/978-3-030-52466-1_5

One of the most prominent examples for the success of cooperatives is the German Cooperative Financial Services Network. The cooperative primary banks, the 875 Volks- and Raiffeisenbanks, represent the network's backbone. Including a number of specialized institutions, for example, the cooperative building society, the cooperative private banking branch and many more, the network employs more than 190,000 people. As of 2019, the assets on the consolidated balance sheet exceed 1,000 billion Euros (Genossenschaftliche FinanzGruppe Volksbanken Raiffeisenbanken 2020).

A popular approach regarding cooperatives studies is the so-called member value concept. This member-centered model is a rather abstract theory that has the aspiration to fit to various types of cooperatives. On the other end of the range, there is an enormous amount of detailed publications from German primary banks and their governing associations. Their statements might be correct to some extent, yet, they do not follow academic criteria. With the present work I want to close that research gap and move in the middle of these two fields. Against this background I elaborate on two guiding research questions that reveal that cooperative banks are role models for a sustainable way of doing financing business in accordance to the UN sustainable development goals:

What are the business practices of cooperative banks?
What constitutes the strategy of cooperative banks?

The chapter starts by embedding the cooperative organizational form in its historical and academic background. By linking my approach to the existing theories, I aim at moving from an abstract to a practical-based grounded theory. My interpretive design is divided into two parts. First of all, I highlight five key themes using a coding tree. This is an activity- and practice-based analysis from 24 in-depth interviews with leaders from German primary banks. The dynamics regarding the business strategy follow in the second part. Through four key insights I turn my illustrative model of the cooperative banks' value creation into a dynamic model. I consider this an essential step for understanding how German cooperative banks contribute to sustainability.

Thereby, I primarily enrich the existing approach on cooperative banks through two models. My first model represents a comprehensive overview of the practices in German cooperative banks. By introducing the dimensions of monetary and non-monetary benefits as well as benefits for members and benefits for non-member clients and the region, I contribute to the appreciation of the cooperative diversity. Secondly, by doing so, I prove that the member value model might not deliver accurate insights for the German cooperative banking sector. My model counts for the shift from member-centered business toward a client- and region-orientated approach. Through my dynamic model, I deliver practice-based insights and starting points for further research. My field work does neither focus on any particular UN development goals nor test any hypotheses. I rather demonstrate that cooperatives contribute in their entirety to sustainability and that they are role models for a sustainable way of doing business. In accordance to the UN aspiration (United Nations 2020), cooperatives combine economic growth, social inclusion and the concern for their environment.

5.2 Historical Background of Cooperative Banks

The present form of cooperative business has a historical background of 200 years. Puusa et al. (2016) argue that the driving force behind this movement was the overcoming of exploitation on the free market. Finding its roots in Great Britain, the pioneers of the cooperative organizational model had the aspiration to decrease the gap between the working and the capitalist class which has been created through the emergence of the industrialization. Seeking for social change, the Welsh businessman Robert Owen called for alternatives to the traditional capitalist working mechanisms. Finding inspiration in his words, in 1844 a group of 28 men from the English North West decided to establish a consumer community for the exchange of daily goods without relying on the free market (Fairbairn 1994). Balnave and Patmore (2009) conclude that this community, called the Rochdale Society of Equitable Pioneers, fought for a more social way of doing business and thus represent the starting point for the cooperative movement. By defining a clear set of rules which organizes their joint venture, they established the unique cooperative governance system (Bello 2005).

Over the course of its existence the principles governing the Rochdale Society have become increasingly specified. Although their original content is strongly connected to the purpose of being a local English consumer community of the nineteenth century, the essence of the principles of the Rochdale Society can still be found in the present cooperative organizations. The governing body of the global cooperative movement, called International Co-operative Alliance, drew on this notion and summarized seven principles for the cooperative movement:

First Principle: Voluntary and Open Membership
Second Principle: Democratic Member Control
Third Principle: Member Economic Participation
Fourth Principle: Autonomy and Independence
Fifth Principle: Education, Training and Information
Sixth Principle: Cooperation among Cooperatives
Seventh Principle: Concern for the Community. (International Co-operative Alliance 2019)

These values are also the foundation for cooperative banking whose history is characterized by long periods of boom and bust. After the industrialization had emerged as the dominant force of the economy, the cooperative movement found countless supporters in large parts of Europe. Local businessmen needed to invest in new machines in order to survive on the increasingly technologized market. Consequently, many families were forced into loans with usurious interests issued by private creditors in order to gain access to working capital (Bundesverband der Deutschen Volksbanken und Raiffeisenbanken 2015). Aiming at the alleviation of this misery, the Saxon politician Hermann Schulze-Delitzsch established a cooperative organization which provided affordable finance to local entrepreneurs. Similarly, Friedrich Wilhelm Raiffeisen founded communities in the rural areas of Germany which enabled the local working class to have quick access to capital and groceries at affordable rates.

Raiffeisen's and Schulze-Delitzsch's ideas and institutions, which can be considered early forms of credit unions, serve as role models for present-day cooperative banking enterprises. Over the course of time the cooperative movement had to deal with a variety of difficulties and setbacks. Although the cooperative businesses in Western Europe were hit hard by World War II, they managed to recover quickly (Martens 2016). Nowadays, cooperative banks do not have to fight against political suppression but need to adjust their business model to the economic circumstances and the clients' expectations. In this regard, the cooperative movement benefitted from the financial crises in the years 2007 and 2008. The business of cooperative banks suffered not as much as that of traditional commercial banks (Vieta and Lionais 2015). Being based on the unique governance structure and the democratic ownership model the cooperative business model benefits from large robustness during crises (International Labour Organization 2018). Analyzing the history of the cooperative movement, Fonteyne (2007) further argues that cooperative organization have always benefitted from the economic and social change.

5.3 The Member Value Concept as Theoretical Foundation

My grounded theory relates to the most popular theory regarding cooperatives in Germany, the member value theory. Cooperative businesses have a different stakeholder construct than commercial enterprises (Gijselinckx 2009). Their members are simultaneously customers, investors, patrons, beneficial owners and citizens of the local region (Limnios et al. 2018). The member value concept was developed in order to count for this unique structure while translating the traditional cooperative principles into a modern approach. This approach has its roots in the German discourse (Gmür and Suter 2012). Theurl (2002) argues that cooperatives create three kinds of value for their members and the region, including direct member value, indirect member value and ideational member value.

The paradox of the member value theory is that nowadays a large number of cooperative banks in Germany have more clients without cooperative shares than members. The practice of early cooperatives to reject any business with outsiders has been altered during the 1970s. In a field study Beuthien et al. (2008) even discover a lack of differentiation between insiders and outsiders when analyzing German primary banks. I take this as starting point to develop a practice-based theory that directly relates to German cooperative banks.

5.4 Research Method

The cooperative governance system and the value creation is a complex phenomenon. The way contemporary cooperative organizations do business does not only depend on their unique historical roots but is also determined by the interpretation of its leading persons. In this sense, the cooperative value creation is a socio-economical phenomenon. I apply an interpretive, practice-based research design. Thereby I aim at expressing the cooperative value creation and emphasizing the special relation to social responsibility and sustainability. Besides reference to existing literature, I use three sources of data for my study:

(a) Semi-structured conversations with experts from German cooperative primary banks
(b) Research memos about observations before, during and after the personal meetings
(c) Information provided by the respective cooperative banks, either accessed through their websites or provided by the conversation partners

Working for DZ PRIVATBANK, the private banking institution within the cooperative network, I can capitalize on my relationships to the primary banks, the Volks- and Raiffeisenbanks. I asked several colleagues who coordinate the cooperation with the primary banks in various parts of Germany to recommend two to four senior leaders of Volks- and Raiffeisenbanks. My gatekeepers are experienced B2B managers who have contact with people from the Volks- and Raiffeisenbanks through both business and personal relationships. In total I used six gatekeepers. Besides informing them about the intention to talk about the cooperative value creation, I did not make any restriction with respect to the banks' size or location. The gatekeepers usually called or e-mailed their contacts. Afterwards, I conducted a follow-up phone call and arranged a meeting. Consequently, the data set consists of 24 in-depth semi-structured conversations with leaders from German cooperative banks who are either general managers or directly responsible for a major division within their banks. CEOs and department heads were chosen as experts since they are well informed about their bank's value creation, decide about the bank's strategy and embody their personal attitude as well as the bank's mission vis-à-vis their employees and further stakeholders. This sampling method created large diversity. Overall, I talked to bankers from seven German states representing banks from 150 million to more than ten billion Euros on the balance sheet.

Meeting in person was an essential step in establishing a trustful relationship to the interviewees as proclaimed by the AOM Code of Ethics (Academy of Management 2019). This was enhanced by the fact that I was recommended by the joint contact, the gatekeeper, and by ensuring that the study is not about the interviewees themselves. I stressed that the data is published in aggregate, anonymized forms.

The conversations were conducted in German, recorded, transcribed and translated into English. Additionally, I attached memos to each interview summarizing common information about the respective bank, observations before, during and after the interview as well as initial conclusions. Besides setting the scene, the aspiration behind these memos is to record key observations. This relates to observations in the respective bank, key statements that were not recorded and further elements, which could not be captured by the audio record.

The conversations took place in the respective expert's office or in the bank's meeting room. All meetings were introduced and concluded by small talk. Overall, I conducted 24 conversations between October 2019 and January 2020. The meetings took between 60 and 120 minutes. The records itself range from 45 to 75 minutes.

The iterative process is also reflected in the conversations' structure, which was based on a questionnaire and individual, detailed questions. I started with relatively open questions. Asking what a typical working day looks like usually served as an icebreaker. As illustrated by Jazarbkowski (2008) I conduct a practice-based study by emphasizing the dynamic relation between the cooperatives' strategy respectively mission and the manifestation in the daily business. Through my interviews I did not observe daily practices, but I encouraged the interviewees to reflect on selected practices. Further into the interview, I became more active by challenging the experts with detailed questions. Toward the end of the interview I presented my previously designed outline of the cooperative value creation. This first-hand feedback helped to develop my overview (see Fig. 5.1), serving as basis for a dynamic, practice-based strategy model (see Fig. 5.2).

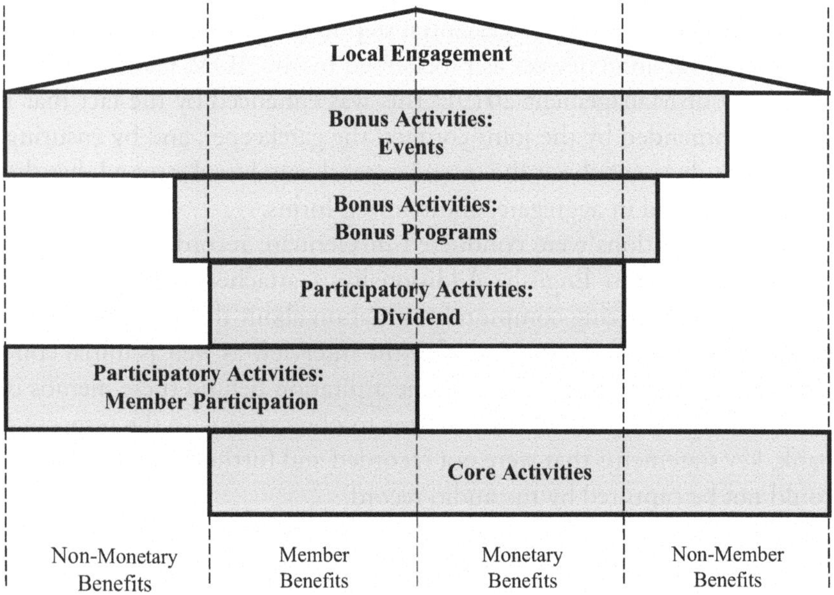

Fig. 5.1 The activities in cooperative banks. (Source: Own illustration)

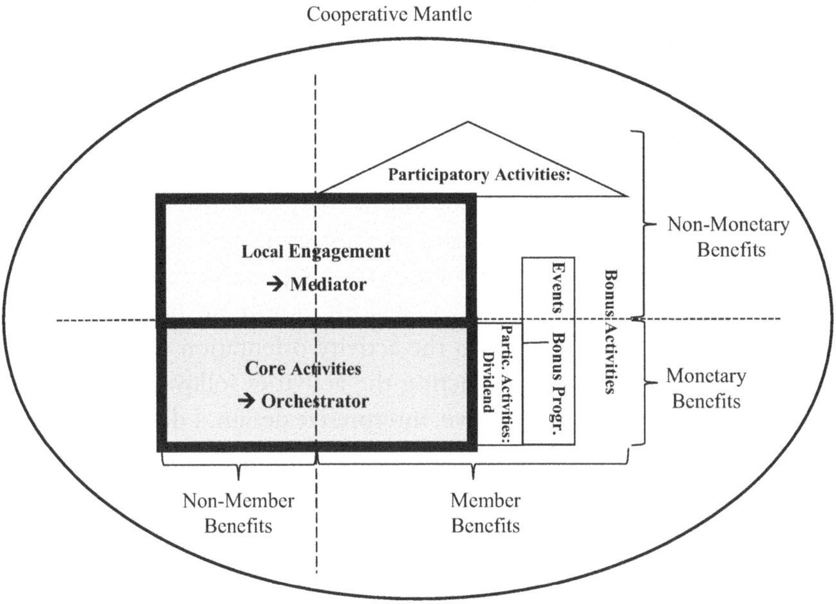

Fig. 5.2 Dynamic model of cooperative banks' strategy. (Source: Own illustration)

The semi-structured interviews are analyzed through the grounded theory approach (Glaser and Strauss 1967). I hereby take the guidelines by Strauss and Corbin (1997) and the applications by Gioia and Chittipeddi (1991) as well as Gioia et al. (2010) as most powerful role models. According to the Gioia method the initial step is the creation of first-order codes. Due to the embeddedness in the historical development and traditional governance structure the author applies selective coding to reveal the meaning of various anecdotes and examples for the cooperative value creation. This might certainly include in vivo codes (Strauss and Corbin 1997), but it is mainly based on in vitro codes. In a second step, I summarized the first-order codes under the five dominant themes, the second-order conceptual categories which I identified throughout the data set. The selective coding process does not only have an exploratory focus by highlighting the practices in cooperative banking but also adds to the strategic understanding by establishing a dynamic theory. The third-order concept produces agile theoretical categories that show the themes' meaning and mechanism.

5.5 Analysis of the Themes

I use a coding tree to summarize my first-order codes under second-order themes. While the first-order categories represent in vitro codes from the interviews, the second-order themes are created by the researcher. These themes reflect the identification of four activity dimensions in cooperative primary banks. Thus, they aim at illustrating practices that led to conclusions about the interpretation of the cooperative mission and the cooperative banks' business strategy. As fifth important theme I identify the role of the employee. Due to the activity-orientation the employees play an important role in conducting the activities following their own set of values. Following an iterative, interpretive design, I did not identify the cooperative promotional mission as distinct theme. The mission is rather a product of the activities in cooperative banks and is filled with life through the interpretation by the employees. Thus, the mission is not seen as an isolated element, but becomes visible through my dynamic model (see Fig. 5.2).

5.5.1 First Theme: Core Activities

The core activities are a distinctive element of the practices by cooperative banks. It refers to the original business purpose of providing financing and advisory services. In this regard, core activities benefit both members and clients without cooperative shares. The cooperatives aim at being lifelong partners for their clients.

> *I am thinking of the example of crafts men. Crafts men who established a company decades ago, who have been member of the Volks- and Raiffeisenbank for decades, who decide about the Volks- and Raiffeisenbank's well-being through the representatives, who talk to their client advisors about all financial topics, and whom the bank can thereby support. Investments, financing, company succession.* (Interview 4)

Early modern cooperatives have rejected any business with outsiders. However, the analysis shows that nowadays there is equal treatment of members and clients-only. Some of the examined banks do not even grant reduced account fees to members. This marks a varying element with regard to the questioned experts. Some banks offer the full range of banking products to all clients. Other banks have created special account models for members or apply different fee schedules for members and non-members. All examined banks have clients with and without cooperative shares.

Despite various functional differences with regard to the range of banking services for their clients, all interviews have a similar practice approach on the core activities. Cooperative banks do not aim at being price-leaders, but rather focus on quality. And this quality aspiration primarily relates to the cooperative customer relationship management. Therefore, good cooperative relationship management and partnership is characterized by six elements according to the interviewees:

Continuity

Cooperative banks are characterized by low fluctuation rates. Most interviewees told that the clients have been dealing with the same advisor for decades. They are very familiar with the clients' families and background.

> *So, the more you know about the clients, the better the conversation finally can be. And if you know about the number of children, how the environment is in general. So, just an example: a colleague of mine, he is now retiring on the 30th of August after 47 years. He has been here for 47 years. 47 years. Think about it.* (Interview 13)

Knowledge

The long-term relationship to the client ensures that the advisor accumulates a large reservoir of knowledge. This knowledge is not only fostered by the personal contact but also by the employees' local embeddedness. As a result, I was able to observe relationship lending processes. Cooperative banks are able to make business decision based on their knowledge about the clients. However, this does not mean that they do not rely on computer-based calculations and legal procedures.

> *We have just returned from a customer, for example. It is about a three million loan. We have existing primary debts of two million. If we do that now … we have told him that he has got our commitment… Well, at another bank… We are now giving one and a half million without security. Why? Because he pays it off very quickly. And he doesn't have to issue new primary debt. We have him under surveillance. But I would like to say that it is not always about interest rates. It is rather about soft facts, interests for provision. Do I have to pledge all my belongings?! Or does my bank trust me?! Trust also means trusting yourself as a bank. The customer has to trust himself, we have to trust ourselves, but we also have to trust him. And that, I think, is certainly important. The requests prove that.* (Interview 3)

Cooperative Network

In order to be a reliable partner in all phases of life, cooperative banks have established a large network. They do not only provide their in-house services but also have partnerships with various other cooperative institutions. These network partners are locally integrated and ensure a hand-in-hand cooperation in order to achieve the clients' satisfaction. According to the interviews and my observations some network partners even have offices inside the primary bank, and their employees are fully integrated.

> *We maintain a very intensive exchange with the network partners, because it is basically a service-orientation within the concept of subsidiarity, that we do not offer all the services ourselves here, but that we receive many services from the network partners and that we work together on the same business case.* (Interview 4)

The demand for high quality is reflected in two aspects. Firstly, the interview partners consider the network partners product providers. The cooperative primary banks are clearly in the lead. The network partners are brought into specific cases on demand of the Volks- and Raiffeisenbank or the client. Some banks even have partnerships with product providers outside the cooperative network. In these cases, the quality orientation with regard to core activities overweighs the loyalty to the cooperative network.

> *However, we [the cooperative network] are not competitive in the range between 250.000 and 750.000 Euros with regard to the leasing division. Against this background, we [as primary bank] have looked for further partners that are not part of the cooperative network. Because once again, the client is first. And at the end of the day the client must feel that we made a competitive offer. Indeed, we focus on the cooperative network. But if the cooperative network is not able to provide it, we have to look for alternatives.* (Interview 1)

Need-Orientation

The large knowledge enables the advisors to comprehensively analyze the client's situation. Cooperative banks are not product driven. They do not sell products for the purpose of making profits. They rather take the clients' perspective and try to fully satisfy them. This also fits to the interviewees' interpretation of the network partners' role. They are the product providers. Yet, the Volks- and Raiffeisenbank decide when to bring a specific product into play. In this context, I could hear several critical statements against possible sales targets and quotas from network partners. Further critique related to a shift of focus away from the Volks- and Raiffeisenbanks and their clients' needs. Cooperative advisory stands for a comprehensive client orientation. The contacts within and beyond the cooperative network enable the advisors to think out of the box and to find the best solution for the client. Yet, many interviewees pointed out that they only sell those products of which they are convinced themselves.

> *And a very, very important point and one of our substantial credos: We want to advise and accompany our clients with regard to their needs, we want to focus on needs instead of provisions.* (Interview 9)

> *I consider myself a helper for the clients. So, it is not like a large bank where a client is left alone with problems. I see it like this: We are there for the clients. The client does not want something from us. We want something from the*

client. And I also help the client whenever he has a problem. And that is how I see the cooperative character. (Interview 2)

I rather reject a deal today because I know it is not good for the client. I provide a precise example. I rejected a loan proposal which would have been feasible because I noticed that the client will get into trouble. I did not conclude this deal and I illustrated the reasons to the client. They were indeed unhappy, but they have understood it. That is an extreme case. But when I feel that the client would be harmed, then I need to interrupt, it would not work. That is how we treat our clients. How much time we invest. What we try to realize. I would argue that we also find solutions for our clients which have nothing to do with the core banking business. Which you might not easily get somewhere else. (Interview 8)

Quickness

While not being price leader, the Volks- and Raiffeisenbank convince with quick solutions. This is fostered by various elements of their setup. Quick solutions are only possible because the relationship manager has large knowledge about the client and the local bank remains relatively short decision-making channels.

That means that if it is urgent, we can get a decision plus a loan agreement within a day. I would say that this does not work at large banks anymore. They clients can directly call me, too. That means that if there are any problems, I can quickly provide a solution. Continuously flexible. Well. We have, I would say, a quick solution for every problem. (Interview 2)

Reliability

The topic of reliability came up in almost every interview. With regard to the customer relationship management reliability has two connotations. First of all, reliability refers to credibility. This means that the clients receive reliable information from their trusted advisors.

And reliability. So, I would say, I say: I check it like this, I check it like this, you will receive an offer. Our clients only receive an offer, if we have managed to do a pre-check beforehand, whether we want to provide a loan to the respec-

tive customer. [...] If you present something which is approved by the client, but you cannot hold your promise then you will not be able to make any further offers. And we have chosen a different path. And this path is, I believe, quite successful because at the end of the day there is a certain reliability. (Interview 1)

The second connotation of reliability refers to solidarity. Being a reliable partner for the clients means that the cooperative bank is always there for the client—especially during difficult times. The bankers often showed me that they treat their clients with patience, solidarity and consideration. Thus, the quality of the relationship becomes apparent especially in times of crisis.

Vice versa, this also means that if you have a long-term business relationship ... you do not let them down as quickly as a large bank. You stay on it for a longer time. You provide support for a longer timer. You try to help through networks and the everything else. (Interview 16)

However, this reliable partnership always works under the premise of help for self-help. I heard several times that the bank wants to support the client to make a living on his own again.

We do not believe in transfers. We just say: Whoever is at the bottom, receives the transfer, he must, indeed, survive. As a metaphor, we give him our hand so that he can stand up. As soon as he is able to stand and walk again, we turn that transfer into a loan. You receive the funds in order to make a living, but you have to pay it back on your own. And this is not primarily in my interest against the background of business making, but it is in your interest so that you can walk with pride. That is cooperative. (Interview 16)

5.5.2 Second Theme: Participatory Activities

The participation is a member's privilege. This reflects the direct democratic structures which allow the members as capital owners to control and govern the decision-making process. Most Volks- and Raiffeisenbanks conduct an annual representatives' meeting. Besides the right to vote in the representatives' election most cooperative banks give their members the chance to attend the local assemblies. These meetings are perfect opportunities for the cooperative bankers to meet their members and to hear about their demands and concerns. The assemblies stir the emotions of both members and employees.

> *So, I regularly experience that sense of community when we have our member assembly where the members appear and spend a day together. And there I see a powerful community. So, the clients who introduce themselves to me, always mention: I am a representative of your institutions. And that shows me that they see the community of representatives of this bank as something special. [...] And I would not say that it is like a family meeting, but you really look forward to seeing one or the other fellow. That is what my clients who are appointed as representatives tell me.* (Interview 11)

> *You notice in every local assembly how committed they are. And you do not have that at any other organization, at any other bank. And it is very intense to experience that. Look at the example I just mentioned. For one person it was about the retirement account because we raised our account fees. And this elderly man stood up: We must create a cheap account for elderly people. [Knocks on the table] If you look at our account models ... It should not be the case that he pays 2,50 Euros for a withdrawal because he does not have any alternatives. ... And I said that this is simply his destiny. I cannot change it. I cannot do everything for everybody. ... Then the other person stood up and said: He does not understand it. We have sufficient opening hours. You must consider how to keep this bank working. ... It costs a lot of money. You get goosebumps. That is so intense.* (Interview 5)

The other part of the participatory activities relates to the dividend. This is a direct monetary benefit that members receive from holding cooperative shares. The redemptions on member shares have not been part of the original cooperative business model. They have been added over the course of time as a product of increased regulatory requirements. While the member assemblies are seen as important opportunity for social exchange and feedback, most interviewees explicitly state that they see the dividend as an add-on.

> *So, I think that it is a secure income at the end of the day. Four percent are far beyond the usual market income. Yet, we limit the shares to 1.000 Euro per*

member. I believe that this is something nice for the members, that they appreciate it. But it is not enough to establish a relationship. (Interview 16)

5.5.3 Third Theme: Bonus Activities

Cooperative banks offer core banking services, participation rights and dividends to their members respectively clients. Additionally, they have also established a whole system of extra benefits which are not directly related to the original business field. In most cases these additional benefits aim at the benefit of members only. However, some interviewees reported that this distinction is not always possible and desired.

To some extent we create tax duties for our clients when conducting hidden profit distribution, or for the members. And that concerns various tax duties. And we cannot allow this for our members. (Interview 15)

There are companies who support our members. There are some advantages if you are member or if you have the member cash card. Some cooperative banks have already implemented this. They receive some discounts, this is one possibility. Otherwise, it is rather tough to give financial benefits when it comes to fees and interests. This is a form of hidden profit distribution which requires special consideration. The main difference really relates to the decision power regarding the bank's strategy. (Interview 8)

The interviewees reported two kinds of bonus activities. First of all, bonus activities have a rather strong focus on monetary benefits when it comes to bonus programs. The mentioned differentiation is easier to implement when issuing member cards or providing discounts for additional services, like insurances.

We have a Volks- and Raiffeisenbank bonus program. That means that members can enjoy certain monetary benefits at local companies or local institutions. They identify themselves through the member card. (Interview 15)

Yet, we offer various kinds of bonus programs. The golden Volks- and Raiffeisenbank card is one example. Members can enjoy shopping benefits, have a better network. That is for sure. (Interview 16)

The second part of the bonus activities relates to events organized by the Volks- and Raiffeisenbanks. Some Volks- and Raiffeisenbanks organize annual member holidays, trips to musicals or an evening at the cinema. This contributes to establishing a sense of community among the members and respectively clients. Against this background, these events combine financial and meta-economic benefits.

> *And we have found various ways of paying this back to the members. This year we, for example, organize another big event, which allows us to establish direct contact to our members, to offer a special event to our members, with various individual elements, which these funds are used for.* (Interview 15)

5.5.4 Fourth Theme: Local Value

The broadest feature in the value creation is represented by the element of local value. This reflects the cooperative aspiration of being a role model for social responsibility. The concern for the local community is closely linked to the member promotion. While the other elements of the value creation have originally aimed at the benefit of the members, the local value creation has always been considered an essential step in fulfilling the comprehensive social responsibility.

> *The Volks- and Raiffeisenbank does many projects every year. Usually through donations to give financial support for social needs or social projects.* (Interview 4)

The cooperative banks' embeddedness is manifested through their close relationships with the local club life. Importantly, the banks do not consider them mere sponsors but rather partners. This means that they have established a trustful relationship to various local clubs and organizations, which is on equal footing and about more than just financial support.

> *The authenticity is ensured by saying that we do not apply any random structures to the clubs, and everybody receives a pre-determined amount. But everybody receives whatever he needs. Where do the people need something?*

We accordingly support them. [...] And if there is any demand, it is not on a level where we say: Hahaha! Condescendingly ... But with authenticity and on equal footing. Where we do not only do business with each other but where we really help each other. (Interview 21)

They are not interested in short-term success, but they want to have a fair partnership. Apart from the product partners it also applies to everybody whom we do business with. Including the carpenter who repairs our windows. You can do cost-cutting there, too, if you order a no-name company online. Or you say that we have a responsibility to work with local craftsmen which deliver good service quality. So that you make sure that they earn enough for making a living for their families and their employees. (Interview 19)

The analysis shows that the local contribution also includes the bank's role as local employer and taxpayer. While financing the drivers of the economy, namely the small and medium enterprises, cooperative banks serve as important local employers, too.

If you look at what the cooperatives give to the public from their earnings, what they give back, what they do when it comes to donations and support, what tax income remains in the region. ... We indeed pay taxes, we pay a lot of taxes. And these are not only the taxes which the bank pays itself but also look at the taxes which are due for each employee which we deduct. No other banking group can compete if I look at what we comprehensively do for the regions. (Interview 8)

Having small decision-making processes, being locally embedded, being a corporate taxpayer in the region. That does not count for large banks. We do a lot for clubs. We are very well known in the region and that is our strength. And our clients like that very much. (Interview 12)

Being locally embedded, cooperatives serve the clients, their families and the whole region. Financial support for local sports clubs and projects like public parks and playgrounds create meta-economic value for the region and imply ideational benefit for the members in their function as inhabitants of the community. Thus, with regard to its effects the local engagement is the most comprehensive activity dimension.

For the municipality as corporate taxpayer, we are the most important employer in our function as large taxpayer, as mentioned we are a very large company in the region. Also for clubs. So actually, for everybody. So, for the club life, donations, financial support. (Interview 12)

5.5.5 Fifth Theme: The Employees' Role

The key for the local focus of cooperative banks is their employees' local embeddedness. They are active members in local clubs and social life. The employees embody the cooperative values and thus serve as multipliers. The experts admitted that they were not motivated by monetary aspects since cooperative banks cannot pay the same wages as large banks. They are rather intrinsically motivated and convinced by the cooperative business model. Overall, cooperative banks' employees are characterized by their ties to the region and their down-to-earthiness.

Many clients do not go to the Volks- and Raiffeisenbank or to the Sparkasse. They go to Mr. J. They go to Mr. S. They go to Mr. M. So, the employees are a very large factor. And if the employees identify themselves with the Volks- and Raiffeisenbank, then you notice that these are the better employees and those employees who make more business. (Interview 2)

I am very down to earth, I know many people from the region with different backgrounds, sport clubs, other cultural institutions. I believe that the key factor in the client business is the personal relationship. And I realized that I can rather benefit from that at a cooperative bank, compared to a large bank where I might work in a region which I do not even know, and every evening I drive home and come back to that region the next morning. (Interview 1)

I think it's our people who make the difference. Because our employees are part of the region in which we live. That is to say, there is not anyone from the distant city of S. Our business area has a diameter of 50 kilometers. But you are advised by somebody who comes from the region. You know that person. Who is possibly involved in the club life himself. And even part of social life. And that's what makes the difference in my opinion. (Interview 23)

This is also reflected in the interviewees' motivation. I noticed that most people like working for a cooperative since they are motivated by the possibilities to promote the clients and the region.

Making a contribution to the region [motivates me]. Making a contribution to the region with regard to the cooperative notion. (Interview 16)

Living in the same region as the clients means that the employees are well informed about the local development and that they directly benefit from enhancing the banks' local commitment. The employees maintain relations with the clients which exceed the business sphere. The interviewees reported that they for example meet their clients at the local bakery which sometimes serves as trigger for further business.

That we can go on Saturdays at 07:30 am—my favorite example—to the local bakery and can talk to our clients without the need to avoid them because we have just ripped him. It is part of our cooperative capabilities that we can do this. (Interview 8)

I cannot leave scorched earth because I have only this one earth. That is why I must ensure that this earth is managed—which is another frequently used term in the cooperative sector—sustainably. I must ensure that we are still able to continue the cooperation in this region in five or ten years' time. (Interview 6)

In addition to that, the managements of cooperative banks try to promote a certain cooperative culture within the bank. This means that the treatment of the employees corresponds to the values that are lived in the relationship to members and clients. Cooperative banks stand for a participatory and sustainable work environment.

We maintain the German test branch of the Volks- and Raiffeisenbanks. So, we have a test branch that was developed together with our regional associations. It is located in the northern part of our market area. And it was developed on the one hand by our managers and on the other hand by our clients and the local employees. That means by those employees who work in the service department, who have daily client contact … together with pro-

> *fessionals, mostly architects, they designed this branch, the test branch. [...] Employees and clients. So, participatory as far as possible. Then, it becomes experienceable.* (Interview 16)

Several interviewees reported that they appreciate that they can express their opinion and integrate their character. Employees at cooperative banks do not have to play-act and they do not have to see their salary as compensation for personal suffering.

> *That is a special business model, and it is a business model—how should I say—which provides a healthy and long-term working environment. You do not have to change your character or play-act. At least at this bank. Here you stay healthy, physiologically and physically. You work for a good thing. We are proud of our culture.* (Interview 16)

> *For me it is essential because the clients notice that the employee is interested in working there, he stands behind his employer. But if I am a mercenary as it is often the case with soccer players, so that I would say I choose my club based on the best salary, and if I do not like it, I will go to the next one. And this has 100 percent influence on the clients. So, this is one of the most important criteria, having a satisfied employee. Because if the employee is satisfied, then it has an influence on the client business. So, that is very essential for me. So, that always depends on how the management lives that, how the management supports it, how the management informs the employees.* (Interview 12)

5.6 The Model of Cooperative Value Creation

My practice-based analysis shows that German cooperative banks' business strategies are characterized by a variety of business activities. Against the background of grounded theory, this model serves as fundament for my dynamic theory.

The German Cooperative Society Act translates the promotional mission into a legal definition. According to §1 cooperative organizations have the purpose of promoting their members' economic, social and cultural interests. Against this background, I introduce two separations in order to illustrate the cooperative activities. First of all, I differ between activities, which benefit the members only, and activities, which benefit all clients, including those without cooperative shares. The second distinction concerns the kind of benefits arising from the respective activities. It draws on the cooperative obligation to promote the economic interests, respectively monetary benefits, and the social as well as cultural interests, respectively meta-economic benefits. As a result, I developed a model of the cooperative value-creating activities (see Fig. 5.1). Importantly, this provides an overview of all activities as identified through the expert interviews. It serves as the basis for my dynamic theory. In short, I was able to observe six different activity dimensions at German cooperative banks. Core activities relate to cooperative advisory, original bank services. These are monetary benefits to all clients. Secondly, participatory activities are separated into the participation of members and the dividend. Both are member privileges. However, the dividend is a monetary benefit while the participation concerns the meta-economic inclusion of the members through local assemblies and respective decision as well as voting rights. Similarly, the dimension of bonus activities is also separated into two parts. The rather monetary element concerns the bonus programs. These discounts on various services within and beyond the cooperative business sphere are monetary benefits aimed at the members. On the other hand, events organized by the cooperative banks generally aim at the members, too. Yet, these mainly meta-economic benefits are often also enjoyed by non-member clients. This is understandable as it would be more difficult to make a strict differentiation regarding events. The final activity dimension relates to the local engagement. Depending on the respective activity this can be targeted at the members or at any person in the local region. The local engagement is very comprehensive including the status as taxpayer and employer as well as the role as partner of local clubs and social institutions. Thus, the local engagement benefits members, non-member clients and all local inhabitants through monetary and meta-economic benefits.

The detailed analysis of my data helps to turn the overview into a dynamic theory. My grounded theory approach reveals the essential key insights for understanding how cooperative banks work and how they contribute to sustainability.

1. Primarily, cooperative banks deliver high-quality, long-term bank services and advisory to all clients. In contrast to their original aspiration, cooperative banks' strategic focus lies on their customers. This includes both members and clients without any cooperative shares.

Our original main task is to create added value for the members and the clients. (Interview 3)

It is not the case that members are first-class clients and clients-only are second-class. That is not the case at all. The customers are all treated equally, and the membership is in many cases an indicator of satisfaction with the bank. (Interview 11)

This implies that the bank's focus is clearly on its original services, namely the provision of banking services.

Thus, focusing on quality in the products you offer, and emphasizing everything you can offer with regard to financial services. That is my approach. And thus, you should rather strengthen the services you offer instead of adding small services at the fringe. (Interview 22)

2. The second strategic focus lies on the local engagement. The promotion of the region fulfills two strategic functions. By doing so, the cooperative bank assumes its social responsibility for their region which is part of the promotional mission and, thus, also part of their DNA. Furthermore, the local engagement positively influences the quality of their core activities. It does not only create knowledge about the region, but it also serves as growth accelerator.

The branch network represents an important part of the business strategy. Maintaining local branches fosters the embeddedness and ensures the local knowledge. Creating or at least maintaining jobs and facilities in various parts of the market area is a contribution to the local competitiveness and prosperity itself. Several interview partners highlighted the importance of this commitment to the respective region in times where large banks seem to focus on the inner cities only. I was able to observe the utilization of the branches during my field work. The bank from interview 4 is in the middle of a shopping mall. The bank from interview

6 shares its ground-floor level with a café. The bank from interview 20—one of the largest cooperative banks in Germany—even established a small city district that does not only host the headquarters but also various restaurants and office spaces.

Nevertheless, as a result of the merger we have 24 branches and we still plan to maintain these 24 branches. So, we are really present in the clients' region. We certainly contribute to that. So, we do not leave the regions as other banks do, but we rather promote the region. (Interview 1)

I argue that we create added value for the region. By being present in the area. By, I would say, providing the financial infrastructure, the ATMs, the branches. (Interview 2)

Especially in times when bakers, butchers and the likes have left, the bank is often one of the last contact points in the region—I indeed know that here, too, the trend is declining due to customer development with regard to branches. Nevertheless, a crucial point is that employees and customers also meet in the villages, meaning away from the head quarter, providing services decentrally. This relates to the branch network that we maintain. (Interview 4)

Of course, we are a promoter of the region. We also have a grocery store within our bank where the people can purchase groceries and everything else that they need for the daily life. And thus, we are somehow a local attraction, meeting point somehow, and the local provider of daily things and services in order to help the clients achieving their goals. (Interview 21)

The local embeddedness enhances the knowledge and also serves as motor for trust. I felt this myself. When I entered the bank branch for interview 2, there were only two persons present. I met a female employee who was just serving a client. She realized that I have an appointment with the CEO whose office is on the second floor. When she went upstairs to tell the CEO's secretary that the interviewer had arrived, she left the client and me for a moment completely alone in the bank's counter hall. I interpret this as symbol for a strong basis of trust with their clients.

3. The participatory activities in terms of member participation are essential for cooperative banks. These activities promote democracy and fulfill various functions. The members serve as long-term creditors providing equity, which is used for enhancing the banks' capability. Moreover,

the members' decision-making power ensures that the long-term strategy fits the demands of the members and their region. Finally, being a cooperative increases the legitimacy when it comes to long-term client orientation and local embeddedness. Although most cooperative banks also serve non-member clients, the interviewees consider the corporate form as cooperative indispensable.

> *So, the eG [German legal term standing for registered cooperative] in our name has indeed a meaning. Otherwise I might have ended up in an AG. And I have to admit, eG means for me that there might be smaller units where you work together. That there is more than profit maximization. Indeed, this is important. But there are more important things in life. Where the clients are satisfied, where I know the clients, too. All these are values which can only be lived by a cooperative bank. Another one cannot do this.* (Interview 13)

This fits with the interpretation of sustainability. Many interviewees stressed that sustainability has more aspects than ecology in their view. Essentially, sustainability relates to the stability of the cooperative organization and its value creation for the clients and the region. The focus on sustainable business relationships instead of profit maximization gives cooperative banks a unique position on the banking market.

> *Treating them adequately. Not only the investor meaning the shareholders but in fact all stakeholders. In my opinion, according to our philosophy this is the fundament of sustainability. And for me this is actually an essential aspect, sustainability. For me sustainability also relates to income. Because we are ultimately income-driven, as we need to make profits to increase our equity, to remain viable. Especially in these times, equity is the most important element.* (Interview 5)

The overall interpretation of sustainability by cooperative banks lays a large focus on economic sustainability. Thus, it is directly linked to generating sustainable income through successful client-orientated key activities. Although not maximizing profits, the economic bottom line influences all cooperative activities. At the end of the day, all activities are linked to the performance of core activities. This is also reflected in upcoming calls for the measurement of the benefits from social engagement. Ultimately, cooperative banks respect the economic bottom line in order to maintain their organization's justification.

> *I am convinced by the fact that this company does not really act for the maximization of profits, for maximizing the investors' capital, but that they have a different purpose. Indeed, I would also admit that we need to make profits, too, in order to sustainably make business. But we have a different main target. And it is really about partnership, about the promotion of the members, about the promotion of the region.* (Interview 15)
>
> *We are in banking competition with all the others and we must deal with that competition. And we must be profitable because there is no alternative.* (Interview 22)

This strive for sustainable income enhances the cooperative mantle. It is not the management's aspiration to do deficient business. At the same time, cooperatives strengthen their governance roots as they feel the benefits of being a cooperative organization. Thus, the long-term existence of the organization of cooperatives with its member-based governance is not at all questioned.

4. The cooperative mission is embedded in the focus on core activities and local engagement. Cooperative banks achieve their goal of promoting the clients and the region by alleviating contemporary miseries.

> *And the original notion was that there are certain miseries or shortages according to Raiffeisen or Schulze-Delitzsch. And today we look for modern miseries and shortages. And we analyze how we can provide support. Also following the principle of help for self-help.* (Interview 15)
>
> *It used to be … we were established to alleviate miseries. There was a shortage. Help for self-help. So, our present task is to find the shortages in the rural regions—we are in a metropolitan area, but we are still rather rural.* (Interview 14)

Through their two dominant practice dimensions, core activities and local engagement, cooperative banks fulfill two roles. When it comes to cooperative advisory to their clients, cooperatives act as orchestrators. They are the house bank for many of their clients accompanying families and companies over decades and generations. When they identify certain client demands, they actively integrate the services of a product provider within the cooperative network or further partners outside the network. By offering long-term, fair and transparent advisory cooperative banks fulfill the need of having a trustful partner who reduces the increased complexity through comprehensive financial services.

> *For me modern miseries—and I see it like this—are indeed in the original banking business. What do we primarily do? We advise our clients. [...] It is our aspiration to provide really client- and need-orientated advisory, and to help the clients, the members to satisfy the need with regard to all financial aspects. I would argue that only few people have an adequate retirement planning. So that we offer optimal advisory in this regard. Only few people have an adequate wealth planning. There is an enormous need for explanations, information and advisory in this regard, too.* (Interview 15)
>
> *The more complex our world becomes, the more people look for local embeddedness, the more people need continuity, the more people look for a trusted setup. And we as cooperative banks can play that role compared to other banks.* (Interview 17)
>
> *But so far, I have found that the financial business is not that simple. Not even for the average customer. So that he says: I'll do it all myself in the future. Regardless of convenience. But I think it's still like this: I want to talk to someone I trust. And because of our regional added value and the regional closeness that is actually inherent in our system, I believe that from this point of view we can play exactly this orchestrator role. And I hope that this will be the case.* (Interview 23)

In addition to that, cooperative banks also strive for the alleviation of miseries beyond financial aspects. Regarding the local engagement, cooperatives act as mediators. Although they do not have as large means as some of their competitors, they deliver an important contribution to the local development. Their most remarkable impact on social welfare does not come from pure financial donations. Cooperative banks stand out when they use their knowledge and networks to bring together politicians, entrepreneurs and citizens to enable joint efforts for the sustainable development of the region. The facilitation of local projects is very efficient because it does not depend on the limited financial resources from cooperatives but is based on their outstanding relationships and networks.

At our bank the cooperative notion is very much manifest in the networking aspect so that we create networks for our clients to connect them. We connect people. We try to unify interests in order to help the company or the individual client enforcing their interests. Together you are stronger. But how does he manage to meet with many people?! That's why we are establishing networks. We see our brand as network bank. And why networking? Because in our opinion we enable people to come together, to unify their interests and to find solutions. We are involved as mediator and we, especially, want to help through financial solutions. Thus, we organize many, many client events. Importantly, we try live this network spirit in the bank by appreciating team work. We introduced that two years ago. Focusing on the team spirit. Why?! To establish internal networks and, thus, to enable the clients to participate in our networks and to network with other participating clients. I think that this is a cooperative task in the region. And we can utilize this very well since we have local connections. It needs time, it needs work to do this. But I think maintaining the network spirit characterizes a cooperative bank. (Interview 22)

I am thinking of a company from our region. They planned to expand. Yet, there was a large citizens' initiative because it also concerned a nature preserve. And as a result, this company was not able to proceed with its investment plans for one and a half years. During an event I was asked if we could somehow help. First of all, I went to the federal government. This did not change much. Yet, another entrepreneur noticed our problem and said: Alright. I am ready to clean the soil. So, to clean the contaminated soil. And thanks to this proposal we managed to get funding from the federal government so that the entrepreneur was able to start with his project after, I believe, four or five months. It happened relatively quickly compared to these one and a half years. And he was able to increase his investments. He was able to build an additional manufacturing building. He was even able to hire an additional employee. And that was only possible through the Volks- and Raiffeisenbank's network to the entrepreneurs. (Interview 17)

In this context, the promotional mission is interpreted with regard to the satisfaction of clients' needs and the overall promotion of the local region.

At the end of the day it [the mission] is about actually helping the clients and the members in the bank ... making their dreams come true. I think that we as cooperative bank through this extreme closeness does not only sell services, but at the end of the day we help the clients. So, the ultimate driving force is to bring the client through every visit closer to fulfilling his dreams. (Interview 21)

Therefore, I need to extend the promotional mission or the member benefits beyond the direct benefit which might be noticed through the dividend or a direct member benefit, I need to achieve this through the development of the community and the prosperity of this region. (Interview 22)

Figure 5.2 shows my grounded theory of the cooperative banks in Germany. I am convinced that it is important to link my theory to existing theories, especially the member value concept which is the dominant approach for German cooperative banking. One major aspect is shared by my grounded theory and the member value theory: Cooperative banks create more than just financial value, namely monetary and non-monetary benefits. This is in accordance to the legal definition which states that cooperatives are supposed to promote their members' economic, social and cultural interests.

However, at same time this reveals one of the biggest differences. While the cooperative law speaks of member promotion, my grounded theory model states that cooperative banks create value for both members and clients without cooperative shares. In fact, most cooperative banks have a client-focus as opposed to a pure member-orientation. Their primary concern is to satisfy all clients with regard to financial services. They do so by acting as orchestrator with regard to core activities. Cooperative banks are not product-centered, neither when it comes to the client relationship management nor regarding the overall strategy. They rather distinguish themselves through the comprehensive advisory of all their clients. In this respect they equally treat member and non-members with continuity, fairness and honesty. My analysis illustrates that they are not focused on price leadership. They rather aim at being quality-leaders by accompanying the clients through all phases of life.

It must sustainably work. I would argue that we are not the one in Germany that pays the most interests or has the lowest prices. But I have the ambition, and that is what I stand in for, that the person who uses our bank as life bank, will get the most out of it. (Interview 3)

While the member value theory puts its focus on the members and their benefits, I apply a different approach. My analysis looks at the practices in cooperative banks. Thus, I illustrate what cooperative banks do, who it benefits and how their various activities are connected to their business strategy. My approach fosters the understanding of the role of the bonus activities. Bonus programs are meant to increase the members' loyalty. Events are organized in order to foster the sense of community. Both activity dimensions are not part of the strategic focus. Similarly, the dividend plays a subordinate role, too. It is a by-product and thus, neither the core of the business strategy nor a leverage for fulfilling the cooperative mission. As illustrated the cooperative organizational form with its member participation structures is essential for the business strategy. The ownership and participation structures with regard to the members serve as roof for the member promotion within and beyond the original business sphere. It serves as underlying notion why a large part of the cooperative activities is concerned with the enhancement of the members' economic, social and cultural interests. Yet, while non-member clients and the whole society are equally in the strategic focus of cooperative banks, they do not have any relations to or benefits from the member participation. But their relationship to the respective bank depends on the existence of the unique cooperative governance and setup, the cooperative mantle. My grounded theory differentiates from the member value concept in various ways.

(a) I apply an activity-based approach interpreting the practices and opinions of leaders from the cooperative primary banks.
(b) Through my dynamic model I illustrate that the cooperative value creation aims at all clients and the whole region.
(c) Furthermore, I am able to explain the strategic focus of cooperative banks which relates to high-quality services for all clients and the alleviation of modern miseries for both their clients and the whole region.

5.7 Cooperative Social Responsibility

It is essential to see the model in relation to the unique character of the cooperative social responsibility in order to understand cooperatives' crucial role in present-day economy and society. Thus, the following section connects the model's key points to the way cooperative banks assume social responsibility. This illustrates that cooperative banks are role models as they harmonize economic sustainability, social inclusion and the responsibility for the local community. This directly corresponds to the aspiration behind the UN developments goals (United Nations 2020).

The aspirations of the cooperative movement have since inception gone beyond the pure economic sphere. Pioneers like Owen considered cooperatives drivers for social change which even have the potential to foster a revolution by the working class (Pezzini 2006). The first consumer communities were clearly positioned as counter model vis-à-vis the capitalism and industrialization. However, over the course of time the revolutionist ideology has been mitigated and replaced by concepts like the Christian solidarity following the ideas of Raiffeisen. This development was caused by changes in the economic, political and social environment. Nowadays, it would be an inconsiderate generalization to attribute cooperatives revolutionist and anti-capitalist aspirations. Nevertheless, cooperative organizations have always thought beyond the creation of economic value (Limnios et al. 2014). Their members are connected to the organization through both economical relationships and emotional attachment (Feng and Hendrikse 2008; Rössl 2017). Against this backdrop, the model of cooperative value creation shows that social considerations are an essential element in the cooperative business model. This is manifested in the official codex of the cooperative movement by the introduction of the sixth principle (see Chap. 5.2). This aspect has nota bene not been added to the cooperative business model over the course of time. Rather, the cooperative social responsibility has always been a part of the cooperative DNA. This concept shares some similarities with the approach on corporate social responsibility. Taking the interpretation of Tirole (2001) as example, both cooperatives and corporates are characterized by a comprehensive mission exceeding the pure economic sphere. Yet, the cooperative and corporate social responsibilities differ in their core. The leaders of the cooperative movement developed a business model, which is based on local embeddedness as well as the support from its members and their communities, 100 years before the academic discourse addressed the social role of enterprises (Rössl 2017; Wychera 1985). This links up to the work of Freeman and Velamuri (2006) who call for a close interrelation between business and ethics. Their model of Company Stakeholder Responsibility promotes a holistic view on the value chain including ethical and social considerations and requires companies to establish substantial knowledge about all stakeholders.

The social responsibility of cooperatives is integrated in their promotional mission, which is inherent in all activities. In this context, the embeddedness does not represent an additional feature but a necessity for the success of cooperatives. Rössl (2017) even argues that the cooperative movement was built on the idea of social responsibility. Cooperatives can only adequately serve the monetary and meta-economic interests of both their clients and the community if they can draw on a large reservoir of social capital. Following the argumentation of Putnam (1995), their sense of responsibility of the broad basis of members and the region fosters the accumulation of social capital. Degli Antonio and Portale (2011) deliver further proof that enterprises which encode and manifest social considerations in their code of conduct are able to gain more social capital. The grounded theory approach shows that the knowledge and networks are essential for successful local engagement. In the case of cooperative banks, the client advisors play a pivotal role by establishing long-term relationships with their clients respectively the members. This relates to my term orchestrator. By providing financing to local entrepreneurs cooperatives stay informed about the developments in their community. Their employees' engagement in the local club life gives cooperative banks an advance in knowledge which they do not only use for the creation of core value, for example as financing partner of new building areas, but also for the improvement of the local value creation. This manifests for example in increased donations to a local kindergarten which requires unforeseen maintenance work.

The knowledge about all their clients and the region represents a sine qua non for the cooperative success. This helps the management board to adapt their comprehensive business strategy including economic and social aspects to the needs of the local community. Drawing on the argumentation of Tuominen et al. (2017) the cooperative ability to accumulate, maintain and capitalize on the knowledge and network relationships represents one of the large competitive advantages. It allows cooperative banks to differ from their competitors when it comes to satisfying the needs of the clients as well as fulfilling social responsibilities. Regarding the creation of local value through the support of local clubs, initiatives and projects, cooperatives do not act as mere sponsors but as long-term partners, as mediators. Their strategy is not linked to isolated contributions to sustainability goals. They rather consider themselves a well-connected and socially responsible partner of both their clients and the region. The roof of the cooperative value creation consists of a strategically grounded and comprehensive commitment to the sustainable development of the region.

5.8 Conclusion and Discussion

Based on 24 in-depth interviews and research memos, I aimed at closing a research gap in the field of cooperative banking. The most popular theory for analyzing cooperative banks is the member value concept. However, illustrating the strategic focus through conversations with leaders from German cooperative primary banks my grounded theory adds a practice-based view to the discourse. The iterative research process moving from a comprehensive description to a dynamic model allows for the following answers to my guiding research questions:

What Are the Business Practices of Cooperative Banks?
The analysis of the primary banks among the German cooperative financial network reveals six activity dimensions. Relating to the original banking business cooperative banks create monetary value through core activities for all clients. Secondly, they offer member privileges through participation and voting rights. These participatory activities relate to the

dividend, too. Cooperative banks are also engaged with a variety of bonus activities, including discounts at local shops and restaurants. This could in some cases be enjoyed by non-member clients, too. Similarly, non-member clients clearly benefit from events organized by cooperative banks. This dimension mainly aims at member benefits. Yet, it adds meta-economic benefits depending on the nature of the respective event. Finally, cooperative banks are socially engaged. The partnerships with clubs and socio-cultural projects as well as donations to institutions and people in need create meta-economic and monetary value for the members, the non-member clients and all local inhabitants.

What Constitutes the Strategy of Cooperative Banks?
The focus of the cooperative banks' business practices exceeds the member sphere. In short, cooperative banks play two important roles. First of all, cooperatives are the orchestrators for all of their clients. In this context, the strategy aims at high-quality banking services and long-term partnership for members and non-member clients. They guide their clients through all financial decisions. In this regard, the relationship manager integrates cooperative network partners or further services whenever this helps to fulfill the clients' needs. Additionally, cooperative banks act as mediators for the region. They assume their social responsibility by exploiting their local networks and connecting people. Through their large amount of local knowledge cooperatives can create a substantial impact by precise financial support and broad meta-economic engagement. This relates, for example, to education about finance, the contribution to local initiatives and the facilitation of crowdfunding.

These questions provide the insights on the cooperative banks' contribution to the UN's sustainable development goals. Cooperatives are role models for social responsibility. This is not the result of an incremental process, but it is part of the cooperative DNA. The embeddedness in the region allows those businesses to be a strong partner for both the clients and the local society. Cooperative social responsibility extends throughout all business areas including the monetary and meta-economic promotion of members, non-member clients as well as the whole community.

They demonstrate an integrated approach of how to build a whole business around the mission of social responsibility. My grounded theory shows that they fulfill their cooperative mission by alleviating modern miseries regarding their clients and the whole region. The cooperative banks' relevance for the UN's sustainable development goals does not only relate to the local value strategy. Cooperatives are also promoters of social inclusion. By embodying a democratic governance model, cooperative banks foster the commitment and the interaction of the local people. Cooperatives prove that democratic organizations are able to be comprehensively and sustainably successful. Regarding the state of theory in the field of value creatin, they prove that there is a way of being successful and creating long-term value without following the common strategy approach of centralizing, profit maximizing and upscaling.

As this analysis focuses on German cooperative banks, inferences are to be made carefully. I reached theoretical saturation regarding my guiding questions. However, further in-depth analysis is required to understand the effects of consolidation, digitalization and market circumstances on the cooperative banks' strategy and value creation. Nevertheless, the elaboration shows that the mission-driven cooperative banks play an important role in achieving the UN's sustainable development goals. They do not focus on a specific goal but contribute to the overall sustainability of their local communities.

References

Academy of Management. 2019. *AOM Code of Ethics*. Last updated November 2019. https://aom.org/About-AOM/AOM-Code-of-Ethics.aspx

Balnave Nikola, and Greg Patmore. "Competition in Retailing: Lessons from the History of Rochdale Consumer Co-operatives in Australia." Paper presented at the Conference of the Academic Association of Historians in Australian and New Zealand Business Schools, Sydney, December 14–15, 2009.

Beuthien Volker, Hanrath Stephanie, and Heinz Weber. 2008. "Mitglieder-Fördermanagement in Genossenschaftsbanken: Analysen, Erläuterungen

und Gestaltungsempfehlungen aus ökonomischer, rechtlicher und steuerlicher Sicht.“ *Marburger Schriften zum Genossenschaftswesen* 106.
Bello Dogarawa. 2005. “The Role of Cooperative Societies in Economic Development.” *Munich Personal RePEc Archive*, Zaria.
Bundesverband der Deutschen Volksbanken und Raiffeisenbanken. 2015. *Basiswissen—Genossenschaftsbanken: Ursprung und Praxis der Genossenschaftsbanken*. Berlin.
Degli Antoni Giacomo, and Elisa Portale. 2011. “The effect of corporate social responsibility on social capital creation in social cooperatives.” *Nonprofit and Voluntary Sector Quarterly* 40(3): 566–582.
Fairbairn Brett. 1994. *The Meaning of Rochdale: The Rochdale Pioneers and the Co-operative Principles*. Centre for the Study of Co-operatives, University of Saskatchewan.
Feng Li, and George Hendrikse. “On the nature of a cooperative: a system of attributes perspective.“ Paper presented at the 12th EAAE Congress People, Food and Environments: Global trends and European Strategies, Gent, 26–29 August, 2008.
Fonteyne Wim. 2007. “Cooperative Banks in Europe: Policy Issues.“ *International Monetary Fund Working Paper 07/159*.
Freeman Edward, and S. Ramakrishna Velamuri. “A New Approach to CSR: Company Stakeholder Responsibility.” In *Corporate Social Responsibility*, edited by Andrew Kakabadse, and Mette Morsing, 9–23. London: Palgrave Macmillan, 2006.
Genossenschaftliche FinanzGruppe Volksbanken Raiffeisenbank. 2020. Die Finanzgruppe. Last updated February 2020. https://www.finanzgruppe.de/finanzgruppe/
Glaser Barney, and Anselm Strauss. 1967. The Discovery of Grounded Theory: Strategies for Qualitative Research. Mill Valley: Sociology Press.
Gijselinckx Caroline. 2009. “Co-operative Stakeholders. Who Counts in Co-operatives, and How. Working Paper on Social and Co-operative Entrepreneurship.” *WP-SCE 09.05*.
Gioia Dennis, and Kumar Chittipeddi. 1991. “Sensemaking and Sensegiving in Strategic Change Initiation.” *Strategic Management Journal* 12(6): 433–448.
Gioia Dennis, Price Kristin, Hamilton Aimee, and James Thomas. 2010. “Forging an Identity: An Insider-outsider Study of Processes Involved in the Formation of Organizational Identity.“ *Administrative Science Quarterly* 55(1): 1–46.

Gmür Markus, and Peter Suter. 2012. "Member Value in Co-operatives." *Working Papers Université de Fribourg*, 444.

Henry Hagen. 2018. "Trends in cooperative legislation: What needs harmonizing?" *Journal of Research on Trade, Management and Economic Development* 5(1): 7–16.

International Co-operative Alliance. 2019. *Guidance Notes to the Co-operative Principles*. Last updated November 2019. https://ica.coop/sites/default/files/basic-page-attachments/guidance-notes-en-221700169.pdf

International Labour Organization. 2018. *Resilience in a Downturn: The power of financial cooperatives*. Last updated November 2019. http://www.ilo.org/empent/Publications/WCMS_207768/lang%2D%2Den/index.htm

Jazarbkowski Paula. 2008. "Shaping Strategy as a Structuration Process." *The Academy of Management Journal* 51(4): 621–650.

Levi Yair, and Peter Davis. 2008. "Cooperatives as the "enfants terribles" of economics: Some implications for the social economy." *Journal of Behavioral and Experimental Economics* 37(6): 2178–2188.

Limnios Elena, Mazzarol Tim, Schilizzi Steven, Iliopoulos Constantine, and Geoffrey Soutar. "Member Loyalty in Co-operatives; The Equity Paradox." Paper presented at the Co-operatives and Mutuals Research and Teaching Conference, Sydney, November 19–20, 2014.

Limnios Elena, Mazzarol Tim, Soutar Geoffrey, and Kadambot Siddique. 2018. "The member wears Four Hats: A member identification framework for cooperative enterprises." *Journal of Co-operative Organization and Management* (6): 20–33.

Martens Holger. "Genossenschaftliche Identität als kulturelles Erbe". In Genossenschaftliche Idendität und Wachstum: Bericht der XVIII. *Internationalen Genossenschaftswissenschaftlichen Tagung IGT 2016 in Luzern*, ed. Franco Taisch, Alexander Jungmeister, and Hilmar Gernet, 306–317. Sankt Gallen: Verlag Raiffeisen Schweiz, 2016.

Pezzini Enzo. "Cooperatives, Good Companies by Definition." Paper presented at The Sixth International Conference on Catholic Social Thought and Management Education, Rome, 5–7 October, 2006.

Putnam Robert. 1995. "Bowling alone: Americas' declining social capital." *Journal of Democracy* 6(1): 65–78.

Puusa Anu, Hokkila Kirsi, and Antti Varis. 2016. "Individuality vs. communality—A new dual role of co-operatives." *Journal of Co-operative Organization and Management* 4: 22–30.

Rössl Dietmar. 2017. "Das gesellschaftlich verantwortliche Agieren von Genossenschaften als Komponente des Membership-Value." *Zeitschrift für das gesamte Genossenschaftswesen* 67(2): 68–83.

Strauss Anselm, and Juliet Corbin. 1997. Grounded Theory in Practice. Thousand Oaks: Sage.

Suter Peter, and Markus Gmür. 2013. "Member Value in Co-operatives." *Working Papers SES*, 444.

Theurl Theresia. "Shareholder Value und genossenschaftlicher Förderauftrag—Zwei unvereinbare strategische Ausrichtungen?" In *Vom Modell zur Umsetzung—Strategische Herausforderungen für Genossenschaften, Münstersche Schriften zur Kooperation, Band 54*, edited by Theresia Theurl, and Rolf Greve, 51–91. Aachen: Shaker, 2002.

Tirole Jean. 2001. "Corporate Governance." *Econometrica* 69 (1): 1–35.

Tuominen Pasi, Syrjä Pasi, Sjörgrén Helena, and Terhi Touminen. 2017. "CSR activities in consumer co-operatives: exploring the case of Finnish S Group co-operatives based on board reporting." *Journal of Co-operative Organization and Management*, 5(2017): 108–117.

United Nations. 2020. *The Sustainable Development Agenda*. Last updated March 2020. https://www.un.org/sustainabledevelopment/development-agenda/

Vieta Marcello, and Doug Lionais. 2015. "Cooperative Advantage for Community Development." *Journal of Entrepreneurial and Organizational Diversity* 4(1): 1–10.

Wychera Robert. "Genossenschaftsideologie und -praxis im Volksbankenverbund." In *Genossenschaften—Die Kooperationsform für den Mittelstand*, edited by Wolfgang Kemmetmüller, 223–238. Wien: Orac, 1985.

Part II

Generating Value Throught CR

6

Emerging Green Values in the UK Energy Sector: Ecotricity as Deep-Green Exemplar

David McQueen and Amelia Turner

6.1 Overview

Sustainability has long been considered to be a key component of corporate social responsibility (CSR) (Eweje and Bathurst 2017) and from 2015 became the explicit, guiding principle for the UN's landmark Sustainable Development Goals (SDGs) which foreground the transformative potential of the private sector (Scheyvens et al. 2016). These goals, and the bedrock tenet of sustainability, are likely to have increasingly urgent relevance for business as growing climate impacts raise the risks of crossing critical ecological tipping points (IPPC 2019). This chapter provides an in-depth case study of a 'deep-green' business, exploring the strong environmental and sustainable values of UK energy firm Ecotricity and its Director, founder and owner Dale Vince. We outline Ecotricity's growth to become one of the UK's largest green-energy providers and

D. McQueen (✉) • A. Turner
Bournemouth University, Bournemouth, UK
e-mail: dmcqueen@bournemouth.ac.uk

F. Farache et al. (eds.), *Values and Corporate Responsibility*, Palgrave Studies in Governance, Leadership and Responsibility,
https://doi.org/10.1007/978-3-030-52466-1_6

show how the company's success is built on a powerful commitment to sustainability and a set of interrelated, green 'activist' values which underpin every aspect of the company's decision-making.

Tracing the history of the company from the mid-1990s when it became the first to offer 'green electricity', the chapter outlines key moments in Ecotricity's expansion, its unique business model, reputation in the market, political lobbying efforts, marketing, communication and social media strategies, as well as the underpinning philosophy informing the growth of the business. The chapter considers Ecotricity's expansion and diversification from clean energy provider to offering a range of sustainable business initiatives including electric car charging stations, grid-scale battery storage, green mobile phone service and vegan school food supplies. It also explores market rivals, regulatory and policy challenges and assesses the extent to which the director's single-minded and uncompromising values have helped secure a loyal, niche customer base. Dale Vince's particular brand of 'citizen entrepreneurship' (Bjerke and Karlsson 2013) may offer a radical template for corporate environmental responsibility (CER) and business leadership as demand grows for green energy, services, products and governance. Vince's high-profile legal manoeuvres around Brexit are briefly considered as part of a highly proactive and interventionist campaigning style which keep him front and centre of a vigorous and politically confrontational communication strategy.

The chapter concludes with a critical discussion of CSR in light of the threat of runaway global warming and the need for immediate and all-inclusive action by citizens, businesses and governments to encompass 'deep decarbonization' of the economy (IPPC 2019). This case study shows that sustainability can take centre stage at every level of business decision-making and strategic planning and that the UN's call on all businesses 'to apply their creativity and innovation to solving sustainable development challenges' (UN 2015) can be met given sufficient will and determination.

6.2 The History of Ecotricity

The Renewable Energy Company (now part of the Ecotricity Group) was founded in 1995 by Director Dale Vince, a former peace activist and new age traveller, originally from Great Yarmouth, Norfolk. Vince, a school dropout at 15, had been living off-grid for several years, including time at a camp at RAF Molesworth to protest against the basing of US cruise missiles there. His converted Air Force trailer (which served as home) was powered using a self-made wind turbine and he built small wind turbines to take to music festivals such as Glastonbury before seeing a gap in the market for this kind of energy (Flintoff 2011). Ecotricity developed an 'embedded supply' model which uses the local grid to match customers to local generation and in 1996 it became the first company in the UK to offer 'green electricity' to a local college in the Gloucester area generated from landfill gas. As the company website states: 'Our mission was and remains to change the way electricity is made and used in Britain'. With help from a loan from Dutch ethical bank Triodos, Ecotricity was able to gradually expand its wind turbine capacity. In 1997, Vince attended the United Nations Convention for Climate Change in Kyoto, Japan, lobbying political and business leaders on the role wind energy could play in combating climate change. Early Ecotricity customers included The Millennium Dome, The Body Shop and Sainsbury's.

In the first few years Ecotricity focused on providing power for businesses, but in 2002, with capacity growing, the company began supplying to 3000 domestic properties rising to 8000 in 2004 and 23,000 by 2006. An 85-metre windmill, the first in the south-east of England, was constructed in 2005 by Ecotricity to supply energy to Green Park Business Park close to junction 11 of the M4. The location meant the turbine became 'possibly the most visible turbine in the world' seen by large numbers of people who had never seen a wind turbine before and, the company argued, this helped to counter rising 'anti-wind scaremongering' (Ecotricity 2017). Ecotricity subsequently became the first company to supply wind-generated electricity to offices in the area, helping Reading Council reduce their CO_2 emissions. In 2007 they opened three new turbines supplying half the power used by the Bristol Port Company at Avonmouth Docks.

By 2008 Ecotricity had installed 51 turbines across the UK and invested £750,000 working with Formula 1 engineers on the first British-built road-going electric supercar, called 'The Nemesis'. In 2009 Ecotricity's engineless 'Greenbird' broke the land speed record for a wind-powered vehicle clocking a speed of 121 mph. Alongside Ecotricity's electric motorbike 'Ion Horse' (with a top speed of 150mph) these developments represented, in the company's words, an effort to challenge negative perceptions of electric vehicles and address one of three 'really big issues we have to face up to, to live post oil—how we power our homes, travel and feed ourselves' (PR Week 2013; Ecotricity 2019b).

Despite the 2008–2009 recession and difficult lending environment Ecotricity continued to grow, adding B&Q in 2009 to the list of 'green chip clients' companies by powering their distribution centre near Worksop with Nottinghamshire's first large-scale wind turbine (Merchant Wind Power 2010). In 2010 Ecotricity diversified by offering a 'Green Gas tariff', making them the first energy company to offer 'bio-gas' made from eco-friendly 'composted' organic waste (Ecotricity 2010). They floated two oversubscribed rounds of 'ecobonds' which together raised £20 million (Edie 2016) and in 2011 also launched their 'Electric Highway'—the UK's first motorway network of charging points for electric vehicles. These were located at Welcome Break service stations enabling electric cars to travel between London, Bristol, Exeter, Birmingham, Manchester, Liverpool and north to the Lake District without running out of power. By 2019 the Electric Highway had 300 chargers for its 50,000 members across 'almost every motorway service station area' in the UK at a cost of £20 m (Campbell 2019).

Ecotricity's social media strategy has helped the company keep in contact with customers and reach out to potential new customers with innovative campaigns that have, amongst other things, aggressively tackled other energy providers for their continued dependence on fossil fuels. For example, in 2012 Ecotricity released a 'Dump the Big Six' viral video, created by Man+Hatchet advertising agency, showing collapsing cooling stacks animated with comical faces which, by 2019, had been seen over 7 million times on YouTube. The video humorously associated the 'Big Six' with polluting and redundant coal-fired energy generation in contrast to the promise of a clean energy future with Ecotricity. When asked if calling for customers to 'Dump the Big Six' was effective, or if it brought any flak or entanglements he regretted, Vince simply noted:

> Very effective. Flak is the measure of impact. No regrets. (Personal communication 2019)

In 2013 Ecotricity launched a 100% green electricity tariff for all customers and made a frack-free commitment to its customers promising not to 'source any of our gas from shale', and 'never invest in fracking'. In 2019 the company claimed to offer 'vegan energy' to over 200,000 customers across Britain, meaning that no animals or animal by-products are involved in the production of its electricity and gas (Ecologist 2019a; Which 2019). The company's Progress Report for 2019 boldly took up Extinction Rebellion's target to become carbon neutral:

> We've become the first business in the world to declare a 'climate emergency'—adopting XR's target of 2025 to become carbon neutral. Carbon zero has been our long-held ambition—and now we've put a date on it.

Identifying the company's corporate goals with that of direct-action climate activists is the most recent indication of the company's radical, deep-green values.

6.3 The UK Energy Market and Renewables Sector

The backdrop to Ecotricity's steady, if modest, growth has been the dramatic increase of renewable capacity in the UK, which tripled in the five years to 2018 to overtake fossil fuels for short periods in 2018–2019. According to research by Dr. Iain Staffell of Imperial College London, electricity generation is decarbonising faster in Britain than anywhere else in the world. However, claims that 'Britain's power system is closer than ever to being fossil-free' (Staffel 2019) made, somewhat ironically, on the

Drax website seem over-optimistic, at best. Available figures show huge fluctuations over time, with fossil fuels making up over 40% (Which 2019) and non-renewable (including nuclear) accounting for around 60% of all supplies in the year to October 2019 (Drax Electric Insights 2019). The need to assess industry-sponsored research with a sceptical eye should mean we treat any selective use of statistics, or stories around the imminent demise of fossil fuels with caution.

In fact, the UK energy market is still dominated by power stations, such as those run by Drax, and energy suppliers which draw very heavily on non-renewable sources as part of a national energy mix. Energy regulator Ofgem (2019b) describes the energy market as being composed of the six largest (British Gas, SSE, nPower, EDF energy, Scottish Power, Eon), seven medium (OVO, Bulb, Shell Energy, Utilita, Utility Warehouse, Octopus Energy, Green Star Energy) and a selection of twelve small suppliers (Ecotricity, Better Energy, Breeze Energy, Bristol Energy, Engie, Good Energy, Green Energy, iSupply, PFP, Robin Hood, Tonik and Zog Energy). Of these only three: Ecotricity, Good Energy and Green Energy UK were given permission in 2019 to charge consumers above the standard variable tariff rates limit set by Ofgem due to their active support for renewable generation (Energy Live News 2019). Many energy suppliers claiming to be supplying 'green energy' do so based solely on the purchase of Renewable Energy Guarantee of Origin (REGO) certificates, which can cost as little as £1.55 per year per customer to purchase. According to *Which* companies such as Green Star Energy, Ovo Energy, Pure Planet, Robin Hood Energy, So Energy, Tonik Energy and Yorkshire Energy all sell 100% renewable tariffs solely backed up by REGO certificates and did not generate renewable electricity themselves or have contracts to buy any renewable electricity directly from generators (The Independent 2019).

Good Energy is, arguably, Ecotricity's closest competitor and in 2017 Ecotricity built up a 25% stake in the company and unsuccessfully attempted to instal Dale Vince and Simon Crowfoot, Managing Director of one of Ecotricity's divisions, on the board of its rival. In 2019 Good Energy had 261,700 customers (Good Energy 2019), although it has a much smaller reach through social media platforms such as Facebook, where Ecotricity have tens of thousands more followers. Good Energy are founded on broadly similar values of care for the environment, although expressed in more 'moderate' and familiar, 'corporate' language:

> Our mission isn't just to provide gas and electricity to our customers; it's to create a structure to help everyone play their part in combating climate change by putting people at the heart of the solution. (Good Energy 2019)

While both pledge to combat climate change as a core goal, Good Energy is less diversified and more focused on the core business of energy and unlike Ecotricity they do not run campaigns on veganism or wider environmental and political issues, for instance. Their Facebook page is less critical of government policy, and when critical it is expressed in more general and less party-political terms with a focus on the need for urgent action in Westminster (Facebook 2019). An example of this is a Good Energy post on 29.04.2019 about the low turnout in the House of Commons for the debate on climate change (Facebook 2019).

With more than a dozen companies offering renewable energy tariffs in 2019, the market for renewable energy is growing but remains volatile in many respects. A government price cap on the unit price of energy was introduced in January 2019 and other, more unwelcome, policy reforms took effect which impacted the renewable energy market. Solarplicity, an energy provider that sourced 100% of its energy from renewables (Which 2019) and which also installed and maintained rooftop solar PV, became the 13th small energy firm to collapse in 2018–2019. This was blamed, in part, on a highly competitive and overcrowded market in which 'high levels of competition, cost volatility and policy uncertainty' (IGov 2019, p. 2) resulted in many suppliers leaving the market or going bankrupt. One element of policy uncertainty was the government's decision to close the solar feed-in tariff scheme (FITs) to new applications after 31 March 2019 without any immediate replacement. This meant those installing new solar panels might not be paid at all for providing electricity to the grid. The resulting uncertainty around a replacement for FITs,[1] in addi-

[1] The UK government confirmed that FITs would be replaced by the Smart Export Guarantee (SEG) from 1 January 2020. The SEG scheme will allow each supplier to set their own tariffs so long as payments are above zero, a provision strongly campaigned against by many MPs and the Solar Trade Association (Solar Guide 2020).

tion to previous cuts in government subsidies for renewables and an effective ban on onshore wind turbines, further damaged market confidence and contributed to ongoing instability and job losses in the renewable energy sector. It is against this somewhat turbulent backdrop that Ecotricity enters the 2020s.

6.4 Ecotricity's Company Structure, Business Model and Growth

Ecotricity is a not-for-dividend, limited company group with a fairly unique business model. Dale Vince as founder Director is the sole owner of Ecotricity, making him ultimately responsible for decisions about the group (Ecotricity 2019a) although day-to-day management is through a team of directors with corporate business backgrounds. While there are no shareholders, the public can invest in Ecobonds which had raised £50 million for the company by 2016 (Solar Power Portal 2016). The company headquarters is based in Stroud, Gloucestershire, where they are one of the biggest employers in the county, with 'more than 800 employees nationwide', according to media reports (Gloucestershire Live 2018), although Ecotricity's own Environmental Footprint Report (Ecotricity 2018) puts the number of employees at 644. Discrepancies in the reported number of employees may be due to the complex nature of the Ecotricity Group which covers over seventy different companies registered with Companies House as outlined in Ecotricity Group's Tax Strategy Statement (Ecotricity Group 2019) which states that the group does 'not promote tax avoidance or aggressive tax planning arrangements'.

Sustainability and fairness are two consistently cited values of Ecotricity which are reflected at different levels in the company. As part of their business model they have a 'bills for mills' initiative which means that much of the money (over 80% in 2012) made from gas and electricity goes directly back into reinvesting and innovating the production of electricity (Facebook 2019). This may be through hybrid renewable energy parks (Ecotricity Wind and Sun Parks Ltd), energy storage, green gas production or through the manufacture of electric motors, generators and transformers (Britwind). Ecotricity have similar system to 'bring the bee back to Britain' with their mobile phone service, called Ecotalks (Ecotalks 2019). The money from phone bills is used to buy up land and return these sites to their natural state to improve habitat for bees. All Ecotricity customers are on the same energy tariff no matter what type of payment, which might be seen as more 'fair', helping reduce fuel poverty that affects over two and a half million people in the UK (Department for Business, Energy, and Industrial Strategy 2019). However, according to *Which*, 'the tariff is far from the cheapest', although the comparison website noted that Ecotricity came 'a respectable join-eighth out of 30 energy companies' and that its customers seem to 'feel happier to pay a little more for a green-focused tariff' (Which 2019).

Since 1995 (when they built their first windmill) Ecotricity has grown in capacity and number of customers with a strong expansion between 2009 and 2017. The number of customers currently stands at approximately 200,000 (Ecotricity 2019a) with hundreds of staff at their Stroud headquarters, although an unspecified number were laid off in 2018 following a restructuring process (Stroud News and Journal 2018). This follows a 'shocking' £23 m loss in 2017, which Vince took 'ultimate responsibility for' and which he attributed to 'accounting errors relating to unbilled amounts in the main', noting that the company had employed a new finance director to help turn things around (Gloucestershire Live 2018). The company, which may have overstretched itself in 2017, went back into profit in 2018. The group gave £416,000 to charity during the 2018 financial year and in 2019 recorded a 16.9% increase in turnover and a 1.4% increase in business and domestic customer numbers (Punchline Gloucester 2019, 2020).

Ecotricity's customer base makes them one of the bigger green-energy companies and while they remain small compared with giants such as British Gas, EDF, SSE or E.ON, the market dominance once enjoyed by the 'Big Six' has seen a marked decline since 2011 with small suppliers now making up 8% of electricity supplied in the UK in 2019 (Ofgem 2019a).

6.5 Customer Care and Critics

The consumer review magazine *Which* gives Ecotricity four out of five and comments on their green values:

> It beat all of the 'Big Six' energy companies and Ecotricity's 70% customer score was nine percentage points higher than the overall average for energy companies in England, Scotland and Wales. (Which 2019)

The highest area they score in is the online customer care which scored 5/5. However, this does not mean the company is without critics. On the customer review website Trustpilot 52% of customers describe the service as 'excellent', but 28% of the reviews are 'bad'. The positive reviews describe a friendly, quick service and good value compared to some of the 'Big Six' providers, for instance, but negative reviews tend to focus on persistent problems with switching accounts, poor customer service and unexpectedly high bills. On the Trustpilot site a representative of Ecotricity has politely replied to almost all the reviews or complaints offering to help with or look into problems that have been described, suggesting the company values good customer experience and makes an effort to redress complaints, especially when aired publicly. This appears to be a more typical response for the smaller energy firms for whom positive reviews are likely to be more important. By contrast, five of the Big Six had between 76% and 95% 'bad reviews' with far lower level of direct replies to customers on Trustpilot from these energy suppliers. Of course, it is possible that the site is being used by unhappy customers as a venue to air grievances and these highly negative reviews may not be representative of the experiences of most customers at any of the energy suppliers.

There have also been criticisms of Ecotricity's Electric Highway. Being first mover into the market for charging stations meant that Ecotricity maintained something of a monopoly, initially. According to *The Financial Times,* many of the more recent charging point operators still struggle to break into the motorway segment because of terms in Electric Highway's contracts with service station groups, lack of interoperability and fragmented system of apps and payment cards. These operators have been critical of Ecotricity for the slow pace of investment and ageing technology. Responding to the criticism, Vince pointed to the upgrading of the network in 2019 which would ensure that '99 percent' of Ecotricity's network was working at any one time. He noted that the Electric Highway had never made a penny in profit: 'We're not about profitability [...] we genuinely did this because we wanted to kick start something' adding that such complaints are the sour grapes of latecomers. 'We welcome honest competition', he said. 'Obviously our competitors will attack us. That's just capitalism in action' (Campbell 2019).

Other complaints on local news website relate to investing in the 'vegan vanity project' football club Forest Green Rovers or the plans to 'concrete over' green fields to build an eco-business and leisure park, revised after refusal of planning permission as a football stadium only. In a comment section below news of redundancies at Ecotricity one member of the public queried the environmental and business case for the proposed Eco Park stadium at a time when the company was laying off workers:

> They claim to be ethical too, and there's nothing ethical around using loopholes in employment law to save you money when eradicating over 10% of their staff with no prior warning or consultation. (Gloucestershire Live 2018)

6.6 Flag Controversy

Other complaints relate to Dale Vince's various political campaigns. On 14 April 2019 a huge 10-metre EU flag was flown from the front of the Ecotricity headquarters in Stroud in celebration at the delay of Brexit. This was described in a Facebook post as a cheeky 'up yours' to hard Brexiteers like Boris Johnson, Nigel Farage and David Davis (Stroud News and Journal 2019). A petition organised by a local teenager Lee Sibley against the flag raised 1240 signatures and the Brexit supporting *Daily Express* reported 'outrage' that the local Council had failed to remove the flag, although no laws were broken. Mr. Sibley was reported as saying:

> This flag is offending many people, including veterans who have signed the petition. […] It's absolutely disgusting as it's also an eyesore, not forgetting health and safety as well. (Daily Express 2019)

More recent political and legal activities by Dale Vince are considered in the final section of this chapter.

6.7 Media, Communications and Values

Ecotricity has an extensive website, comprising 1270 registered web pages[2] on Google with a well-designed and easily navigable interface. It has a news section and a business section which include information about how to get a quote, the different tariffs and services available as well as a section focusing on the company's values. Ecotricity makes extensive use of social media platforms, including Facebook (73 K+ followers), Twitter (32 K+ followers) and Instagram (9 K+ followers), some aspects of which are managed by a company called Falcon Management. They also have a regularly updated YouTube channel (11 K+ followers) with videos that cover environmentally related topics such as energy, transport, food and nature. The company has been able to draw on the creative resources required to produce over two hundred carefully-crafted videos on themes such as energy, transport, food and nature, reflecting Ecotricity's deep-green values. Alongside but sometimes separately from these communications Vince makes extensive use of Facebook (9 K+ followers) and Twitter (15 K+ followers), in particular, to publicise numerous ventures and discuss a range of issues from Forest Green Rovers to his joint legal interventions around Brexit. In 2019 a new podcast 'Zercarbonista' was added to the suite of communication channels and dozens of media interviews Ecotricity's Director was contributing to, as the urgency of the climate crisis gained greater news coverage against a backdrop of global protests.

Value patterns communicated on social media by Ecotricity have been consistent since the company's first Facebook posting in June, 2009,

[2] At the time of writing (September 2019).

reflecting the company's deep-green ethos and Dale Vince's vision for a green economy. Ecotricity's public communications stress that environmental and communal responsibility comes first, in contrast to more profit-driven competitors such as British Gas or NPower. Few of their posts appear overtly aimed at recruiting new customers and there is, in fact, a huge range of issues covered in the posts ranging from fracking and government energy policy to company-led initiatives around electric car charging points, to land bought and set aside for wild flowers and bees. Major issues covered between 2009 and 2019 on Facebook, for instance, include fracking, associations/friends of Ecotricity, government energy policy, veganism and wildlife conservation.

Ecotricity's communications often contain a sense of urgency drawing on phrases such as 'climate crisis' rather than 'climate change' to emphasise the importance of urgent action, although this mirrors a wider shift in public discourse towards the use of terms like 'climate emergency'. This has happened particularly, as *The Guardian's* environment editor notes (in marking the change to that newspaper's house style guide), since May 2019 when Swedish teenager Greta Thunberg, who inspired school strikes for climate around the globe, argued:

> Can we all now call it what it is: climate breakdown, climate crisis, climate emergency, ecological breakdown, ecological crisis and ecological emergency? (cited Carrington 2019)

Although Ecotricity's online communications contain few obvious direct bids for new customers there is a sense of joining the fight against climate breakdown with the company, rather than being complicit in the damage being done by other energy providers. This message of an urgent need to 'join the fight' is neatly summed up in the image of Dale Vince in a First World War Lord Kitchener recruiting pose, pointing at the reader of Ecotricity's 2019 Progress Report against the company's green and white Union Jack logo above the strapline 'Green Britain needs YOU'. The headline for the short, online report is simply, '12 Years to Save the Planet'.

Ecotricity's Facebook and Twitter feeds are usually updated on a daily basis, sometimes several times a day. On some occasions the company has posted over a dozen times, for instance, on 2/07/2019 when they posted 11 times about WOMAD. This included pictures, videos and tweets about updates and information on their involvement with the event.

The focus of Ecotricity posts range over a number of themes that sometimes reflect political developments in the UK and beyond. For example, there were a flurry of posts on fracking in 2018 when there was relatively heavy media coverage and social media discourse around the issue, especially related to protests against drilling in parts of Lancashire and Yorkshire. Some of the posts have an anti-establishment tenor, such as a post on 15/09/2017 about protesting: 'the fracking giants in government and industry'. This not only illustrates a value of environmentalism but also unchanging and uncompromising values, even in the face of a determined and well-funded energy sector with (at that time) full government support.

Criticism of government policy is not limited to social media posts. In a news feature on the Ecotricity website posted in 2015, Dale Vince complains:

> [...] the government has rigged the market in favour of fossil fuels. That's why we're calling on the Conservatives to level the playing field for energy generation in Britain—to remove the subsidies for fossil fuels just as they have done for wind and solar power. Those stealth fossil fuel subsidies add up to £1000 a year for each household; compare that to just £100 a year for renewable energy, which now provides 25% of Britain's electricity—that's £100 well spent and a big part of the reason why we're so confident that with a level playing field renewable energy would thrive.

Such direct criticism of national government policy is unusual in the corporate world and reflects the campaigning style which characterises much of Dale Vince's communications.

Although they don't get as many interactions, self-education and the personal changes people can make to have a greener lifestyle is also a consistent theme in Ecotricity's communications. Examples include support for and partnership with the organisation Green Tourism, or advice about recycling plastic by using 'eco bricks'. The benefits of a vegan diet are also a recurring issue, such as vegan sausage roll recipes or information about supplying vegan food to schools. When asked about his decision to be a vegan and the company's communications around this Vince indicated how important he believes this issue is:

> Being vegan is a moral issue first and foremost for me, subsequently the impact of meat and dairy on human health came into view (a few decades ago) and more recently the impact on climate change—so three great reasons to stop eating animals and their bodily functions—animal rights, human health and climate change. Any one reason is good enough, all three are overwhelming. No serious environmental person or organisation can not endorse the move away from meat and dairy—it's essential if we are to fight climate change. But some are still on the fence. XR for example—radical in so many ways, reticent about giving up meat. (Personal communication 2019)

This reinforces their value system that fundamental attitude change in society is needed if we are going to save the planet. Veganism and more sustainable food, transport and energy on a personal and policy level are part of their vision for 2030.

Ecotricity's Instagram posts have seen the most evolution since their first post in November, 2014. In 2014 the posts were mostly about nature and not apparently directly related to promoting the company or its causes. Over time their posts have become more branded and tightly focused. Firstly, on raising awareness about changes people can make in their homes and the importance of reducing carbon emissions. One way they do this is by publishing infographics, such as a post from 30/11/2017 on the many benefits of urban trees. Then there is emphasis on the need for political action with a substantial number of posts calling for policy change. There is support for policies that may affect public behaviour such as a 'cow tax' (tax on meat farming), or which are legally binding such as carbon limits on corporations. All have a critical tone with some militant rhetoric, for example, 'system change not climate change' (2019, Instagram).

Looking at values in social media posts, mentions of fairness and equality appear frequently throughout their social media discourse and are projected as intrinsic to their billing system. The language used reflects a sense of care for their customers which, surveys show, is often found wanting in bigger corporate companies:

> At Ecotricity, all of our customers pay the same so they can choose the payment method that works for them and not feel that they are losing out as a result. We feel that's a much fairer system and it's one that works for us and our customers. (Facebook 2014)

There is a sense of the importance of good customer care and this is also evident in Vince's frequent criticism of monopolies that overcharge customers.

The overarching goals and values of Ecotricity's communications reveal an underlying belief in the need for profound social, economic and institutional change. They try and achieve this by promoting key issues such as the need to act on the climate crisis, to promote wildlife conservation, to champion carbon neutral technologies and strategies and to impact future government policy. The key issues occur persistently throughout their social media campaigns and are intrinsic to the company itself, indicating that Ecotricity sees itself as more than just a green-energy company, but positions itself as a radical organisation with revolutionary, 'deep-green' values. Asked how much involvement he has in his company's social media and if Ecotricity planned and coordinated their communications over the year, Vince replied:

> I have a significant role in this and I try to make sure that it all reflects our values and views. Much of what we do is reactive, we have no calendar of events that I am aware of—but I don't do everything. (Personal communications 2019)

The posts, as a whole, cover a wide range of demographics, yet, it is reasonably clear who they are targeting in each individual post—often quite specific groups, such as vegetarians and vegans, or businesses that want to go green. This reflects the value of changing all of society, even though some of their posts support more marginal or countercultural lifestyles (such as veganism). Holistic solutions which stress the need for action on a range of fronts by individuals, businesses and governments are characteristic of Ecotricity's communications. A major theme is inclusive change that people need to come together for the better. There is a sense of almost incidental advertising for Ecotricity, amidst the campaigning and educational material, or links to other organisations.

6.8 Partnerships

Previous research on CSR partnerships suggests mutually beneficial partnerships between corporations and non-profit organisations, civil society and various governmental organisations can often be successful (Albareda et al. 2007). Nevertheless, there are often significant issues aligning business interests which are rooted in profit and economic growth and NGOs and charitable sectors, in particular, where sustainability, workers and community rights or ethical values take priority (Wadham 2009; Bingham and Walters 2013). Such issues of alignment do not, generally, appear to hinder Ecotricity's various partnerships.

One way in which Ecotricity reaches new customers and raises awareness of its green business is through strategic sponsorship. This ranges from financial support for Forest Green Rovers, described by FIFA as 'the world's greenest football club', to collaborations with charities, campaign groups and wildlife conservation organisations. Over 140 organisations Ecotricity works with or provides power to are listed on their partner page, including eight conservation trusts, six vegan groups, six animal rights organisations, four transition towns, various pressure groups such as CND, Greenpeace, Friends of the Earth, the festival WOMAD and several ethical consumer groups or progressive magazines, such as *Red Pepper* and *Juno*. These partnerships offer an opportunity for people belonging to other ethical, progressive or environmentally-focused organisations to learn about Ecotricity's vision of a 'Green Britain' and potentially become a customer, sometimes with incentive offers of cash donations to the partner organisation. As Burton et al. (2017) have noted, such sponsorship and cause-related marketing can be transactional and simply oriented towards building brand awareness. However, the degree to which Ecotricity under Dale Vince has become involved with some of these partners suggests a more long-term commitment above and beyond the financial bottom line, particularly where sustainability objectives of each party clearly align.

An example of such commitment would be Forest Green Rovers FC (FGR), of which Vince is Chairman and owner. FGR has received frequent coverage and publicity through Ecotricity's website and social media coverage since 2010 when the club ran into financial difficulties and Ecotricity became involved. Under Vince's stewardship FGR set themselves the task of becoming 'the most sustainable football club in Britain, probably the world' including a pesticide- and chemical-free pitch, solar panels, ultra-low energy LED floodlights, recycled rainwater irrigation system, electric carpool, bamboo kit and vegan food for players, staff and fans (Sustainability in Sport n.d.; FGR 2019). Ownership of FGR has proved an effective way to raise awareness of sustainability values and provides marketing and campaigning synergies for Ecotricity with widespread media coverage and publicity, especially locally where coverage of football games is a regular feature of the news.

Amongst Ecotricity's closest partnerships, the three most mentioned on their social media and news article history are, the RSPB, the Vegan Society and Sea Shepherd. On social media Ecotricity have shared content from these organisations, mentioned them in posts and named them as partners of the month. They also appear in news articles on Ecotricity's website and these organisations also share stories and links back to the company. The RSPB, for instance, have a page explaining who their partners are and a search on RSPB website for 'Ecotricity' reveals five articles, although Ecotricity are mentioned more on the RSPB Facebook page, such as this comment on 29 March:

> Our RSPB members have helped to save 10,000 tonnes of CO_2 by switching to green energy and we want to say a big thank you! (Facebook 2019)

The link with RSPB, a well-established and non-controversial institution, was strengthened when in 2016 Ecotricity built a windmill supplying electricity to their Headquarters in Sandy, Bedfordshire. This close association with RSPB helps give Ecotricity a sense of being trustworthy and embedded in mainstream values and causes whilst helping to debunk some of the myths around the impact of windfarms on birdlife. Having

RSPB endorse Ecotricity acts as a counter argument to a recurring criticism of wind turbines and increases the appeal to middle England.

Out of the three, the Vegan Society carries the most content and articles about Ecotricity, all positive, including a description of the company as 'the world's only official vegan energy supplier' (The Vegan Society 2019). Sea Shepherd has the least online content relating to their partner and sponsor (Dale Vince is an Honorary Patron of Sea Shepherd). Of all Ecotricity's partners, Sea Shepherd could be considered the most controversial as they employ direct-action tactics, such as ramming ships and removing fishing gear. Sea Shepherd's more single-minded focus on direct-action tactics to confront illegal activities and protect wildlife in the world's oceans is, perhaps, indicative of a more militant dimension to Vince's bedrock, environmental values. It is these strongly-held values which has spurred him to invest in numerous conservation initiatives alongside the core green-energy supply business and take on a more public, interventionist and explicitly political campaigning role than most CEOs would be comfortable with. Asked about the campaigning dimension to Ecotricity's communications, Vince admitted:

> Yes, much of what we do is campaigning—we are trying to change the world, using business as a medium, and football more recently. (Personal communications 2019)

6.9 Party-Political Support

Lobbying and funding of political parties has long been a concern for critical research into the disproportionate influence of corporations over government policy and law-making process in the US (Drutman 2015), the UK (Miller and Dinan 2008; Cave and Rowell 2014) and across the globe (Beder 2006, 2019; McMenamin 2013). Bauer (2014) has drawn on CSR and lobbying research to develop a normative model of 'responsible lobbying' incorporating stakeholders' and broader society's interests within a transparent and democratic process. Her paper points to problems of transparency and accountability and that symmetric two-way-communication with stakeholders may be desirable, but that 'moving policy issues to the open public sphere is not always possible' (p. 68).

From a sustainability perspective Ecotricity can be shown to be carrying out 'responsible lobbying' by pushing the major parties for greater support for renewable energy and to end subsidies and tax relief for the fossil fuel sector. There is a degree of transparency in the funding of political parties, partly due to British laws regarding disclosure of party funding. It is through Ecotricity's funding of three parties that Dale Vince was subject to negative commentary about financial backing for the Labour Party, in particular, who supported government subsidies for the renewable sector (see The Telegraph 2015; The Independent 2015). The issue of transparency and democratic accountability of Vince's lobbying efforts is more difficult to assess given lack of shareholder oversight and that, as Bauer (2014) has pointed out, policy discussion between corporations and political decision-makers usually takes place behind closed doors.

Ecotricity's funding of and 'ethical partnerships' with UK political parties, as with its other charity and organisational partnerships also appears to have a tactical and marketing role (access to potential new customers), alongside an influence and lobbying rationale. Promotional deals with the Green Party and Liberal Democrats mean that when someone signs up to Ecotricity they donate £50 to these parties.

While Ecotricity has been critical of the Conservative and Conservative-Lib Dem coalition governments, there are indications that they align themselves with particular Labour, Green Party and Liberal Democrat policies. There have been various posts supportive of Labour proposals, such as one in March 2019 with a picture supporting Labour's zero carbon housing standards. They have also mentioned joint events with the Green Party such as at WOMAD Q&A and a link to the Green Party from Ecotricity's partner page states:

> We both agree that Britain needs to ditch fracking and choose green energy, for any hope of a sustainable future. We need a world where we can take real care of our planet, our wildlife, and our people. And together, Britain's greenest energy company and the greenest political party can help deliver that.

In fact, Ecotricity have made donations to Labour, the Green Party and the Liberal Democrats as all three parties support subsidies for renewables. In November 2013 they donated £20,000 to the Green Party and £250,000 to the Labour Party in 2015 to help prevent, 'an existential threat from a second-term Tory government' (The Guardian 2018). In an article in *The Guardian* Dale Vince explained how he felt let down by the coalition:

> We've watched the coalition government systematically undermine not just the renewable energy industry in Britain but the whole green economy and, by default, efforts to combat climate change.

Records at The Electoral Commission show the Liberal Democrats received £50,000 in 2015 from Ecotricity, of which £20,000 was to the party in Kingston-upon-Thames constituency which Ed Davey, pro-renewables Secretary of State for Energy and Climate Change, had lost. This shows a strong tactical dimension to these donations, which include a further £20,000 to the Lib Dems in 2016 and tens of thousands of pounds donated regularly to The Labour Party between 2014 and 2018, but none to the Green Party since 2013. These donations have led to hostile coverage in the press. A critical report in *The Telegraph* in 2015 noted that Dale Vince had received a £3.2 m loan from his own company and described the revelation 'as potentially embarrassing for Mr Miliband'.

6.10 Mutual Three-Way Party Support for Ecotricity

Dale Vince's support over time for three political parties has paid some dividends, at least in terms of endorsement for Ecotricity. On the Liberal Democrats website, for instance, there is a section that talks about the partnership:

> Our partnership with Ecotricity is about hitting our climate targets, it's about building more green energy, and it's about changing the way energy is made and used in Britain. (Liberal Democrats 2017)

The content is positively framed, explaining what the company does and why the Lib Dems see it as a good cause. There are similar messages from the Green Party, with positive support on their social media encouraging members of the public to switch to Ecotricity. The Labour Party have also positively endorsed Ecotricity and Dale Vince who they invited to speak on the theme of a Green New Deal and Renewable Energy at various Labour Party events in 2019. Asked about his support, over the past decade, for three parties Vince responded:

> They are all progressive parties when it comes to issues like social justice—and more relevantly Renewable Energy. Where there is a relationship there is a chance to be heard on issues like RE and to make a difference to policy. That has happened with the Labour Party, according to them. (Personal communication 2019)

Lobbying appears to have been effective in this case, from his perspective at least, and through his Twitter feed and Facebook posts in 2018–2019, Vince has shown very strong support for Labour's Declaration for a Green Industrial Revolution. He has also shown fierce opposition to Brexit and the Conservative Party under the leadership of Boris Johnson, in particular. The degree of alignment in Labour Party and Dale Vince's is an example of what Burton et al. (2017) describe as 'co-branded tweets' which enable the joint promotion of the cause and help engage customers in awareness of the issues and developing mutual support for both partners.

6.11 Brexit Legal Challenge

On the question of Brexit, Dale Vince made national headlines in 2019 for funding a legal challenge in the Court of Session in Edinburgh to consider if Boris Johnson could be imprisoned if he defied the so-called Benn Act passed in Parliament in September and pursued a 'no-deal' Brexit. Vince, described in many of the media headlines as a 'multimillionaire environmentalist', said:

> That we can anticipate law-breaking by our prime minister is incredible [...] There is a remedy to that through the courts, which is an injunction to prevent that law-breaking from taking place. (Al Jazeera 2019)

Prime Minister Johnson subsequently sent a photocopy of an unsigned letter to Brussels asking the EU for a Brexit delay after his deal was not approved in Parliament. He also sent another accompanying letter saying he did not support an extension which appeared designed to frustrate the Benn Act. The EU responded to the letters by accepting the initial request for an extension. On 21 October judges at Scotland's highest civil court maintained pressure on Boris Johnson by delaying their ruling—this time until the 'obligations under the 2019 Act have been complied with in full' (*IGov* 2019; The Financial Times 2019). A running commentary on the progress of this successful legal challenge could be followed through Dale Vince's Twitter and Facebook posts. A sense of mischievous pleasure could be detected in several of these posts which celebrating blocking the will of the Prime Minister, for whom it is very clear Dale Vince has no respect. This tweet from 12 September was somewhat typical:

> Dale Vince @DaleVince
>
> Our legal action is a sign of the times perhaps, I'm an ex hippie traveller who has to take an old Etonian PM to court to ensure he abides by the law.

This could be added to many other mocking posts which showed Boris Johnson as a dodgy car salesman, or as a bull being led by the nose by a Scottish judge. A photo on his Twitter feed of a smiling Dale Vince pointing approvingly at a poster on the Global Climate Strike march of 20 September 2019 proclaimed 'F**K Boris' (a confrontational post that remains on Vince's feed despite overwhelmingly negative comments). These examples all stray very far from the norms of CSR communications and show Ecotricity's founder and director as a take-no-prisoners environmental and political activist as much as a business leader. For more than twenty years, somewhat remarkably, he has successfully managed to combine the two.

6.12 Summary of Values

The deep-green value system of Ecotricity has been a constant through their public communications over the past two decades. Their Facebook and social media communications imply that the company is, first and foremost, for environmental sustainability through a concern with developing a green, de-carbonised economy. Explicit values include the need for a clean energy revolution in Britain; sustainability; economic and environmental improvement and fairness. Implicit values include a critique of neoliberalism and Thatcherite free-market values which form a common thread within the company's communications. In a video on YouTube, Vince expresses concern at the impacts and uncontrolled force of capitalism:

> capitalism has become a force of evil ... it's above all else, isn't it? Above people, above the planet. (cited The Ecologist 2019b)

These are unusual sentiments from a 'multimillionaire' businessman, who describes Ecotricity as 'a corporate alter ego' in terms of its values (personal communication 2019). When asked about the phrase 'people and planet before profit' and competing against less ethical companies, Vince elaborates on some of the choices made by the company:

> The word profit is a bit uncomfortable for me, I feel it's a dirty word or concept. This phrase is all well and good, but I wonder if it's from the CSR department of some big org. Making money is essential to being able to do our work—but we exist for our mission and make money to fulfil that, normal companies exist to make money and might chip in a bit to a good cause—the essential difference is posed by the question—do you live to eat or eat to live? We eat to live. How you make money is also important, but it ought to be obvious enough not to do that at the expense of people or the environment.
>
> It's never a problem operating in the way that we do, the opportunities that are closed to us are of our own choosing. Not buying energy from industrial farming for example or supplying companies we don't consider ethical, like

> McDonalds. We lose nothing when we make these choices, we keep our principles. (Personal communication 2019)

Aligned with criticism of the 'free market' is a call for an end to state support for fossil fuels and greater intervention through government policies or directives in the fight against climate change. When asked if it is possible for governments to regulate or intervene in the market so that capitalism can become a sustainable force for good, Vince argues:

> Governments intervene wherever they want for the outcome they want. The rules of capitalism are set by us, they are not laws of physics. Governments can and should change the rules for business, competition will always be within the rules (except for cheating) if the rules focus on money so does the competition, if the rules focus on other issues, so must the competition. It's totally possible to set the rules so that companies must for example adopt ISO14000 and pursue a zero carbon target. At the moment companies first priority is to shareholders, it's in company law, this should change and the tax system should be used to reward environmental outcomes and penalise 'business as usual'. (Personal communication 2019)

The value of and necessity for government intervention may be linked to a distrust in the motives of big business. There is a sense of disgust with the mess other corporations have made with fracking, plastic and farming for meat, for instance. Dale Vince's impatience with the government's support for the fossil fuel sector means that much of his online communications are very critical indeed of government policy. This example from a Facebook post on 19.07.2019:

> Our Alveston windpark in South Gloucestershire could be our last in England unless we see a change in government policy and they lift the ban on onshore wind. (Facebook 2019)

The urgent need for a clean energy revolution is one of the fundamental and consistent messages of Ecotricity. It is within their DNA and outlined clearly in (*Ecotricity's 2030 Vision for a Green Britain* which argues that Britain's power must go through:

> A revolution that spreads all the way down from the Big Six to British families. (Ecotricity 2015)

In statements made in their reports and website there is support for a shift in policy to influence the public's behaviour. A good example of this would be the 'cow tax', in their 2030 vision. This is a proposed tax on meat products with the intention of shifting public habits towards having a more low-carbon, vegan diet (Ecotricity's 2030 vision for a Green Britain). Other policies include no VAT on electric cars, a Carbon Minister and so-called Quantitative Greening. This suggests that Ecotricity believe that people won't change quickly enough and that corporations are not ethical enough to be left to free-market forces alone.

Dale's visit to Downing Street in July 2019 to work on EV charging was described as 'positive', although he did hint that the work done was token due to the short life span of Theresa May's government. He was pleased with the announcement that houses would, in future, be built with charging points, but there is a sardonic tone that might be regarded as highly unusual for a company lobbying a sitting government.

> I nearly didn't go, because I thought it might be a waste of a day but. (Facebook 2019)

This reflects the general attitude of Vince towards the Conservative government which is, often, critical, frustrated and mistrustful. In 2019 he appeared at Labour Party's 'Rebuilding Britain' event in Stroud where he gave a speech about the climate crisis and the importance of change. This reflected the value of deep ecology and radical change that appears to be a driving force for Ecotricity under his leadership. The discourse was not so much party political in its nature, although, the context of it being a Labour event made it clear where he hoped a future government might be led from. Whether Vince is a loyal Labour supporter, or has simply thrown his weight behind the party which had the most realistic chance to make changes he believes are urgently needed remains to be seen. Perhaps more important than his party affiliation is the focus of his campaigning efforts which was with Labour's touted New Green Deal in the run up to the December 2019 election. This New Deal has its roots in the Green New Deal Group formed in 2007 by Caroline Lucas from the Green Party, amongst others. Since then other influential environmentalists, including Dale Vince, have played an important role in shaping and advancing in the public discourse around the climate emergency and raising its importance in the news agenda. When asked about the impact of his public-facing lobbying, Vince placed his contribution within a broader dialogue on these issues:

> If you assume our aim in doing this is to effect change, then I would say yes it has worked to varying degrees over the years. It's about being part of the discussion, airing alternative viewpoints and through that hopefully changing outcomes. (Personal communication 2019)

With Ecotricity, green business strategy and corporate environmental responsibility go hand in hand. The company's various research and development initiatives and innovations (in energy, transport and, more recently, food) alongside proactive partnerships, campaigning communications and strong, uncompromising values and leadership have won Dale Vince many friends and enemies; a loyal, if niche customer base and a public profile and political influence far beyond what a company of Ecotricity's size might expect.

In the next decade, such qualities and deep-green values may come to pose a challenge to traditional CSR practices and point the way towards a more root-and-branch approach to sustainability for organisations. In fact, the term Corporate Social Responsibility is one Vince describes in very unflattering terms:

> I recognise it as BS. Any company that has to have such a thing is inherently a bad company, and CSR is window dressing. (Personal communication 2019)

This attitude may be dismissed as overly cynical, but it is in step with much public sentiment about corporate greenwashing should perhaps ring alarm bells for those who would defend CSR in practice. When asked about the values of Ecotricity and how these have helped/hindered the growth of the company, Vince responded:

> Green values can't ever hinder, in my opinion. And I'd rather have a small green company than a large not green one, for obvious reasons. The world is moving this way, ten or twenty years from now the things we do will be far more mainstream—we've already seen that in Energy, Transport and Food, our three big areas of work—renewable energy has become mainstream, electric cars are on the verge and plant based living has really taken off in the last few years. Decades ago these were fringe ideas. (Personal communication 2019)

6.13 Conclusion

Ecotricity is a highly unusual company in many respects. It is unusual because uncompromising, deep-green values appear to dictate the organisation's growth strategy, communications and relationship to a small, but loyal customer base. Ecotricity has made a convincing claim to put planet before profit and the sustainable values it champions seem to have attracted enough like-minded energy users to support their vision. While the price of green energy may sometimes be marginally higher for consumers, particularly as renewable subsidies have been cut, the 'externalities', or true cost of other energy sources has yet to be faced by governments or built realistically into customer's bills. There has only been space here to briefly sketch UK policy-makers' inadequate and often perverse response to the looming climate catastrophe. This poor leadership from the UK government has been thrown into stark relief by the efforts of undaunted individuals and entrepreneurs within pockets of the private sector, including at Ecotricity, Good Energy and other small energy providers. These companies, and those that lead them, have shown that clean energy is not only possible but, given a level playing field, could very quickly replace our dangerous dependence on fossil fuels. Until now, only a fraction of the millions of energy users has been prepared, if necessary, to pay a small supplement to power their homes and businesses using green energy. An end to hidden subsidies and tax breaks for fossil fuels and nuclear power would reveal renewable energy to be significantly cheaper in a competitive market and consumers would quickly make the shift away from unsustainable energy sources on which the larger energy companies still depend. It is clear from existing research (see Brown et al. 2018) that 100% renewable energy is not only possible but already exists in several parts of the world.[3] A review of the available technology and the UK's natural resources shows that with enough political will and investment every consumer could switch to renewable energy and put Britain on course to meet its declared commitments to the Paris Agreement required for a sustainable, low-carbon future.

Vince's single-minded focus on an ethical, deep-green business model have sustained Ecotricity through the first twenty-five years of its history and helped it prosper in a crowded and insecure market. As an early pioneer in the green-energy sector he has also shown that providing 100% renewable energy to customers at a competitive price is both possible and profitable. The company has communicated publicly and lobbied aggressively against a perceived tilt by Conservative governments towards fracking, fossil fuel subsidies and deep cuts to renewable energy subsidies. Dale Vince has built a reputation in the market as an outspoken, campaigning, politically engaged and radical activist for clean energy and a sustainable economy. Leading Ecotricity in a way that has sometimes caused discomfort and offence, Vince's leadership style and takeover efforts with competitors may strike many as sharp-elbowed and perhaps autocratic. However, since 1995 he has slowly built up a dynamic, innovative and robust group of companies at Ecotricity. In the rapidly expanding area of renewable energy supply in the UK he has been able to rely on strong customer loyalty through an increasingly difficult trading environment where recent government decisions appear designed to frustrate rather than help the green-energy sector.

This chapter has drawn on detailed discussion of British energy provider Ecotricity—its history, sustainable innovations, communications and values alongside personal insights from its founder and Director Dale Vince. We have shown how a 'deep-green' business has operated successfully for twenty-five years and considered some of the uncompromising values and important impacts this relatively small company has

[3] These include Mecklenburg-Vorpommern and Schleswig-Holstein in Germany, South Island in New Zealand, Orkney in Scotland and Samsø along with many other parts of Denmark (Brown et al. 2018, p. 842).

had. Trying to imagine a larger company taking on such values today is difficult and yet imagining may be the first necessary step. We have been warned that the world must dramatically accelerate the transition towards clean energy now to prevent greenhouse gas emissions exceeding levels which scientists agree will lead to irreversible and catastrophic climate change (New York Times 2018). The threat of runaway global warming and the need for immediate action by businesses to encompass 'deep decarbonization' of the economy (IPPC 2019) give greater urgency for businesses to take on greater environmental responsibility; and develop and diffuse environmentally friendly technologies (see UN Global Compact 2019). This case study may offer indicators as to what kind of business and business leadership is required for the crisis we all face.

References

Albareda, Laura, Josep M. Lozano, and Tamyko Ysa. "Public Policies on Corporate Social Responsibility: The Role of Governments in Europe." *Journal of Business Ethics* 74, no. 4 (September 15, 2007): 391–407.

Al Jazeera. 2019. Campaigners in court bid to make Johnson obey Brexit law. *Al Jazeera*. 3rd October. Available at: https://www.aljazeera.com/news/2019/10/campaigners-court-bid-johnson-obey-brexit-law-191003160843050.html. Accessed 15/10/2019.

Bauer, Theresa. 2014. Responsible Lobbying: A Multidimensional Model. In: *Journal of Corporate Citizenship*. JCC 53 March 2014.

Beder, Sharon. 2006. *Free Market Missionaries: The Corporate Manipulation of Community Values*. Routledge, London.

Beder, Sharon. 2019. *Suiting Themselves: How Corporations Drive the Global Agenda*. Routledge, London.

Bingham, Timothy, and Geoff Walters. 2013. "Financial Sustainability Within UK Charities: Community Sport Trusts and Corporate Social Responsibility Partnerships." *Voluntas: International Journal of Voluntary & Nonprofit Organizations* 24 (3): 606–29.

Brown, T.W., T. Bischof-Niemz, K. Blok, C. Breyer, H. Lund, and B.V. Mathiesen. 2018. "Response to 'Burden of Proof: A Comprehensive Review of the Feasibility of 100% Renewable-Electricity Systems.'" *Renewable & Sustainable Energy Reviews 92* (September): 834–47.

Bjerke, Bjorn, and Karlsson, Mathias. 2013. *Social Entrepreneurship: To Act as If and Make a Difference*. Cheltenham, Gloucestershire: Edward Elgar Publishing Limited.

Burton, Suzan, Alena Soboleva, Kate Daellenbach, Debra Basil, Terry Beckman, and Sameer Deshpande. "Helping Those Who Help Us: Co-Branded and Co-Created Twitter Promotion in CSR Partnerships." *Journal of Brand Management* 24, no. 4 (August 2017): 322–33.

Carrington, Damian. 2019. Why the Guardian is changing the language it uses about the environment. *The Guardian*. 17th May. Available at: https://www.theguardian.com/environment/2019/may/17/why-the-guardian-is-changing-the-language-it-uses-about-the-environment. Accessed 17/10/2019.

Campbell, Peter. 2019. UK pioneer of electric car charging points faces barrage of criticism. *Financial Times* January 3. Available at: https://www.ft.com/content/e39f5bd6-0537-11e9-99df-6183d3002ee1. Accessed 9th October 2019.

Cave, Tamasin, and Rowell, Andrew. 2014. *A quiet word: lobbying, crony capitalism and broken politics in Britain*. London: The Bodley Head.

Department for Business, Energy & Industrial Strategy. 2019. Annual fuel poverty statistics report: 2019 Available at: https://www.gov.uk/government/statistics/annual-fuel-poverty-statistics-report-2019

Drax Electric Insights. 2019. Available at: https://electricinsights.co.uk/#/dashboard?period=1-year&start=2019-01-01&&_k=lmhd7w. Accessed October 31, 2019

Drutman, Lee. 2015. *The Business of America Is Lobbying: How Corporations Became Politicized and Politics Became More Corporate*. Oxford University Press.

Ecotalks. 2019. *Giving land back to nature*. Ecotricity. Available at: https://www.ecotalk.co.uk/our-story/giving-land-back-to-nature. Accessed September 12, 2019.

Ecologist. 2019a. *Where the gas is greener.* 9th January. Available at: theecologist.org. Accessed October 29, 2019.

Ecologist. 2019b. *Capitalism 'has become a force of evil'* Available at: https://theecologist.org/2019/feb/13/capitalism-has-become-force-evil. Accessed October 29, 2019.

Ecotricity. 2010. *Ecotricity customers cooking on UK's first Green Gas*. Available at: https://www.ecotricity.co.uk/news/news-archive/2010/ecotricity-customers-cooking-on-uk-s-first-green-gas. Accessed October 10, 2019.

Ecotricity. 2017. *Our history: 2005*. Available at: https://www.ecotricity.co.uk/about-ecotricity/our-history/2005. Accessed October 10, 2019.

Ecotricity. 2015. *Ecotricity's 2030 Vision for a Green Britain*. Available at: https://www.ecotricity.co.uk/content/download/2298/13081. Accessed October 30, 2019.

Ecotricity. 2018. *Our Environmental Footprint Report 2018*. Available at: https://www.ecotricity.co.uk/content/download/10014/152088. Accessed October 31, 2019.

Ecotricity. 2019a. *About Ecotricity*. Available at: https://www.ecotricity.co.uk/about-ecotricity/the-ecotricity-group. Accessed August 21, 2019.

Ecotricity, 2019b. *Greenbird*. Available at: https://www.ecotricity.co.uk/about-ecotricity/eco-labs/greenbird. Accessed: October 10, 2019.

Edie. 2016. *Ecotricity launches new 'Ecobond' amidst acquisition of Good Energy shares*. Available at: https://www.edie.net/news/10/Ecotricity-launches-new-Ecobond-amidst-rumoured-Good-Energy-acquisition/.

Energy Live News. 2019. *Ecotricity, Good Energy and Green Energy UK can charge consumers above the standard variable tariff rates limit set by Ofgem*. August 1st. Available at: https://www.energylivenews.com/2019/08/01/ofgem-confirms-permanent-energy-price-cap-exemptions-for-three-green-suppliers/

Ecotricity Group. 2019. Ecotricity Group's Tax Strategy Statement. Available at: https://www.ecotricity.co.uk/content/download/8138/file/EcotricityGroupTaxStrategyStatement2019.pdf. Accessed October 30, 2019.

Eweje, Gabriel, and Bathurst, Ralph, eds. 2017. *CSR, Sustainability, and Leadership*. Florence: Routledge. Accessed August 21, 2019. ProQuest Ebook Central.

Express. 2019. Fury at EU flag on eco building despite 1,000-plus petition—'Absolutely disgusting. *The Daily Express*. 22 June. https://www.express.co.uk/news/uk/1144009/brexit-news-eu-flag-stroud-gloucestershire-lee-sibley-dale-vince-ecotricity

The Financial Times. 2019. Scottish court keeps alive pressure on Boris Johnson over Brexit delay. *The Financial Times*. 21st October. Available at: https://www.ft.com/content/7678c2f4-f3f7-11e9-b018-3ef8794b17c6. Accessed 2/11/2019.

Facebook. 2014. *Ecotricity 5 February 2014*. Available at: https://www.facebook.com/ecotricity/posts/10152210929331153.

Facebook. 2019. *Good Energy 29 April 2019*. https://www.facebook.com/goodenergy.co.uk/posts/10161677640900174

Flintoff, John-Paul. 2011. Power to the people: Dale Vince, green energy pioneer. *The Telegraph*. 27th May 2011. Available at: https://www.telegraph.co.

uk/news/8537788/Power-to-the-people-Dale-Vince-green-energy-pioneer.html. Accessed 19/9/2019.

Forest Green Rovers. 2019. *FGR dazzles with world's first bamboo football kit*. 5th July. Available at: https://www.fgr.co.uk/news/july-2019/fgr-dazzles-with-world-s-first-bamboo-football-kit. Accessed 12 October 2019.

Good Energy. 2019. Half-Year Report 2019. Available at: https://s22.q4cdn.com/772923126/files/doc_financials/interim_reports/10/2019-Interims.pdf. Accessed 15/10/2019.

The Guardian 2018. Solarplicity becomes 13th energy supplier to collapse since 2018. *The Guardian*. August 13. Available at: https://www.theguardian.com/business/2019/aug/13/solarplicity-energy-supplier-collapse Accessed: October 10, 2019.

Gloucestershire Live 2018 'It's my responsibility': The leaked Dale Vince email to at-risk Ecotricity staff which speaks of £23m loss. *Gloucestershire Live* 16 June. Available at: https://www.gloucestershirelive.co.uk/news/gloucester-news/its-responsibility-leaked-dale-vince-1680779. Accessed: October 10, 2019.

IGov 2019. *Changing actor dynamics and emerging value propositions in the UK electricity retail market*. University of Exeter's Energy Policy Group. Available at: http://projects.exeter.ac.uk/igov/wp-content/uploads/2019/01/IGov-BM-Analysis-report.pdf. Accessed: October 9, 2019.

The Independent. 2019. Energy suppliers claim to sell '100% renewable' electricity without producing any green power. 27th September. Available at: https://www.independent.co.uk/news/business/news/renewable-energy-suppliers-green-electricity-which-research-a9123566.html. Accessed 12/10/2019.

IPPC. 2019. Landmark United in Science report informs Climate Action Summit. Available at: https://www.ipcc.ch/2019/09/22/united-in-science-report-climate-summit/ Accessed: October 7, 2019.

Liberal Democrats. 2017. *Switch to the Greenest energy company in Britain and they'll donate £50 a year to the Lib Dems*. Available at: https://www.libdems.org.uk/switch-ecotricity-save-money. Accessed October 30, 2019.

McMenamin, Iain 2013. *If Money Talks, What Does it Say?: Corruption and Business Financing of Political Parties*. OUP, Oxford.

Merchant Wind Power. 2010. *B&Q goes wind powered*. Available at: Green power making headlines. http://www.merchantwindpower.co.uk/home/mwp-news/b-q-goes-wind-powered.

Miller, David and Dinan, William. 2008. *A century of spin: How public relations became the cutting edge of corporate power*. Pluto Press.

The New York Times. 2018. *The World Still Isn't Meeting Its Climate Goals.* Available at: https://www.nytimes.com/interactive/2018/12/07/climate/world-emissions-paris-goals-not-on-track.html. Accessed October 30, 2019.

Ofgem. 2019a. Electricity supply market shares by company: Domestic (GB). Accessed 23/08/2019 at: https://www.ofgem.gov.uk/data-portal/electricity-supply-market-shares-company-domestic-gb

Ofgem. 2019b. Gas supply market shares by company: Domestic (GB). Accessed 23/08/2019 at: https://www.ofgem.gov.uk/data-portal/gas-supply-market-shares-company-domestic-gb

PR Week. 2013. Ecotricity Founder Dale Vince Talks the Talk and Walks the Walk. *PR Week.* 20th November. Available at: https://www.prweek.com/article/1220600/ecotricity-founder-dale-vince-talks-talk-walks-walk. Accessed 19/10/2019.

Scheyvens, Regina; Banks Glenn and Hughes, Emma. 2016. The Private Sector and the SDGs: The Need to Move Beyond 'Business as Usual'. *Sustainable Development.* 24:6. Available at: https://onlinelibrary.wiley.com/doi/full/10.1002/sd.1623

Punchline Gloucester. 2019. Firm's accounts reveal £50 million increase in turnover. *Punchline Gloucester.* Accessed 16/04/2020 at: https://www.punchline-gloucester.com/articles/aanews/stroud-gloucestershire-green-energy-business-ecotricity-50-million-increase-in-turnover-2018-dale-vi

Punchline Gloucester. 2020. Turnover growth fails to blow green energy firm into profit. *Punchline Gloucester.* Accessed 16/04/2020 at: https://www.punchline-gloucester.com/articles/aanews/turnover-growth-fails-to-blow-gloucestershire-green-energy-firm-ecotricity-into-profit

Solar Guide. 2020. Smart Export Guarantee to Replace FiT From 2020.

Staffel, Iain. 2019. Britain's power system is closer than ever to being fossil-free. *Electric Insights Quarterly*—Q2 2019. Drax. Available at: https://electricinsights.co.uk/#/reports/report-2019-q2/detail/britains-power-system-is-closer-than-ever-to-being-fossil-free?_k=98yehj

Stroud News and Journal. 2018. Available at: https://www.stroudnewsandjournal.co.uk/news/16271126.job-losses-at-ecotricity/. Accessed 27/08/2019.

Stroud News and Journal 2019. *Dale Vince hangs massive EU flag from Ecotricity HQ to celebrate Brexit delay. Stroud News and Journal.* April 14.

Sustainability in Sport. n.d. *Forest Green Rovers.* Available at: http://www.sustainabilityinsport.com/case-studies/forest-green-rovers. Accessed 12 October 2019.

Solar Power Portal. 2016. *Ecotricity raises over £12 million from latest ecobond.* Available at: https://www.solarpowerportal.co.uk/news/ecotricity_raises_over_12_million_from_latest_ecobond_4891. Accessed October 30, 2019.

The Independent. 2015. *General Election 2015: Green energy tycoon spreads bets with campaign donations.* Available at: https://www.independent.co.uk/news/uk/politics/generalelection/general-election-2015-green-energy-tycoon-spreads-his-bets-with-campaign-donations-10217107.html. Accessed October 30, 2019.

The Telegraph 2015. *The wind tycoon, the donations to Labour and £36m in subsidies.* Available at: https://www.telegraph.co.uk/news/earth/environment/11413504/The-wind-tycoon-the-donations-to-Labour-and-36m-in-subsidies.html. Accessed October 30, 2019.

UN. 2015. Transforming our world: the 2030 Agenda for Sustainable Development. Available at: https://sustainabledevelopment.un.org/post2015/transformingourworld. Accessed 27/08/2019.

UN Global Compact. 2019. *The power of principles.* Available at: https://www.unglobalcompact.org/what-is-gc/mission/principles. Accessed October 30, 2019.

The Vegan Society. 2019. *An energy company like no other.* Available at: https://www.vegansociety.com/society/whos-involved/partners/ecotricity. Accessed 10 October 2019.

Wadham, Helen. 2009. "Talking across Boundaries: Business and NGO Perspectives on CSR, Sustainable Development and Partnership." *Journal of Corporate Citizenship*, no. 34: 57.

Which. 2019. *How green is your energy tariff?* 27 September. Available at: https://www.which.co.uk/news/2019/09/how-green-is-your-energy-tariff/

7

A Conceptual Framework of Strategic Corporate Social Responsibility: A Model for Fulfilment of Societal Needs While Increasing Business Financial Performance

Adrian A. Baumgartner

7.1 Introduction

Business sector representatives have increasingly stopped viewing corporate social responsibility (CSR) as a burden and have started embracing the idea that it can be an additional competitive advantage that might lead to increase of financial performance (Ubrežiová et al. 2013, 2903). The increasing interest in CSR can be tracked by the exponential growth, from 10 in 1990 to several thousands in 2012 (Okoye 2009), in the number of articles on the topic. This availability of various CSR-related definitions and concepts also leads to a certain amount of uncertainty for researchers to deal with.

A. A. Baumgartner (✉)
Hong Kong, Hong Kong SAR

F. Farache et al. (eds.), *Values and Corporate Responsibility*, Palgrave Studies in Governance, Leadership and Responsibility,
https://doi.org/10.1007/978-3-030-52466-1_7

One of the most prominent implications in the extensive CSR-related debates relates to the motivation of corporations to act in a socially responsible manner and the connection between the social activities of companies and their financial performance (Schaltegger and Burritt 2018, 241).

According to the results of a major study, conducted by UN Global Compact and Accenture in 2019, on the attitude of company CEOs towards sustainability, "for the first time ever, the aggregate number of CEOs reporting sustainability as 'important' or 'very important' has gone down (from 97% in 2016 to 94% in 2019) and one in three CEOs (29%) do not believe that—even with increased commitment and action—business can play a critical role in contributing to the Global Goals" (Apurv 2019, 32). This finding shows the importance of creating a business case for CSR in the corporate sector. As a consequence, the business community has begun paying attention to the idea of creating shared value (CSV) as proposed by Porter and Kramer (2011, 5), aimed at exploring whether companies can enhance their economic value by addressing and advancing the social conditions of their stakeholders.

In this paper, the authors analysed not only the impact of the socially responsible behaviour of companies but also examined the reasons and motivations for corporations to behave in a socially responsible way. Understanding these motivating factors is crucial for creating a connection between a company's values, goals and corporate responsibility. Building a connection between a company's core business values and CSR will be a crucial factor for helping the business sector achieve Sustainable Development Goals (SDG) by 2030. "Instead of dabbling in all of the SDGs, businesses can more effectively contribute if they pick the ones that are most relevant to their core operations and make strong commitments to achieving those goals" (Apurv 2019, 32).

While building upon existing research in the field of CSR and related academic concepts, this paper goes further and proposes a conceptual framework that incorporates the CSV theory—something that has been largely ignored by existing literature. This work begins with an overview and discussion of different CSR concepts. Special attention is paid to the interplay between CSR and corporate financial performance (CFP) in the corporate sector. In the following section, factors that foster corporate CSR activities are analysed. The main outcome of this work is a conceptual strategic CSR (SCSR) framework, enhanced with a set of propositions constructed with the support of existing academic literature, business debates and the author's contributions.

7.2 CSR and CFP: Debates and Related Concepts

The *New York Times* article by Milton Friedman, in which he claimed that "there is one and only one social responsibility of business—to use its resources and engage in activities designed to increase its profits so long as it stays within the rules of the game, which is to say, engages in open and free competition without deception or fraud" (Friedman 1970, par. 31), split academics and practitioners into two major groups. There are ongoing debates regarding relations between CSR and CFP, with a substantial number of both allies and opponents of Friedman's theory as well as those who stand in the middle. For the purpose of this research, some of the relevant viewpoints will be considered and analysed.

Among some of the prominent opponents of Friedman's vision of CSR are McWilliams and Siegel (2001, 117), who defined CSR "as the actions that appear to further some social good beyond the interest of the firm and which is required by the law". They argued that a corporation has obligations other than those stated in their mission and values and has to devote resources to social causes that go beyond their business model. Matten and Moon (2008, 405), besides providing a similar vision of CSR, went even further by specifying CSR actions as being clearly articulated and communicated policies and practices "that reflect business responsibility for some of the wider societal good".

Carroll and Shabana (2010, 85) proposed a different and more precise CSR definition that takes into account not only corporations but also society. They referred to Carroll's (1979) original four-part social responsibility definition, stating that "the social responsibility of business encompasses the economic, legal, ethical, and discretionary philanthropic expectations that society has of organizations at a given point in time" (Carroll and Shabana 2010, 89). In accordance with this definition, corporations have an obligation to react to and fulfil the unmet needs of society without expecting any benefits in return.

While mentioning business responsibility towards society, none of the definitions specify what exactly constitutes societal expectations but rather use references to the interests of the companies' stakeholders (Elms 2006, 203; Gangone and Gănescu 2014, 539). Considering the fact that stakeholders' interests often contradict each other, existing CSR definitions provide no specific explanation of what kind of measures companies can include (Baden and Harwood 2013, 15).

While referencing the business itself—or society—as the triggers for the CSR (Acar et al. 2001, 51; Baden and Harwood 2013, 11), what most definitions are missing is the strategic aspect, which should be of utmost importance when talking about the business environment.

Since society began to reconsider the balance between wealth generation and ethical considerations, we can observe numerous attempts by researchers and businesses to measure CSR. "Corporate social responsibility, once a do-gooding sideshow, is now seen as a mainstream. But as yet too few companies are doing it well" (Whadcock 2008, 1). Considering that the attempts aimed at measuring CSR still have not resulted in a clear methodology, it is assumed that the strategic approach to CSR can become a valuable contribution to resolution of *the actual purpose of CSR* debates (Werther and Chandler 2010, 40).

In support of a strategic approach to CSR, Porter and Kramer (2006, 2) argued that CSR should not be used just to comply with community standards but applied strategically to gain a competitive advantage, with the activities being part of a business model. Hence, CSR activities are not just a philanthropic reaction but a clear strategy to gain a competitive position and create profit. Matten and Moon (2008, 404) support this vision by providing implicit and explicit forms of CSR. Implicit CSR refers to corporations' role within the wider formal and informal institutions for societal interests and concerns, consisting of values, norms and rules that result in requirements for addressing stakeholder issues. On the other hand, explicit CSR refers to corporate policies that assume and articulate responsibility for societal interests (Matten and Moon 2008, 410).

Another paradigm, which addresses the current business debate about tackling social issues and argues that charity and philanthropy alone can no longer solve the world's problems, is referred to as *impact investing* (Rodin and Brandenburg 2014, 3–4). Bugg-Levine and Emerson (2011, 5) defined impact investments as "investments that pursue financial returns while intentionally addressing social and environmental challenges". In contrast to philanthropists, impact investors also seek financial return in addition to generating social or environmental impact. Porter and Kramer (2011, 5) argued that this type of business is more powerful than charity and is an unmatched source of funding for satisfying society's needs.

In this regard, the concept of creating shared value (CSV) as proposed by Porter and Kramer (2011), which has gained significant traction in the business community over the last five years, seems to be of particular interest and importance. In their research, the authors define CSV "as the policies and operating practices that enhance the competitiveness of a company while simultaneously advancing the economic and social conditions in the communities in which it operates" (Porter and Kramer 2011, 6). CSV reshapes conventional stereotypes by stating that the market is defined not just by economic needs but to a large extent by societal needs and that unmet societal needs can lead to significant internal costs for the companies.

On the other hand, by advancing their technologies or management, technology companies can benefit from innovations and more advanced management processes that, besides meeting societal needs, can help the company benefit in the long term. In other words, Porter and Kramer (2011, 8) argued that corporations should create financial value in a way that also creates value for societies by addressing their needs. CSV as an activity should be related to a firm's business model and not be targeted only on doing good for both society and the environment. Porter and Kramer (2011, 4) argued that such businesses are more powerful than charities and can better address pressing issues as long as they act as businesses and not charitable donors.

In this research, the authors arrived at a classic definition of CSR (CCSR) with a strategic approach and implications of CSV and proposed a definition of strategic CSR (SCSR), defined as a corporation's clearly articulated and communicated policies and practices to gain competitive advantage by addressing society's unmet needs.

The definition of SCSR proposed by the authors of this research addresses two important implications, addressing both economic value (EV) and society value (SV) and resulting in benefits for both the company and its stakeholders.

First, SCSR is clearly embedded in a corporation's mission, values and business model and is targeted at gaining a competitive advantage. This implication argues with the proponents of Friedman's theory, who believe that social responsibility activities can bind the company's resources, limit its intended growth and endanger its competitive position (Barnett 2007, 795). Nonetheless, this observation makes sense only for social investments that are not in line with the corporation's business model (i.e. CCSR activities). If this argument is combined with the SCSR definition, it can be concluded that a firm can increase its CFP or EV by engaging in SCSR activities. This definition also addresses concerns regarding the business case for CSR, which many researchers and practitioners are struggling with.

Second, this implication addresses the relationship between the SCSR definition and societal needs. By providing a service or product that meets a need or a requirement of the society, the company at the same time increases social welfare or societal value (SV) by satisfying those needs through the product or service. As a consequence, by meeting societal needs, companies tend to increase the trust between the corporation and its stakeholders (Fombrun et al. 2002), which subsequently increases revenue by attracting customers who either buy more or are willing to pay a premium (McWilliams and Siegel 2001, 120; Barnett 2007, 796).

7.3 SCSR Conceptual Framework

The main section of this paper describes a conceptual framework for SCSR, which incorporates two subsequently represented models: the decision model and the performance model. The decision model represents an analysis of the drivers behind a company's motivation to act in a socially responsible manner and to create shared value. This model defines stakeholder pressure as the independent variable and the SCSR activity of the corporation as the outcome or dependent variable. In the performance model, SCSR activity transforms into an independent variable, which leads to an increased EV and SV, both dependent variables.

Throughout the conceptual framework, various institutional, organisational and individual factors related to the socially responsible behaviour of companies are analysed and formulated in the form of a proposition for future research.

7.3.1 SCSR Decision Model

The Dependent Variable: SCSR Activities

A company's SCSR activities constitute the dependent variable of the SCSR decision model and represent an outcome of the decision model.

The Independent Variable: A Company's Stakeholders

Stakeholders play an important role in the company's achievement of its objectives as they drive the strategic decision of a corporation (Freeman et al. 2010, 95). Based on the stakeholder theory, Matten and Moon (2008, 409) argued that stakeholders define the social responsibility activities of a corporation. In line with these arguments, Aguilera et al. (2007, 10) showed that stakeholders apply pressure and influence social change and responsibility through direct strategic decisions (e.g. managers or employees) or indirect exercises of power (e.g. shareholder, customers, governments or media). According to Elms (2006, 204), stakeholders' responsibility is always two-way and thus the goal of each company should not be to reduce the "misery induced by capitalism" (Elms 2006, 204) but to promote a desire for ethical business among stakeholders.

Both internal and external stakeholders might push the company into socially responsible behaviour. Those stakeholders who value ethical business practices will be more willing to collaborate with companies that ethically conduct business. The same reasoning is applied to the corporations: By seeing high societal demand for the ethical business practices, the business realises that by addressing this demand they might get a competitive advantage in the form of lower employee turnover, lower purchase prices or higher client loyalty (Elms 2006, 205).

Therefore, consumers, by purchasing products or services from only socially responsible companies, can stimulate positive social change in the business community (Sen and Bhattacharya 2001, 225). At the same time, shareholders also have the ability to pressure corporations into behaving in a more socially responsible way (Kurtz 2008, 250). Therefore, the first SCSR driver proposition can be formulated as follows:

> *Proposition DM_a1: Powerful and socially oriented stakeholders can pressure a corporation into engaging in SCSR activities.*

Moderating Variables: Instrumental Motivation and Financial Resources

The impact of stakeholder pressure on a corporation's SCSR activities is moderated by several factors. The first important moderator of the effectiveness of shareholder pressure on forcing a corporation to behave in a socially responsible manner is a corporation's instrumental motivation, that is, the source of most decisions made in an organisation. Bansal and Roth (2000, 731) found that CSR activities increase based on a corporation's motivation or, in other words, the perception of the possible impact of CSR. CSR is perceived as desirable for the business as long as it leads to a competitive advantage, increased competitiveness, lower transaction costs and better CFP. Furthermore, corporations also act based on normative reasons, which include the sense of corporate responsibility and duty towards their stakeholders (Bansal and Roth 2000, 731). Hence, it can be argued that corporations perform SCSR activities based on their instrumental motivation, which is defined as a moderator of SCSR activities and can be formulated in the form of the following proposition:

Proposition DM_b1: The positive impact of stakeholder pressure on the corporation's SCSR activities will be amplified if the corporation's instrumental motivation to perform SCSR activities increases.

Considering the fact that the motivation of a corporation to do SCSR activities is based on an expected increase of CFP, Campbell (2007, 945) stated that companies with weak financial performance are less likely to engage in socially responsible activities. These corporations have limited resources and thus might be unwilling to invest these resources in social responsibility activities (Waddock and Graves 1997, 5). On the other hand, lower capital constraints allow a company to make growth-oriented investments, such as strategic SCSR activities. In this regard, the next moderator affecting company's SCSR activities can be formulated as follows:

Proposition DM_b2: The positive impact of stakeholder pressure on the corporation's SCSR activities will be amplified if the corporation has no capital constraints and has sufficient financial resources available to invest in SCSR activities.

7.3.2 SCSR Performance Model

Dependent Variables (Outcome): Economic Value and Societal Value

Over the course of the last few years, multiple studies aimed at revealing the CSR–CFP correlation. Some studies have proven a positive correlation between social responsibility and EV (Margolis et al. 2007, 2; Orlitzky et al. 2003, 403; Flammer 2015, 2549; Waddock and Graves 1997, 3). Tsoutsoura's (2004, 2) study used extensive data from most SandP 500 companies over the 1996–2000 five-year period, which revealed signs of positive CSR-CFP correlation. The results of Peloza's (2009) meta-analyses, however, revealed a positive relationship between CSP and financial performance, while still taking into consideration that "the business case for corporate social performance is somewhat unclear:

the relationship is relatively weak, questions of causality are unanswered and the measures used to examine the business case are inconsistent" (Peloza 2009, 1531–1532).

The authors of this research believe that inconsistent results can be obtained due to the different factors used to define CSR. As CSR is a topic that embraces multiple dimensions represented by environmental, social and governance (ESG) factors and rated by external agencies or with self-designed indicators, the number of various simplified input factors varies significantly across studies, resulting in inconsistent results. This proves an observation made by Baden and Harwood (2013, 15) regarding existing methodological difficulties in establishing cause and relation between the two matters.

It can be concluded that existing literature is divided about the impact of CSR on CFP but that a majority of studies found a positive association, although they are inconsistent. This leads to the first outcome proposition:

Proposition PM_a1: SCSR activities lead to increased CFP or EV of the corporation.

According to Porter and Kramer's (2011, 6) CSV theory, a company can increase its EV and simultaneously address its SV by offering a product or service that meets society's unmet needs. Therefore, society's welfare, or SV, increases as a result of SCSR activities.

An impressive example of creation of profit by addressing society's needs comes from India, where the multinational media company Thomson Reuters has developed a promising monthly service for farmers. By paying a fee of just $5 a quarter, local farmers receive latest information about the weather and crop pricing as well as agricultural advice. According to early research results, the service reaches about 2 million farmers, of which 60% increased their income while some even managed to triple their incomes. "As capitalism begins to work in poorer communities, new opportunities for economic development and social progress increase exponentially" (Porter and Kramer 2011, 8).

Thus, the second outcome proposition is based on CSC theory and can be formulated as follows:

Proposition PM_a2: SCSR activities lead to an increase in society's welfare or SV.

This correlation has been mostly overlooked by academic literature, presumably due to the fact that it is difficult to find a measurement for SV that can be used to test the proposition.

Independent Variable: SCSR Activities

While representing a dependent variable (outcome) in the decision model, SCSR activity emerges as the independent variable of the performance model.

Moderators: Stakeholders' CSR Awareness, Strong Intangible Resources, Healthy Economic Environment

In order for a corporation to benefit from SCSR activities, it has to inform its stakeholders about relevant socially oriented activities. Thus, socially responsible employees can be hired in case the market is aware of the company's socially responsible activities. Similarly, socially oriented customers can start buying from a related company only if they know about its socially responsible behaviour. Servaes and Tamayo (2013, 1045) found that firms with high customer awareness could benefit from socially responsible activities. However, firms with low customer awareness experience a negative impact on CFP from socially responsible activities. In other words, the customer relationship only improves if customers know about the socially responsible activities of a company. Furthermore, they need to believe that the company is truly acting in a socially responsible manner and that the behaviour is not just a public relations activity (Sen et al. 2006, 164). In this regard, the first moderating proposition can be formulated as follows:

Proposition PM_b1: The positive impact of SCSR activities on EV and SV will be amplified if the corporation's stakeholders are aware of these activities and believe they are genuine.

In addition to stakeholder awareness, the existing literature refers to intangible resources as a moderator. Aspects such as innovation (e.g. Klassen and Whybark 1999, 599), human resources (e.g. Russo and Harrison 2005, 582), corporate reputation (e.g. Strong et al. 2001, 219) and organisational culture (e.g. Howard-Grenville and Hoffman 2003, 70) constitute a company's intangible resources. Surroca et al. (2010, 463), while analysing 599 companies, despite not finding a direct relationship between social responsibility and CFP, revealed an indirect relationship between a firm's intangible resources and CFP. Thus, intangible resources can be another moderator, which leads to the next proposition:

Proposition PM_b2: The positive impact of SCSR activities on EV and SV will be amplified if the corporation has strong intangible resources.

The following moderator is based on the changing economic context and environment of a company. When factors in the economic environment take the negative form of hyperinflation, high interest rates, low productivity or scarce resources, they negatively influence a company's growth and the ability to make profit. Considering the fact that low profitable companies are unwilling to invest in socially related activities, negative economic environment is considered the next moderator relevant for the outcome of SCSR activities.

Proposition PM_b3: The positive impact of SCSR activities on EV and SV will be amplified if the corporation operates in a healthy economic environment.

Mediators: Stakeholders' Relationship and Corporate Reputation

A company can manage its SCSR activities depending on the relations between its stakeholders. Orlitzky et al. (2003, 403) found that a corporation that performs socially responsible activities enjoys better stakeholder relationships, which impacts CFP. Employees, as particular stakeholder representatives, are considered to play one of the most important roles in a corporation's engagement in socially responsible activities.

A socially responsible company attracts employees who share the same values and provides them with a feeling of a better self-identification with the company. In return, the company obtains more motivated and engaged employees, which results in a lower turnover and thus reduces costs for the company (Flammer and Luo 2017, 163). This is in line with Griffeth et al.'s (2000, 484) argument that CSR positively impacts performance by reducing employee turnover. Finally, managers and employees are the ones who implement the practices and act in a socially responsible manner in daily business. Therefore, employees determine the impact on EV and SV. This paper argues that a company's relationship with its managers and employees mediates the outcome of SCSR activities.

Proposition PM_c1: SCSR activities strengthen stakeholder relationships.

Proposition PM_d1: Strengthened stakeholder relationships have a positive impact on EV and SV.

Another important factor that mediates the outcome of SCSR activities is a corporation's reputation. According to Brammer and Pavelin (2006, 435), CSR activities improve corporate reputation, which in turn leads to positive financial performance (Orlitzky et al. 2003, 403). In this light, corporate reputation is considered an outcome of socially responsible activities and a predictor of financial performance, which leads to the second mediating propositions.

Proposition PM_c2: SCSR activities have a positive impact on the corporation's reputation.

Proposition PM_d2: Better corporate reputation has a positive impact on EV and SV.

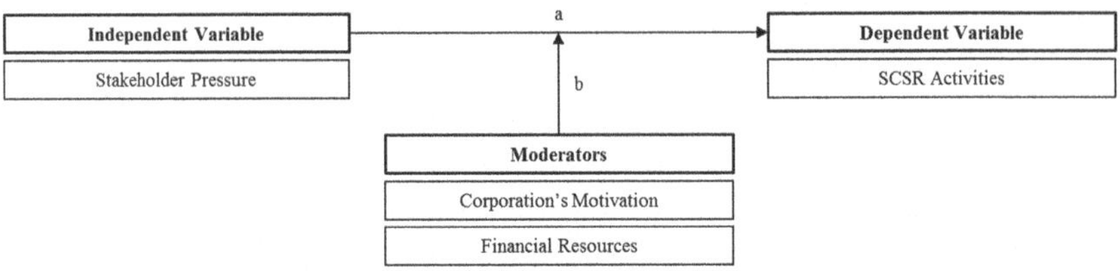

Fig. 7.1 Strategic corporate social responsibility (SCSR) decision model

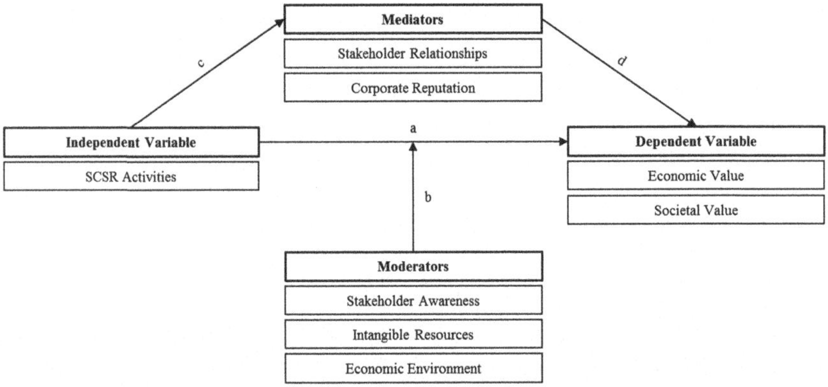

Fig. 7.2 Strategic corporate social responsibility (SCSR) performance model

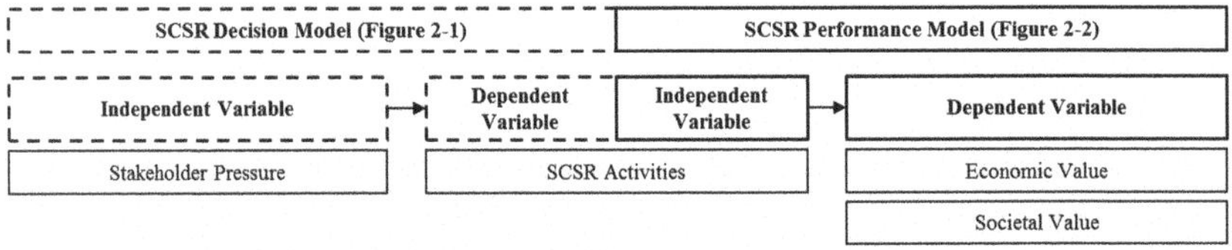

Fig. 7.3 Conceptual strategic corporate social responsibility (SCSR) framework

Table 7.1 Terminologies of social responsibility

Academic theories		
Philanthropy and charity	**Classical corporate social responsibility (CCSR)**	**Strategic corporate social responsibility (SCSR)**
"An unconditional transfer of cash or other assets to an entity or a settlement or cancellation of its liabilities in a voluntary non-reciprocal transfer by another entity acting other than as an owner"(Godfrey 2005, p. 778).	"The social responsibility of business encompasses the economic, legal, ethical, and discretionary expectations that society has of organizations at a given point in time" (Carroll 1979, p. 500).	A corporation's clearly articulated and communicated policies and practices to gain a competitive advantage by addressing its society's unmet needs.

Business concepts	
Creating shared value (CSV)	**Impact investing**
"Policies and operating practices that enhance the competitiveness of a company while simultaneously advancing the economic and social conditions in the communities in which it operates" (Porter and Kramer 2011, p. 6).	"Investments that pursue financial returns while intentionally addressing social and environmental challenges" (Bugg-Levine and Emerson 2011, p. 5). ⇒ Proxy to test CSV and thus SCSR in the business community

Table 7.2 Propositions of the strategic corporate social responsibility (SCSR) decision model

(a) Independent variable ⇒ dependent variable	
DM_a1	*Powerful and socially oriented stakeholders can pressure a corporation into engaging in SCSR activities.*
(b) Moderators	
DM_b1	*The positive impact of stakeholder pressure on the corporation's SCSR activities will be amplified if the corporation's instrumental motivation to perform SCSR activities increases.*
DM_b2	*The positive impact of stakeholder pressure on the corporation's SCSR activities will be amplified if the corporation has no capital constraints and has sufficient financial resources available to invest in SCSR activities.*

Table 7.3 Propositions of the strategic corporate social responsibility (SCSR) performance model

(a) Independent variable ⇒ dependent variable	
PM_a1	*SCSR activities lead to increased CFP or EV of the corporation.*
PM_a2	*SCSR activities lead to an increase in societies welfare or SV.*
(b) Moderators of independent variable ⇒ dependent variable	
PM_b1	*The positive impact of SCSR activities on EV and SV will be amplified if the corporation's stakeholders are aware of these activities and believe they are genuine.*
PM_b2	*The positive impact of SCSR activities on EV and SV will be amplified if the corporation has strong intangible resources.*
PM_b3	*The positive impact of SCSR activities on EV and SV will be amplified if the corporation operates in a healthy economic environment.*
(c) Independent variable ⇒mediators	
PM_c1	*SCSR activities strengthen stakeholder relationships.*
PM_c2	*SCSR activities have a positive impact on the corporation's reputation.*
(d) Mediators ⇒ dependent variable	
PM_d1	*Strengthened stakeholder relationships have a positive impact on EV and SV.*
PM_d2	*Better corporate reputation has a positive impact on EV and SV.*

7.3.3 Conceptual SCSR Framework

Figs. 7.1 and 7.2 provide the decision and performance model. Together, they form a holistic SCSR framework, as shown in Fig. 7.3 in a simplified version without moderation or mediation effects. As described in this section, this framework demonstrates that SCSR activities are driven or predicted by external stakeholder pressure. The outcome or result of these activities is an increase in EV and SV. Tables 7.2 and 7.3 provide an overview of the proposition of the two models described in this section.

7.4 Conclusion

The social obligations of corporations have long been debated. One of the most prominent places in these debates is taken by attempts to analyse the connection between CSR and financial performance of the business. Various studies aimed at revealing the CSR–CFP connection provide valuable arguments both in favour and against this tandem. Instead of joining one side or the other, this paper bridges both views by addressing the debates in the light of SCSR. Combining the classical CSR definition, which claims that the company's main responsibility is to address the needs of all its stakeholders, and a new CSV phenomenon, SCSR presents a valuable framework that provides companies an opportunity to address societal needs by means that are an integrated part of the company's mission, values and business model.

The proposed CSR framework analyses how a company, by strategically implementing CSR, can move towards increased economic and societal value, what resources are required and which factors influence the process and contribute to the successful outcome.

Building on the idea of CSV proposed by Porter and Kramer (2011), this research argues that there should not be a choice between social responsibility or financial prosperity of the business but rather, by pursuing SCSR activities, a company can gain a competitive advantage and increase revenues by addressing its society's needs.

7.4.1 Limitations and Future Research

The present work is built on the foundation of both theoretical and empirical work. In light of the recommendations proposed by Sekaran and Bougie (2016, 72), such a theoretical framework provides the necessary foundation for future empirical work.

In conjunction with this is one of the core limitations of empirical work in regard to SCSR: Due to the number of stakeholders, processes and structures involved and the resulting complexity, empirical analyses typically only focus on a small selection of aspects, rarely being able to take into consideration a holistic model like the one proposed within this paper. Thus, the empirical verification of a model such as the one proposed might need a multitude of papers based on different studies and samples.

References

Acar, William, Kenneth E. Aupperle, and Ronald M. Lowy. 2001. "An Empirical Exploration of Measures of Social Responsibility Across the Spectrum of Organizational Types." *The International Journal of Organizational Analysis* 9 (1): 26–57.

Aguilera, Ruth V., Deborah E. Rupp, Cynthia A. Williams, and Jyoti Ganapathi. 2007. "Putting the S Back in Corporate Social Responsibility: A Multilevel Theory of Social Change in Organizations." *Academy of Management Review* 32 (3): 836–863.

Gupta, Apurv. September 2019. "The UN Global Compact—Accenture CEO Study on Sustainability: Architects of a Better World." Accenture and United Nations Global Compact. Accessed October 20, 2019. https://www.accenture.com/_acnmedia/pdf-109/accenture-ungc-ceo-study.pdf#zoom=50.

Baden, Denise, and Ian A. Harwood. 2013. "Terminology Matters: A Critical Exploration of Corporate Social Responsibility Terms." *Journal of Business Ethics* 116 (3): 615–627.

Bansal, Pratima, and Kendall Roth. 2000. "Why Companies Go Green: A Model of Ecological Responsiveness." *Academy of Management Journal* 43 (4): 717–736.

Barnett, Michael L. 2007. "Stakeholder Influence Capacity and the Variability of Financial Returns to Corporate Social Responsibility." *Academy of Management Review* 32 (3): 794–816.

Brammer, Stephen J., and Stephen Pavelin. 2006. "Corporate Reputation and Social Performance: The Importance of Fit." *Journal of Management Studies* 43 (3): 435–455.

Bugg-Levine, Antony, and Jed Emerson. 2011. "Impact Investing: Transforming How We Make Money While Making a Difference." *Innovations: Technology, Governance, Globalization* 6 (3): 9–18.

Campbell, John L. 2007. "Why Would Corporations Behave in Socially Responsible Ways? An Institutional Theory of Corporate Social Responsibility." *Academy of Management Review* 32 (3): 946–967.

Carroll, Archie B. 1979. "A Three-Dimensional Conceptual Model of Corporate Performance." *Academy of Management Review* 4 (4): 497–505.

Carroll, Archie B., and Kareem M. Shabana. 2010. "The Business Case for Corporate Social Responsibility: A Review of Concepts, Research and Practice." *International Journal of Management Reviews* 12 (1): 85–105.

Elms, Heather. 2006. "Corporate (and Stakeholder) Responsibility in Central and Eastern Europe." *International Journal of Emerging Markets* 1 (3): 203–211.

Flammer, Caroline. 2015. "Does Corporate Social Responsibility Lead to Superior Financial Performance? A Regression Discontinuity Approach." *Management Science* 61 (11): 2549–2568.

Flammer, Caroline, and Jiao Luo. 2017. "Corporate Social Responsibility as an Employee Governance Tool: Evidence from a Quasi-experiment." *Strategic Management Journal* 38 (2): 163–183.

Freeman, R. Edward, Jeffrey S. Harrison, Andrew C. Wicks, Bidhan L. Parmar, and Simone De Colle. 2010. *Stakeholder Theory: The State of the Art.* Cambridge: Cambridge University Press.

Friedman, Milton. 1970. "The Social Responsibility of Business is to Increase Profits". *The New York Times Magazine*, September 13, 1970.

Fombrun, Charles J., Naomi A. Gardberg, Michael L. Barnett. 2002. "Opportunity Platforms and Safety Nets: Corporate Citizenship and Reputational Risk." *Business and Society Review* 105 (1): 85–106.

Gangone, Andreea-Daniela, and Mariana-Cristina Gănescu. 2014. "Corporate Social Responsibility in Emerging and Developing Economies in Central and Eastern Europe—A Measurement Model from the Stakeholder Theory Perspective." *Economic Research-Ekonomska Istraživanja* 27 (1): 539–558.

Griffeth, Rodger W., Peter W. Hom, and Stefan Gaertner. 2000. "A Meta-analysis of Antecedents and Correlates of Employee Turnover: Update, Moderator Tests, and Research Implications for the Next Millennium." *Journal of Management* 26 (3): 463–488.

Godfrey, Paul C. 2005. "The Relationship Between Corporate Philanthropy And Shareholder Wealth: A Risk Management Perspective." *Academy of Management Review* 30 (4): 777–798.

Howard-Grenville, Jennifer A., and Andrew J. Hoffman. 2003. "The Importance of Cultural Framing to the Success of Social Initiatives in Business." *Academy of Management Perspectives* 17 (2): 70–84.

Klassen, Robert D., and D. Clay Whybark. 1999. "The Impact of Environmental Technologies on Manufacturing Performance." *Academy of Management Journal* 42 (6): 599–615.

Kurtz, Lloyd. 2008. "Socially Responsible Investment and Shareholder Activism." In *The Oxford Handbook of CSR*, edited by Andrew Crane, Dirk Matten, Abagail McWilliams, Jeremy Moon, and Donald S. Siegel, 249–280. Oxford: Oxford University Press.

Margolis, Joshua D., Hillary Anger Elfenbein, and James P. Walsh. 2007. *Does it Pay to Be Good? A Meta-analysis and Redirection of Research on the Relationship Between Corporate Social and Financial Performance*. Cambridge: Harvard Kennedy School.

Matten, Dirk, and Jeremy Moon. 2008. "'Implicit' and 'Explicit' CSR: A Conceptual Framework for a Comparative Understanding of Corporate Social Responsibility." *Academy of Management Review* 33 (2): 404–424.

McWilliams, Abagail, and Donald Siegel. 2001. "Corporate Social Responsibility: A Theory of the Firm Perspective." *Academy of Management Review* 26 (1): 117–127.

Okoye, Adaeze. 2009. "Theorising corporate social responsibility as an essentially contested concept: is a definition necessary?" *Journal of Business Ethics* 89 (4): 613–627.

Orlitzky, Marc, Frank L. Schmidt, and Sara L. Rynes. 2003. "Corporate Social and Financial Performance: A Meta-analysis." *Organization Studies* 24 (3): 403–441.

Peloza, John. 2009. "The Challenge of Measuring Financial Impacts from Investments in Corporate Social Performance." *Journal of Management* 35 (6): 1518–1541.

Porter, Michael E., and Mark R. Kramer. 2006. "The Link Between Competitive Advantage and Corporate Social Responsibility." *Harvard Business Review* 84 (12): 78–92.

Porter, Michael E., and Mark R. Kramer. 2011. "Creating Shared Value." *Harvard Business Review* 89 (1–2): 62–77.

Rodin, Judith, and Margot Brandenburg. 2014. *The Power of Impact Investing: Putting Markets to Work for Profit and Global Good*. Philadelphia: Wharton Digital Press.

Russo, Michael V., and Niran S. Harrison. 2005. "Organizational Design and Environmental Performance: Clues from the Electronics Industry." *Academy of Management Journal* 48 (4): 582–593.

Schaltegger, Stefan, and Roger Burritt. 2018. "Business Cases and Corporate Engagement with Sustainability: Differentiating Ethical Motivations." *Journal of Business Ethics* 147 (2): 241–259.

Sekaran, Uma, and Roger Bougie. 2016. *Research Methods for Business: A Skill Building Approach*. Hoboken: John Wiley & Sons.

Sen, Sankar, and Chitra Bhanu Bhattacharya. 2001. "Does Doing Good Always Lead to Doing Better? Consumer Reactions to Corporate Social Responsibility." *Journal of Marketing Research* 38 (2): 225–243.

Sen, Sankar, Chitra Bhanu Bhattacharya, and Daniel Korschun. 2006. "The Role of Corporate Social Responsibility in Strengthening Multiple Stakeholder Relationships: A Field Experiment." *Journal of the Academy of Marketing Science* 34 (2): 158–166.

Servaes, Henri, and Ane Tamayo. 2013. "The Impact of Corporate Social Responsibility on Firm Value: The Role of Customer Awareness." *Management Science* 59 (5): 1045–1061.

Strong, Kelly C., Richard C. Ringer, and Steven A. Taylor. 2001. "THE* Rules of Stakeholder Satisfaction (* Timeliness, Honesty, Empathy)." *Journal of Business Ethics* 32 (3): 219–230.

Surroca, Jordi, Josep A. Tribó, and Sandra Waddock. 2010. "Corporate Responsibility and Financial Performance: The Role of Intangible Resources." *Strategic Management Journal* 31 (5): 463–490.

Tsoutsoura, Margarita. *Corporate Social Responsibility and Financial Performance*. Berkeley: University of California Press, 2004.

Ubrežiová, Iveta, Lýdia Stankovič, Bohuslava Mihalčová, and Andrea Ubrežiová. 2013. "Perception of Corporate Social Responsibility in Companies of Eastern Slovakia Region in 2009 and 2010." *Acta Universitatis Agriculturae et Silviculturae Mendelianae Brunensis* 61 (7): 2903–2910.

Waddock, Sandra A., and Samuel B. Graves. 1997. "The Corporate Social Performance–Financial Performance Link." *Strategic Management Journal* 18 (4): 303–319.

Whadcock, Ian. 2008. "Just Good Business." *The Economist*, January 19, 2008.

Werther, William B., Jr., and David Chandler. 2010. *Strategic Corporate Social Responsibility: Stakeholders in a Global Environment*. Sage.

8

CSR Strategies for (Re)gaining Legitimacy

Florian Weber and Kerstin Fehre

8.1 Introduction

A 2009 article in *The Economist*, "Germany's Flawed Corporate Governance," reported that "[b]ig companies such as Deutsche Bank, Deutsche Telekom, Deutsche Bahn and Lidl have been caught spying on workers, journalists or board members. Siemens has confessed to bribing customers and MAN is being investigated for the same" (The Economist 2009, p. 55). These are only a few examples of corporate misconduct, expressing an imbalance between value and values management. These corporate scandals violate Suchman's (1995, p. 574) definition of

F. Weber (✉)
Karlsruhe Institute of Management, Karlsruhe, Germany
e-mail: florian.weber@partner.kit.edu

K. Fehre
Vlerick Business School, Brussels, Belgium
e-mail: kerstin.fehre@vlerick.com

F. Farache et al. (eds.), *Values and Corporate Responsibility*, Palgrave Studies in Governance, Leadership and Responsibility,
https://doi.org/10.1007/978-3-030-52466-1_8

legitimacy as behavior that is "desirable, proper, or appropriate within some socially constructed system of norms, values, beliefs, and definitions" and are a major reason why corporate legitimacy is in decline (Castelló and Lozano 2011). In this article, we examine the question of whether corporate social responsibility (CSR)—addressing stakeholder needs—can act as a vehicle for (re)gaining legitimacy.

Although the definition of CSR varies from one author to another (Dahlsrud 2008), all seem to agree that CSR is about the voluntary adoption of non-financial responsibilities—through activity and communication. CSR activity (CSRA) addresses the interests of different stakeholder groups and includes, for example, employee health care, charitable giving, waste reduction and eco-efficient product innovations, sustainable growth, or diversity programs. Communication about CSR issues (CSRC) is a means of broadcasting to stakeholders senior management's stance on a range of social issues and management's plans for addressing these issues. Insofar, both—CSRA and CSRC—underpin that values are core of corporate agenda and that management is committed to the sustainable development goals. Departing from decoupling theory (Elsbach and Sutton 1992; Westphal and Zajac 2001), firstly, we focus on the legitimacy effects of CSRA and CSRC separately, and secondly, we concentrate on combinations of the CSRA and CSRC components that constitute a given CSR strategy for legitimacy.

In the rich academic debate about CSR that has transpired in recent decades (Garriga and Melé 2004), only a few studies have examined the relation between CSRA and CSRC. These few studies, moreover, were conducted from an accounting perspective that views communication as a record of past performance; that is, CSRA and CSRC are two different but interchangeable means of CSR operationalization (Han and Hansen 2012). In contrast to the accounting perspective, several researchers have taken a strategic perspective (Gao et al. 2016). Following their argumentation, communication is used with intention; that is, the sender of the information thoroughly considers what to communicate, selectively places the messages, and in doing so, steers the company. Discrepancies between CSRA and CSRC then become common. Moreover, these discrepancies become strategic themselves and have a forward-looking character, such as regarding stakeholder satisfaction. So far, this is a merely theoretical debate; empirical findings that contribute to a better understanding of the interplay between CSRA and CSRC, coupled with new insights into the effectiveness of CSR strategies for legitimacy, are missing.

The distinction allows to combine CSRA and CSRC into three CSR strategies (shown in Fig. 8.1) and to analyze the legitimacy effect associated with each strategy:

1. be rather than seem, which means that CSRA is high, whereas CSRC is low;
2. walk the talk, which means that CSRA and CSRC are more or less equal; and
3. make it shine, which means that CSRA is low, whereas CSRC is high.

This results in better insights into the interrelatedness of CSR inputs and outcomes and in clearer guidelines for CSR management, both aspects identified as research lacunae by Aguinis and Glavas (2012).

In summary, the main research question of this study is as follows: Does CSR, in general, affect legitimacy? This question can be disaggregated into the following, more fine-grained questions: Does CSRA affect legitimacy? Does CSRC affect legitimacy? Can CSR strategies (defined in terms of combinations of CSRA and CSRC) be distinguished according to their effectiveness in legitimacy acquisition?

8.2 Theory and Hypotheses Development

8.2.1 CSR Through the Legitimacy Theory Lens

Although there are several definitions of CSR, the element of voluntariness figures centrally in most (Dahlsrud 2008). Therefore, CSR effectively reflects a company's level of commitment to broader social values and objectives beyond the company's bottom line. Legitimacy is defined in terms of a company's desirability and appropriateness in the eyes of society (Suchman 1995). "Society allows organizations to operate as long as they are perceived to fulfill the needs of society and to benefit society" (Panwar et al. 2014, p. 483).

Because CSR is concerned with how a business performs regarding social objectives and legitimacy is concerned with how society views business, legitimacy theory provides an ideal backdrop for the study of CSR. According to legitimacy theory, companies must comply with certain rules, norms, and societal expectations in order to (re)gain legitimacy. Only companies that conform to the formal and informal expectations of society are given a social license-to-operate, that is, are seen as acceptable, appropriate, and desirable by their multiple direct and indirect stakeholders (Suchman 1995). In this perspective, legitimacy is an essential prerequisite without which companies could not exist.

The number of direct and indirect stakeholders has increased as a result of globalization, which, in turn, has resulted in a larger number of expectations to be met (Jones and Fleming 2003). Modern businesses "are supposed to have activities which are congruent with social values and also to communicate that their activities are congruent with such values" (Branco and Rodrigues 2007, p. 82). Companies respond to these demands with CSRA and CSRC.

8.2.2 CSRA

Stakeholders and society in general expect companies to take on responsibilities beyond their bottom line and to engage in projects with objectives unrelated to profit-making. For example, Matten and Moon (2008) described a change in the European institutional framework that resulted in the requirement for more explicit CSR. Companies that take a multifaceted approach to CSRA address multiple stakeholder groups. The more a company invests in CSRA, the higher the number of stakeholder groups positively impacted, and the larger the effect on legitimacy. Therefore, we formulated the following hypothesis:

Hypothesis 1a:
The greater a company's CSRA, the greater the legitimacy of that company.

8.2.3 CSRC

Communication is a way to manage a firm's relationship with the public and to influence the firm's public perception (Beelitz and Merkl-Davies 2012; Matten and Moon 2008; Neu et al. 1998). However, stakeholders and society assume that companies overstate their CSR awareness through CSRC (Nielsen and Thomsen 2007). As widely accepted in the academic literature, increased and activity-detached levels of CSRC are seen negatively as an indicator of greenwashing—a term introduced by environmentalist Jay Westerveld in 1986 (Becker-Olsen and Potucek 2013)—instead of positively as signaling (Mahoney et al. 2013). This idea of de-legitimation through CSR rhetoric leads to the following hypothesis:

Hypothesis 1b:
The greater a company's CSRC, the lower the legitimacy of that company.

8.2.4 CSR Strategies for Legitimacy

CSRA and CSRC are cornerstones of company legitimacy, long-term sustainability, and profitability. As discussed by Cho et al. (2015), a given company's approach to CSR is not a random outcome, but the result of strategic managerial decision making. Two mismatched combinations of CSRA and CSRC, as well as the residual walk the talk strategy, make up the limiting set of feasible strategies (shown in Fig. 8.1). Each strategy is expected to have a different impact on legitimacy.

A company gains legitimacy by performing CSRA and destroys legitimacy with excessive CSRC. Therefore, the be rather than seem strategy that combines high levels of CSRA and low levels of CSRC is hypothesized to result in increased legitimacy. This idea is in line with the findings that many corporate activities are not reported at all (Jenkins 2004). If CSRA is not accompanied by communication, then they are referred to as "sunken" or "silent" and are not be detected unless the public and/or

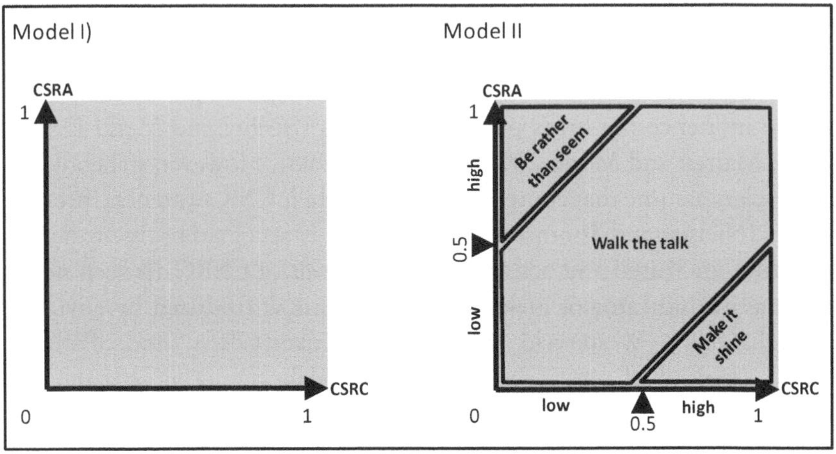

Fig. 8.1 Conceptualization of the study

stakeholders actively inquire about the activities. Based on these considerations, we propose the following hypothesis:

Hypothesis 2a:
A high CSRA and low CSRC strategy leads to increased legitimacy of that company.

In contrast, combinations of low levels of CSRA and high levels of CSRC are assumed to result in little legitimacy. This strategy is what we call the make it shine strategy. Some company leaders might be inclined to broadcast CSR messages that are unsubstantiated by any corresponding activity or to communicate a skewed portrayal of events that omits negative aspects and overstates positive aspects (O'Donovan 2002). When practiced in this abusive form, CSR is fundamentally no different from mere image management or advertising (McWilliams and Siegel 2011). Such behavior has drawn sharp criticism from stakeholders and society (Vlachos et al. 2009). Therefore, we propose the following hypothesis:

Hypothesis 2b:
A low CSRA and high CSRC strategy leads to decreased legitimacy.

The high CSRA levels and high CSRC levels resonate with the call for "CSR seriousness," which means that to gain legitimacy activity should be matched with communication (Aguilera et al. 2007, p. 855). Simultaneous investments in CSRA and CSRC, without favoring one strategy component over another, are presumed to result in intermediate levels of legitimacy. Thus, the corresponding walk the talk strategy is employed for comparison purposes.

8.3 Methods and Model Design

8.3.1 Sample

The study sample consisted of the 110 largest German companies listed on the HDAX stock market index (Deutsche Börse AG 2013). Data were collected from 2004 to 2012, comprising a full economic cycle of upturns and downturns, and the 2008–2009 financial crisis. The financial crisis is relevant to this study, as public perceptions of capitalism worsened due to this crisis, and legitimacy decreased during this period (Lin-Hi 2010).

8.3.2 Method

Following Kabanoff et al. (1995), in this study we employed word count analyses (a form of content analyses) using computers to operationalize CSRC, as well as for the measurement of legitimacy. Short et al. (2010) name the high reliability in the analysis process and the possibility of studying a large number of documents as two major advantages of computer-aided text analysis (CATA). Another strongpoint of CATA is that it provides a means of quantifying qualitative information (Duriau et al. 2007).

8.3.3 Dependent Variable: Legitimacy

Press articles on the sample companies from 2004 to 2012 formed the basis for the operationalization of legitimacy in this study. The press plays an important role in society as distributor of information (Luo et al. 2012; Pollock and Rindova 2003), with a "broad reach and influence on readers" (Alex Bitektine 2011, p. 154). Consequently, press articles can be considered an accurate reflection of company legitimacy (Bednar 2012; Deephouse and Carter 2005).

Concretely, legitimacy was measured from press articles in the LexisNexis press database (Luo et al. 2012) by applying the German Language News filter. In total, 149,965 articles were analyzed for all companies over the nine-year sample period. The procedure was as follows: First, all press articles were tokenized into single words using RapidMiner software. Second, a proven list of positive and negative sentiment words in the German language (SentiWS developed by Remus et al. (2010)) was applied to the press data. Third, each article was assessed as either favorable or unfavorable based on the previous. Last, for each company year a coefficient of imbalance was calculated using the following formula:

$$\mathrm{LEG}_{ij} = \frac{p_{ij} - n_{ij}}{g_{ij}},$$

with LEG for legitimacy, p for number of positive articles, n for number of negative articles, g for total number of articles (p + n), i for company, and j for year. A value of −1 signaled low legitimacy whereas a value of +1 signaled high legitimacy.

8.3.4 Independent Variables

CSRA

As Godfrey and Hatch (2007, p. 88) stated, "CSR activity is not one comprehensive activity but rather a collective name for many different activities." Therefore, it makes sense to apply an index that covers the broad field of CSRAs. In general, CSR ratings measure a company's CSR capability with an evaluation of firm characteristics in a predefined set of points, comparable to a financial rating (e.g., Attig et al. 2013). Chatterji et al. (2009) found that ratings are appropriate proxies for CSRA and are good in summing up past performance.

We used the ASSET4 ESG database, which systematically verifies facts about CSRAs and rates firms according to their CSRAs. The inclusion of driver and outcome variables is one of the strengths of the ASSET4 ESG approach: Driver variables demarcate the existence versus non-existence of company-internal rules regarding CSR practices (e.g., codes of conduct), and outcome variables focus on quantifiable information (such as emission values, remuneration, etc.) (Cheng et al. 2014).

CSRC

Neu et al. (1998, p. 269) pointed out that annual reports offer a "unique opportunity to design a particular organizational image." This is especially true in terms of CEO letters to shareholders, which are relevant to many user groups, such as employees, customers, and society in general (Hooghiemstra 2010). As these letters are a voluntary part of the annual report, managers use the letters to express their attention to and to highlight topics that are of high personal relevance (Branco and Rodrigues 2005). Therefore, in this study, CSRC was operationalized based on CEO letters to shareholders in the company annual reports.

For all sample firms, the letters to the shareholders were collected and tokenized into single words. Each word was assigned to one of the four CSR areas (social, environment, economic, or governance) by agreement of three independent coders. To ensure reliability, Cohen's (1968) kappa was calculated; the values were all above 80% suggesting that intercoder reliability can be assumed (Banerjee et al. 1999). This two-stage procedure resulted in a comprehensive CSR dictionary of 2213 words, which then was applied to the CEO letters of the sample companies. The number of hits for each CEO letter was counted and finally divided by the letter's length. As annual reports are published ex post, we lagged the

CSRC variable by one period to ensure that the values for CSRA, CSRC, and legitimacy correspond to the same year.

CSR Strategies

The CSR strategies were calculated from combinations of CSRA and CSRC as follows: First, CSRA and CSRC values were percentile ranked by year. Second, the sum of CSRA and CSRC was allowed to vary around the respective matrix corner point by the value 0.5 at most (see Fig. 8.1). Technically, this is done by three defining conditions for each of the two mismatch strategies as follows; the walk the talk is the residual strategy.

	Be rather than seem	Walk the talk	Make it shine
1.	$A > 0.5$	Residual	$A < 0.5$
2.	$C < 0.5$	Category	$C > 0.5$
3.	$A - C > 0.5$		$C - A > 0.5$

with A for the CSRA percentile rank and C for the CSRC percentile rank. Strategies were assigned to each company year based on these criteria.

8.3.5 Control Variables

Company age, company size, and performance were introduced as standard control variables. To account for potential macroeconomic influences on legitimacy, additional year and industry dummies were included.

8.3.6 Model Specification and Validity

We used multiple regression analyses to test the hypotheses. As the data were longitudinal and had a panel structure, fixed-effects estimators were used in accordance with the results of the Sargan (1958)-Hansen (1982) test statistic, which is a robust version of the Hausman (1978) test. We further tested for autocorrelation using Wooldridge's (2002) test for autocorrelation in panel data models, for panel heteroskedasticity using Levene's (1960) test, and for multicollinearity by checking the maximum variance inflation factors (VIFs). The test results and the VIFs are reported for each model in Table 8.2. To correct for autocorrelation and heteroskedasticity, we clustered standard errors at the firm level according to White (1980). The VIFs did not indicate any problems with multicollinearity (O'Brien 2007). We handled the issue of missing data for the CSRA variable by dropping incomplete observations. Finally, we standardized the CSRA, CSRC, and legitimacy variables via a z-transformation in order to make them comparable.

8.4 Results and Discussion

The descriptive statistics and the correlation matrix are shown in Table 8.1. The significant correlations between the key variables suggest that the research questions addressed in this study are relevant.

8.4.1 Neither CSRA Nor CSRC Matter on Their Own

The model 1 results are presented in Table 8.2. Neither CSRA nor CSRC on its own has a strong effect on legitimacy. The betas for both variables were positive but far from being statistically significant. Therefore, neither Hypothesis 1a nor Hypothesis 1b was supported. For CSRA, this result resonates with Aguilera et al.'s (2007) proposition that stakeholders' evaluations of CSRAs are context-sensitive. For CSRC, this result resonates with Clarke and Gibson-Sweet's (1999) findings for a sample of 100 British companies.

8.4.2 The Right CSR Strategy as a Combination of CSRA and CSRC Matters

The classification of various combinations of CSRA and CSRC yielded more detailed insights into their interplay. The results indicate that the hypothesized differentiation of the strategies is true: The all action and no communication strategy had a higher positive impact on legitimacy compared with the residual walk the talk strategy. Thus, Hypothesis 2a was

Table 8.1 Descriptive statistics and correlation matrix

Variable	Obs	Mean	SD	Min	Max	1	2	3	4	5	6
1 Legitimacy	589	−0.06	0.28	−0.81	0.80	1.0000					
2 CSRA	589	58.31	22.21	7.69	95.04	−0.1391	1.0000				
						0.0007					
3 CSRC	589	5.97	2.14	1.73	13.33	0.2012	0.1689	1.0000			
						0.0000	0.0000				
4 Age	589	111.46	74.30	7.00	443.00	−0.0606	0.2023	0.1140	1.0000		
						0.1417	0.0000	0.0056			
5 Size [employees (ln)]	589	10.09	1.65	1.39	13.22	−0.1177	0.6118	0.2613	0.1307	1.0000	
						0.0042	0.0000	0.0000	0.0015		
6 Profitability [ROA]	589	3.67	6.84	−51.70	34.76	0.4226	0.0538	0.2338	−0.0294	0.0196	1.0000
						0.0000	0.1921	0.0000	0.4765	0.6354	

Table shows pairwise correlations following Pearson
The second line indicates the respective *p*-values

Table 8.2 Effect of CSRA and CSRC combinations on legitimacy

	Model I			Model II		
	Coeff. (*p*-value)	Sign.	*t*-stat.	Coeff. (*p*-value)	Sign.	*t*-stat.
CSRA	0.0231 *(0.7267)*		0.35	−0.0464 *(0.4571)*		−0.75
CSRC	0.0434 *(0.3065)*		1.03	0.1202 *(0.0099)*	***	2.64
Be rather than seem-dummy				0.1989 *(0.0690)*	*	1.84
Make it shine-dummy				*−0.3604* *(0.0500)*	*	−1.99
Age	−0.0336 *(0.0379)*	**	−2.11	−0.0317 *(0.0443)*	**	−2.04
Size [employees (ln)]	−0.2628 *(0.1941)*		−1.31	−0.2900 *(0.1499)*		−1.45
Profitability [ROA]	0.0369 *(0.0000)*	***	4.70	0.0356 *(0.0000)*	***	4.68
Constant	6.2322 *(0.0040)*	***	2.96	6.3164 *(0.0026)*	***	3.11
Year effects significant	Yes			Yes		
N	589			589		
R2	0.2907			0.3039		
Heteroscedasticity (Levene)	Yes		(0.0000)	Yes		(0.0000)
Autocorrelation (Woodridge)	No		(0.2433)	No		(0.1882)
Maximum VIF	2.28			2.92		

Walk the talk-dummy omitted
Cluster-robust standard errors according to White (1980) used
*** $p < 0.01$; ** $p < 0.05$; * $p < 0.10$

supported ($p = 0.0695$). The high CSRC and low CSRA strategy emerged as the worst strategy for acquiring legitimacy. The strategy had a significant negative impact on legitimacy compared with the walk the talk strategy. Thus, Hypothesis 2b was supported ($p = 0.0500$). Overall, the results provide evidence that the be rather than seem strategy is more effective than the make it shine strategy in (re)gaining legitimacy.

8.4.3 Robustness of the Results

We performed several robustness checks of the results: First, we modified the legitimacy variable and calculated the Janis-Fadner coefficient of imbalance. Janis and Fadner (1943) offer a quantitative text analysis tool that is applicable to a wide range of communications media and is accepted in media research (Bansal and Clelland 2004). Second, we varied the legitimacy variable introducing a minimum number of 24 press articles, thus ensuring that the legitimacy value was not random. Third, we checked diverse alternative operationalizations of the control. Fourth, we included the number of press articles as an additional control variable to ensure that the dependent variable reflected legitimacy and not media attention. Fifth, we estimated the models again but excluded observations from the finance, insurance, and real estate industry sector, which was the industry most badly hit by the 2008–2009 financial crisis. Finally, we made adjustments to model 2 and defined the CSR strategies more narrowly and relied on a 33% threshold (instead of the default 50% threshold). For all models, we also examined the alternative random-effects estimators to improve confidence in the findings.

In general, the robustness analyses confirmed the results. Only one difference was remarkable: The make it shine strategy effect became slightly more negative throughout the alternative calculations, whereas the be rather than seem strategy effect became slightly less positive when the minimum press coverage threshold was introduced, when sales were measured as DAX30 membership, or when the 33% threshold was used. The number of press articles had a statistically significant negative effect on legitimacy but did not alter the main results.

8.5 Discussion

The debate over CSR strategies thus far has been limited to questions of whether CSRAs should form an integral part of the management agenda (McWilliams and Siegel 2011) and whether CSRC is good for financial performance. In practice, however, CSR strategies integrate the CSRA and CSRC dimensions—company leaders have to think about both elements in a single stroke. The present results suggest that there is a fundamental difference among the effectiveness of the high CSRA and low CSRC strategy, the high CSRC and low CSRA strategy, and the residual corridor strategy for enhancing legitimacy. Extreme levels of CSRC (whether high or low) awaken public interest and draw attention from outside stakeholders. As soon as these inquiring stakeholders notice a gap between CSRA and CSRC the company's legitimacy is impacted. The be rather than seem strategy results in higher legitimacy, while the make it shine strategy seems to result in lower legitimacy. The statistically significant negative effect of the make it shine strategy resonates with the debate on illegitimacy (e.g., Hudson 2008), with core stigma as the strongest (and almost irreversible) form of illegitimacy. Society is able to observe CSRA and CSRC and to detect different CSR strategies. This finding disagrees with findings in previous studies that people have difficulty distinguishing cheap talk from core activity (see, e.g., Skarmeas and Leonidou 2013). Nevertheless, the finding makes sense in the context of the present study, which focused on media legitimacy (Bitektine and Haack 2014): The media are responsible for discovering inconsistencies between corporate activity and communication like a "watchdog" (Bednar 2012).

Firms more and more engage in CSR and put effort in contributing to sustainability goals. This study is the first in which the impact of CSRA and CSRC on social legitimacy was empirically differentiated, resulting from decoupling theory (Elsbach and Sutton 1992; Westphal and Zajac 2001). The strategic perspective implicitly taken is in sharp contrast to the accounting perspective that is characterized by the claim of fit between activity and disclosure (Aguilera et al. 2007). In this study, we showed that the two extremes of either all communication and no action (make it shine) or all action and no communication (be rather than seem) have fundamentally different effects on legitimacy, while the walk the talk strategy that invests equally in activity and communication appears to have little impact. The be rather than seem strategy appears to be the most effective strategy for improving legitimacy.

8.6 Conclusion

Numerous scandals have challenged the social legitimacy of corporations. As CSR strategies are designed to improve a company's social standing, they could serve as vehicles for improving a company's social legitimacy. Little research exists on the impact of CSR strategies on company legitimacy. In the present empirical study, this gap was filled by the differentiation between CSRA and CSRC and by the derivation of effective CSR strategies for legitimacy from combinations of the two CSR dimensions.

From a research perspective, the findings show that empirical investigations of CSR impacts should be performed using the strategic perspective of CSRC, which explicitly draws a distinction between CSRA and CSRC. Researchers should be more explicit about which dimension of CSR—CSRA or CSRC—they are studying. When examining the two together, researchers have to account for the methodological pluralism and different measures in CSRA versus CSRC research (Aguinis and Glavas 2012; Cheng et al. 2014): There is no simple ready-to-use CSR operationalization. In future research, increased methodological transparency and precision will enhance the academic debate and yield new findings on CSR.

From a management perspective, legitimacy is essential to a company's long-term sustainability and success. To best achieve this legitimacy, management must find the right balance between CSRA and CSRC. According to our results, a company's management may consider pursuing a be rather than seem strategy or a strategy that balances CSRA and CSRC and avoid the make it shine strategy altogether. However, companies must, of course, interpret the findings of this study in light of the specific challenges, opportunities, and constraints faced in their immediate operational environments. As noted by Scherer et al. (2013), there often is no single best legitimacy strategy—especially in fragmented environments. More comprehensive insights into the CSR-versus-strategy interplay help to better integrate the contribution to the sustainable development goals into corporate strategy.

8.6.1 Limitations and Further Research

When interpreting the findings of this study, the methodological limitation of press sentiment as measure of legitimacy should be kept in mind. For example, questionnaires could be a more direct means of gaining insight into how companies are perceived by individuals (micro legitimacy) and—extrapolating from there—by society (macro legitimacy) (Bitektine and Haack 2014).

With regard to the CSRC construct, our intention was rather to analyze the importance and strategic aspect of CSR, that is, finally the attention paid to CSR as a strategic outcome. Additional research is required to introduce alternative forms of multi-directional communication.

We (in line with the Global Reporting Initiative (2013)) distinguish four pillars of CSR: social, environment, economic, and governance issues. However, CSR is a multifaceted phenomenon with nuances extending beyond those examined in this study. The CSRA versus CSRC debate stands to benefit greatly from more research on unexplored aspects of CSR and their connection to social legitimacy.

Once we have a deeper understanding of such fine-grained issues, we will have a more complete and nuanced understanding of how CSR affects legitimacy and thus will be in a position to take the logical next step of investigating how legitimacy, in turn, impacts financial performance. Many studies have investigated this link in recent decades (see Orlitzky et al. (2003) for an overview). However, these studies neglected the fine distinctions drawn in the present study and have, likely as a result of this neglect, produced mixed and inconclusive findings.

References

Aguilera, R. V., D. E. Rupp, C. A. Williams, & J. Ganapathi. (2007). Putting the S Back in Corporate Social Responsibility: A Multilevel Theory of Social Change in Organizations. *Academy of Management Review*, *32*(3), 836–863.

Aguinis, H., & Glavas, A. (2012). What We Know and Don't Know About Corporate Social Responsibility: A Review and Research Agenda. *Journal of Management*, *38*(4), 932–968.

Attig, N., El Ghoul, S., Guedhami, O., & Suh, J. (2013). Corporate Social Responsibility and Credit Ratings. *Journal of Business Ethics, 117*(4), 679–694. https://doi.org/10.1007/s10551-013-1714-2

Banerjee, M., Capozzoli, M., McSweeney, L., & Sinha, D. (1999). Beyond Kappa: A Review of Interrater Agreement Measure. *Canadian Journal of Statistics, 27*(1), 3–23.

Bansal, P., & Clelland, I. (2004). Talking Trash: Legitimacy, Impression Management, and Unsystematic Risk in the Context of the Natural Environment. *Academy of Management Journal, 47*(1), 93–103.

Becker-Olsen, K., & Potucek, S. (2013). Greenwashing. In S. O. Idowu, N. Capaldi, L. Zu, & A. Das Gupta (Eds.), *Encyclopedia of Corporate Social Responsibility* (pp. 1318–1323). Berlin and New York: Springer. https://doi.org/10.1007/978-3-642-28036-8\textunderscore

Bednar, M. K. (2012). Watchdog or Lapdog? A Behavioral View of the Media as a Corporate Governance Mechanism. *Academy of Management Journal, 55*(1), 131–150.

Beelitz, A., & Merkl-Davies, D. M. (2012). Using Discourse to Restore Organisational Legitimacy: "CEO-speak" After an Incident in a German Nuclear Power Plant. *Journal of Business Ethics, 108*(1), 101–120.

Bitektine, A., & Haack, P. (2014). The "Macro" and the "Micro" of Legitimacy: Toward a Multilevel Theory of the Legitimacy Process. *Academy of Management Review, 40*(1), 49–75. https://doi.org/10.5465/amr.2013.0318

Bitektine, A. (2011). Towards a Theory of Social Judgments of Organizations: The Case of Legitimacy, Reputation, and Status. *Academy of Management Review, 36*(1), 151–179.

Branco, M. C., & Rodrigues, L. L. (2005). An Exploratory Study of Social Responsibility Disclosure on the Internet by Portuguese Listed Companies. *Social Responsibility Journal, 1*(1/2), 81–90. https://doi.org/10.1108/eb045798

Branco, M. C., & Rodrigues, L. L. (2007). Issues in Corporate Social and Environmental Reporting Research: An Overview. *Issues in Social and Environmental Accounting, 1*(1), 72–90.

Castelló, I., & Lozano, J. M. (2011). Searching for New Forms of Legitimacy Through Corporate Responsibility Rhetoric. *Journal of Business Ethics, 100*(1), 11–29.

Chatterji, A. K., Levine, D. I., & Toffel, M. W. (2009). How Well Do Social Ratings Actually Measure Corporate Social Responsibility. *Journal of Economics and Management Strategy, 18*(1), 125–169.

Cheng, B., Ioannou, I., & Serafeim, G. (2014). Corporate Social Responsibility and Access to Finance. *Strategic Management Journal, 35*(1), 1–23.

Cho, C. H., Laine, M., Roberts, R. W., & Rodrigue, M. (2015). Organized Hypocrisy, Organizational Façades, and Sustainability Reporting. *Accounting, Organizations and Society, 40*, 78–94. https://doi.org/10.1016/j.aos.2014.12.003

Clarke, J., & Gibson-Sweet, M. (1999). The Use of Corporate Social Disclosures in the Management of Reputation and Legitimacy: A Cross Sectoral Analysis of UK Top 100 Companies. *Business Ethics: A European Review, 8*(1), 5–13. https://doi.org/10.1111/1467-8608.00120

Cohen, J. (1968). Weighted Kappa: Nominal Scale Agreement Provision for Scaled Disagreement or Partial Credit. *Psychological Bulletin, 70*(4), 213–220.

Dahlsrud, A. (2008). How Corporate Social Responsibility is Defined: An Analysis of 37 Definitions. *Corporate Social Responsibility and Environmental Management, 15*(1), 1–13. https://doi.org/10.1002/csr.132

Deephouse, D. L., & Carter, S. M. (2005). An Examination of Differences between Organizational Legitimacy and Organizational Reputation. *Journal of Management Studies, 42*(2), 329–360.

Deutsche Börse AG. (2013). *Leitfaden zu den Aktienindizes der Deutschen Börse: Version 6.18, Januar 2013*. Frankfurt am Main. Retrieved from http://www.dax-indices.com/DE/MediaLibrary/Document/Equity_L_6_18_d.pdf

Duriau, V. J., Reger, R. K., & Pfarrer, M. D. (2007). A Content Analysis of the Content Analysis Literature in Organizations Studies: Research Themes, Data Sources, and Methodological Refinements. *Organizational Research Methods, 10*(1), 5–34.

Elsbach, K. D., & Sutton, R. I. (1992). Acquiring Organizational Legitimacy through Illegitimate Action—A Marriage of Institutional and Impression Management Theories. *Academy of Management Journal, 35*(4), 699–738.

Gao, H., Yu, T., & Cannella, A. A. (2016). The Use of Public Language in Strategy: A Multidisciplinary Review and Research Agenda. *Journal of Management, 42*(1), 21–54. https://doi.org/10.1177/0149206315615675

Garriga, E., & Melé, D. (2004). Corporate Social Responsibility Theories: Mapping the Territory. *Journal of Business Ethics, 53*(1–2), 51–71.

Global Reporting Initiative. (2013). *G4—Sustainability Reporting Standards: Reporting Principles and Standard Disclosures*. Amsterdam.

Godfrey, P. C., & Hatch, N. W. (2007). Researching Corporate Social Responsibility: An Agenda for the 21st Century. *Journal of Business Ethics, 70*(1), 87–98.

Han, X., & Hansen, E. (2012). Corporate Social Responsibility Implementation in the Global Forest Sector. *Journal of Corporate Citizenship, 47*, 101–118.

Hansen, L. P. (1982). Large Sample Properties of Generalized Method of Moments Estimators. *Econometrica, 50*(4), 1029. https://doi.org/10.2307/1912775

Hausman, J. A. (1978). Specification Tests in Econometrics. *Econometrica, 46*(6), 1251–1271.

Hooghiemstra, R. (2010). Letters to the Shareholders: A Content Analysis Comparison of Letters Written by CEOs in the United States and Japan. *The International Journal of Accounting, 45*(3), 275–300.

Hudson, B. A. (2008). Against All Odds: A Consideration of Cores Stigmatized Organizations. *Academy of Management Review, 33*(1), 252–266.

Janis, I. L., & Fadner, R. H. (1943). A Code of Imbalance for Content Analysis. *Psychometrika, 8*(2), 105–119.

Jenkins, H. (2004). A Critique of Conventional CSR Theory: AN SME Perspective. *Journal of General Management, 29*(4), 37–57.

Jones, M. T., & Fleming, P. (2003). Unpacking Complexity Through Critical Stakeholder Analysis The Case of Globalization. *Business & Society, 42*(4), 430–454. https://doi.org/10.1177/0007650303259070

Kabanoff, B., Waldersee, R., & Cohen, M. (1995). Espoused Values and Organizational Change Themes. *Academy of Management Journal, 38*(4), 1075–1104.

Levene, H. (1960). Robust Tests for Equality of Variances. In I. Olkin (Ed.), *Contributions to Probability and Statistics* (pp. 278–292). Palo Alto, CA: Stanford University Press.

Lin-Hi, N. (2010). The Problem of a Narrow-Minded Interpretation of CSR: Why CSR has Nothing to Do with Philanthropy. *Ramon Llull Journal of Applied Ethics, 1*(1), 79–95.

Luo, J., Meier, S., & Oberholzer-Gee, F. (2012). No News is Good News: CSR Strategy and Newspaper Coverage of Negative Firm Events. *Working Paper 12-091, Harvard Business School.*

Mahoney, L. S., Thorne, L., Cecil, L., & LaGore, W. (2013). A Research Note on Standalone Corporate Social Responsibility Reports: Signaling or Greenwashing? *Critical Perspectives on Accounting, 24*(4–5), 350–359. https://doi.org/10.1016/j.cpa.2012.09.008

Matten, D., & Moon, J. (2008). "Implicit" and "Explicit" CSR—A Conceptual Framework for a Comparative Understanding of Corporate Social Responsibility. *Academy of Management Review, 33*(2), 404–424.

McWilliams, A., & Siegel, D. S. (2011). Creating and Capturing Value: Strategic Corporate Social Responsibility, Resource-Based Theory, and Sustainable Competitive Advantage. *Journal of Management, 37*(5), 1480–1495.

Neu, D., Warsame, H., & Pedwell, K. (1998). Managing Public Impressions: Environmental Disclosures in Annual Reports. *Accounting, Organizations and Society, 23*(3), 265–282.

Nielsen, A. E., & Thomsen, C. (2007). Reporting CSR—What and How to Say It? *Corporate Communications: An International Journal, 12*(1), 25–40.

O'Brien, R. M. (2007). A Caution Regarding Rules of Thumb for Variance Inflation Factors. *Quality & Quantity, 41*(5), 673–690. https://doi.org/10.1007/s11135-006-9018-6

O'Donovan, G. (2002). Environmental Disclosures in the Annual Report—Extending the Applicability and Predictive Power of Legitimacy Theory. *Accounting, Auditing & Accountability Journal, 15*(3), 344–371.

Orlitzky, M., Schmidt, F. L., & Rynes, S. L. (2003). Corporate Social and Financial Performance: A Meta-Analysis. *Organization Studies, 24*(3), 403–441.

Panwar, R., Paul, K., Nybakk, E., Hansen, E., & Thompson, D. (2014). The Legitimacy of CSR Actions of Publicly Traded Companies Versus Family-Owned Companies. *Journal of Business Ethics, 125*(3), 481–496. https://doi.org/10.1007/s10551-013-1933-6

Pollock, T. G., & Rindova, V. P. (2003). Media Legitimation Effects in the Market for Initial Public Offerings. *Academy of Management Journal, 46*(5), 631–642.

Remus, R., Quasthoff, U., & Heyer, G. (2010). SentiWS—A Publicly Available German Language Resource for Sentiment Analysis. In N. Calzolari, K. Choukri, B. Maegaard, J. Mariani, J. Odijk, S. Piperidis et al. (Eds.), *Proceedings of the 7th International Conference on Language Resources and Evaluation* (pp. 1168–1171). Paris: ELRA.

Sargan, J. D. (1958). The Estimation of Economic Relationships using Instrumental Variables. *Econometrica, 26*(3), 393. https://doi.org/10.2307/1907619

Scherer, A. G., Palazzo, G., & Seidl, D. (2013). Managing Legitimacy in Complex and Heterogeneous Environments: Sustainable Development in a Globalized World. *Journal of Management Studies, 50*(2), 259–284. https://doi.org/10.1111/joms.12014

Short, J. C., Broberg, J. C., Cogliser, C. C., & Brigham, K. H. (2010). Construct Validation Using Computer-Aided Text Analysis (CATA): An Illustration

Using Entrepreneurial Orientation. *Organizational Research Methods, 13*(2), 320–347.

Skarmeas, D., & Leonidou, C. N. (2013). When Consumers Doubt, Watch Out! The Role of CSR Skepticism. *Journal of Business Research, 66*(10), 1831–1838.

Suchman, M. C. (1995). Managing Legitimacy: Strategic and Institutional Approaches. *Academy of Management Review, 20*(3), 571–610.

The Economist. (2009). Germany's Flawed Corporate Governance: Boards Behaving Badly: Why the Leading Citizens of Corporate Germany are So Scandal-Prone. *The Economist, 392*(8643), 55.

Vlachos, P. A., Tsamakos, A., Vrechopoulos, A. P., & Avramidis, P. K. (2009). Corporate Social Responsibility: Attributions, Loyalty, and the Mediating Role of Trust. *Journal of the Academy of Marketing Science, 37*(2), 170–180.

Westphal, J. D., & Zajac, E. J. (2001). Decoupling Policy from Practice: The Case of Stock Repurchase Programs. *Administrative Science Quarterly, 46*(2), 202. https://doi.org/10.2307/2667086

White, H. (1980). A Heteroskedasticity-Consistent Covariance Matrix Estimator and a Direct Test for Heteroskedasticity. *Econometrica, 48*(4), 817. https://doi.org/10.2307/1912934

Wooldridge, J. M. (2002). *Econometric Analysis of Cross Section and Panel Data* (2nd ed.). Cambridge, MA: The MIT Press.

9

Cultural and Educational Imprints on the Entrepreneurial Mindset: Romanian Insights

Anca-Teodora Șerban-Oprescu

9.1 Introduction

This chapter aims to explore how culture and education in Romania influence and encourage entrepreneurship, entrepreneurial values along with ethical and socially responsible behavior in business. The material provides an empirical analysis of the impact of cultural and educational values on the entrepreneurial mindset and concludes that Romanians still need to have a more profound understanding of the core values that make for ethical and socially responsible behavior in independent ventures. This outcome is based on arguments provided by an analysis of the impact of cultural and educational factors and/or values on the entrepreneurial spirit. Building and expanding upon a previous study by Şerban-Oprescu and Curea (2015), the present paper focuses on three main aspects: (1)

A.-T. Şerban-Oprescu (✉)
School of International Business and Economics, Bucharest University of Economic Studies, Bucharest, Romania
e-mail: teodora.oprescu@rei.ase.ro

F. Farache et al. (eds.), *Values and Corporate Responsibility*, Palgrave Studies in Governance, Leadership and Responsibility,
https://doi.org/10.1007/978-3-030-52466-1_9

the connection between education and entrepreneurship, (2) risk aversion in entrepreneurship, and (3) ethics, social responsibility, and entrepreneurship.

An overview of the literature focusing on components that influence entrepreneurial mindset and behavior (Scherer et al. 1989; Reitan 1996; Autio et al. 1997; Honig and Davidsson 2000; Mitchell et al. 2017; Truls 2002; Engle et al. 2010) shows that education proves to be an important asset which allows students to reach their potential and assert entrepreneurial capabilities. Scholars argued that there might be a weak correlation between education and entrepreneurship, as entrepreneurs are perceived to have an education level below the average of general population (Jacobowitz and Vidler 1982; Shetty 2004). More recent studies, however, assert that people who are more advanced in their formal studies display greater willingness to set up a business when compared to people with less formal studies (Bates 1995; Dunn and Holtz-Eakin 2000). To confirm this further, Robinson and Sexton (1994) conclude that business owners display a level of education above average. Likewise, Vesa (2010) quoting Pajarinen et al. (2006) contends that business owners with good educational training are more creative, keep pace with business trends, and are prone to apply new technology. Education is, therefore, linked to personal and professional growth, to acquiring skills and changing attitudes toward a constructive view of entrepreneurship. Nevertheless, the imprint of education on willingness to start up and develop business is somewhat less tested (Donckels 1991; Krueger and Brazeal 1994; Krueger et al. 2000). Reviewing a decade of literature on entrepreneurship education, Dainow (1986) concluded that, albeit the praise of the merits of education, there is still much work to be done in order to integrate suitable methodologies to collect and analyze data. The argument is reinforced by Donckels (1991), Krueger and Brazeal (1994), Gorman et al. (1997), and McMullan et al. (2002) who each highlight the need for more in-depth research and the lack of studies assessing the impact of education on entrepreneurship. In the presented context of previous observation that the descriptive and exploratory methodologies are not enough to offer a comprehensive view of the phenomenon, the present study brings forward a working framework meant to gauge the influence of education on entrepreneurship.

As with any heavily studied topic, researchers and authors have described entrepreneurship in detail, as well as the distinct traits of character that are relevant for entrepreneurs (Cooper et al. 1997; Brandstätter 1997; Stewart and Roth 2001; Collins et al. 2004). Among the traits most often mentioned are motivation for high achievement, need for control, intrinsic control, autonomy, confidence, enterprise, enthusiasm, creativity, perseverance, single-mindedness, determination, competitive edge, and risk-taking (Deakins et al. 1999; Cromie 2000). According to researchers (Schumpeter 1934; Kilby 1971), one of the key aspects of entrepreneurship is risk-bearing; risk-taking propensity is considered to be a feature of entrepreneur behavior. Nevertheless, entrepreneurs' propensity for risk-taking has been the subject of controversy. Brockhaus (1980) argues against the traditional point of view with an empirical study which shows that there is no relevant variance in the risk-taking features of managers, entrepreneurs, and the general public. On the other hand, another study (Carland et al. 2007) concludes that entrepreneurs, whose interests are profit and growth, are more likely to display greater affinity for risk-taking than managers or small business owners, whose primary interests are family oriented. In support of these findings, Stewart Jr. and Roth (2001) concluded, based on a psychometric meta-analysis of the literature, that the risk-taking tendency of entrepreneurs is greater than to that of managers. This short review demonstrates that existing studies have not reached a commonly accepted conclusion on whether entrepreneurs display a higher risk propensity. Moreover, studies that bring together and connect educational and cultural accumulative input with the entrepreneurs' propensity for risk-taking are very scarce. In this regard, the present work opens up the research to the less explored area of identifying the manner in which perception of the business environment, as shaped by cultural and educational accumulations, imprints on the entrepreneurial mindset and how these might relate to the risk-bearing and risk-taking propensity.

Although the scholarly interest in the entrepreneurship-ethics link is rather popular, increased attention to this issue led to a substantial body of knowledge. According to Harris et al. (2009, 2011), studies on ethics and entrepreneurship are divided into three primary areas of investigation: entrepreneurship and society, entrepreneurial ethics, and social venturing. Our main concern here refers to the ethical perception and action of entrepreneurs, as recent studies suggest that ethics and entrepreneurship are connected (Buchholz and Rosenthal 2005) while moral imagination and suitable strategies are prerequisites for entrepreneurial success (Dunham 2010). Other studies indicate that there is more focus on ethical behavior among entrepreneurs (Bucar and Hisrich 2001) and they reveal advanced moral reasoning (Teal and Carroll 1999).

Nevertheless, other research suggests that entrepreneurs are more tempted to avoid situations that would require ethical behavior (Bhide 1996). Longenecker et al. (1988, 1989) suggest that entrepreneurs are focused on financial outcome, even when this fails to respect norms of fairness. The entrepreneurs' propensity for rule-breaking is analyzed by Brenkert (2009), who investigates the ethical tension that rule-breaking creates. More recent research into entrepreneurship and ethics has shifted direction toward two topics in particular: (1) how entrepreneurs make ethical decisions and (2) the ethical dilemmas of entrepreneurs. Following the first research direction, using mixed methods of study, Bryant (2009) explores the impact of cognitive factors on entrepreneurs' moral awareness and reveals an intricate connection between social cognitive dynamics and sensitivity to moral issues. The second research direction is exemplified by Chau and Siu (2000) who argue that business environment pressures may have a deep effect upon ethical decision-making processes and a profound impact on the ethical standards of entrepreneurs (De Clercq and Dakhli 2009). Furthermore, as Payne and Joyner (2006) argue, entrepreneurs are dealing with ethical dilemmas with respect to personal values, employee well-being, organizational culture, client experience, and external liability. The notion of external liability automatically leads to corporate social responsibility (CSR) and how CSR is undoubtedly influenced and shaped by the values of entrepreneurs and managers or business people, in general. It is already known that culture and education have an essential role in the personal makeup of values. These personal values translate into managers' and business persons' style and have direct impact on attitude, on behavior, and, further, on corporate social responsibility (Hemingway and Maclagan 2004). As early as 2004, and already looking at previous research, the two authors conclude that this link between personal values and inclination toward a heightened sense of social responsibility is a less studied area. A year later, in 2005, Hemingway contends that personal values may be an incentive for corporate social entrepreneurship. However, the abovementioned authors do not debate the possible influence of certain personal values as those, for example, measured by the Schwartz values instrument on attitudes toward corporate ethics and social responsibility. Nevertheless it is obvious that high personal values are positively associated with good ethics and social responsibility. Furthermore, as argued by Shafer and Simmons (2007, p. 272) the values of ethical universalism, such as social justice, equality, protecting the environment, and harmony with nature, have a direct connection to corporate ethics and social responsibility. As further discussed by Shafer and Simmons (2007, p. 273), a great deal of social responsibility initiatives are linked to matters such as social justice, or equality. It is also largely recognized that values such as preserving a world of beauty and protecting the environment are associated with social responsibility, corporate involvement with the community, and impact on the environment. In their study from 2004, Hemingway and Maclagan make reference to another value category, namely, self-transcendence, benevolence, which should also be associated with ethical and socially responsible behavior. These translate into various forms of philanthropy, which is a trait of social responsibility.

Relying and building on the work of Rokeach (1973), Schwartz (1992, 1994) tries to identify universal values that are to be found in most cultures and comes up with the Schwartz value instrument which includes benevolence values, with items such as being helpful, truthful, loyal, accountable, and forgiving, that are in alignment with an altruistic and ethical behavior. Such individuals with high priority for ethical and altruistic conduct are bound to strongly support ethics and social responsibility in a business context, as noticed by Shafer and Simmons (2007, p. 272). The theoretical framings and empirical results revealed by these studies are directing to future studies designed to provide in-depth knowledge on the ethical mindset of entrepreneurs. In addition, although research connecting entrepreneurship and ethics continues to grow substantial research effort is vital to follow the rhythm of real-life business setting. Our study engages in an analysis of the link between ethical and socially responsible behavior and entrepreneurship from the perspective of the perception that the individual has on the business environment, a perception influenced and altered by his/her educational and cultural values.

9.2 Methodology and Results

In line with the evidence charted in the literature review and identified knowledge gaps, the present paper starts from the following assumptions:

(a) There is no significant connection between education and entrepreneurial spirit among Romanian business leaders or managers.
(b) Lack of financial and entrepreneurial education is connected with lower entrepreneurial enthusiasm.
(c) There is a strong correlation between the assessment of entrepreneurial spirit and the perception of the difficulties of starting a business.
(d) Assessments are highly subjective when evaluating behaviors from a business ethics perspective.

An empirical research via survey was conducted in order to test these assumptions.

The empirical study involved the administration of a survey consisting of 17 items measured on a 5-point Likert scale. The questionnaire was administered in paper-pencil version to 86 respondents, mainly entrepreneurs and managers from Romania. The selected sample consists of respondents who interact with the Romanian business environment as entrepreneurs or managers and who, thus, have the experience and expertise necessary to provide relevant answers to the questions asked in the survey. The items were grouped according to areas of interest related to the perceptions about the risk of the Romanian business environment, the entrepreneurial spirit, as well as assessments regarding the ethical behavior in the field of activity.

The first set of items aimed at revealing data on the demographic and occupational characteristics of the respondents. The following questions, identified, on the one hand, important data on occupation, age, and level of education, and, on the other hand, data on business owned or managed by respondents.

The majority of the respondents (47 from 86) have business in Romania, either on their own (16 respondents) or in association with other partners (31). In addition, a significant number of those surveyed are self-employed (11) or have a small individual or family business (13). A particular category of the respondents is made up of managers (15) who, although do not own their own businesses, are directly involved in the Romanian business environment and deal directly with the management of companies. The overwhelming majority (82 respondents) of those surveyed are graduates of higher studies at bachelor's degree, master's degree, or other postgraduate courses. In general, respondents older than 35 years old say that they have graduated postgraduate courses because at the time of their studies the university system was not developed at master's degree level. Very few of the respondents (4) did not graduate from university education, being among those who declare that they own a small family business or a business in their own name. Regarding age, most respondents (30) are between 35 and 44 years old, and another significant part (21) are between 25 and 34 years old. At the same time, the survey was answered by 16 people under the age of 25 and 19 individuals between 45 and 54 years old.

Regarding the businesses owned or managed as manager, data concerns the number of existing employees, the annual turnover, and the field of activity of the respective companies. Most of the companies owned/managed have a maximum number of employees of 25 persons. There are very few companies with a large number of employees owned by the respondents, and the few companies that have more than 50 employees are mostly managed by respondents as managers, not as owners. The same is true in the case of turnover, where most companies owned by the respondents can be classified in the category of small- and medium-sized companies, and some companies with an annual turnover of more than 500,000 euros are managed by respondents as managers, not owners. Most respondents (53) own or manage companies that come from the trade-services sector and IT which are among the most dynamic sectors of the Romanian economy.

The entrepreneurial spirit shown by the people who answered the survey and the most important contributions to its formation were analyzed through a series of items that tried to highlight the contribution of the family environment and education to the development of the entrepreneurial spirit.

Following the analysis of the answers received regarding the respondents' evaluation of the entrepreneurial spirit, it is possible to identify interesting elements that either confirm or refute results previously obtained and presented in specialized literature. Thus, many respondents consider that they have a developed (29 respondents) and a very developed (14) entrepreneurial spirit, but at the same time, a significant number of respondents consider that their entrepreneurial spirit is average (30) or even poorly developed (8) and very poorly developed (5). Therefore, it is found that the proportion of those who think they have a developed entrepreneurial spirit is approximately equal to those who are not convinced of their entrepreneurial spirit. Data gathered reveals that, in the Romanian business environment, there is still very little confidence in the entrepreneurial spirit that can be attributed to family and education when it comes to the formation of this spirit. The statement is supported by the data that encompasses the contributions of family and education to the formation of the entrepreneurial spirit. A significant majority of respondents consider the contribution of the family environment to the development of their entrepreneurial spirit as small (38 respondents) and very small (20). Part of the explanation for these results can be identified in the answers given in previous contexts, where the respondents emphasized the lack of entrepreneurial behaviors displayed among family members; the lack of such role models can be understood in the context of the Eastern European, specifically Romanian, pre-and post-transition socio-economic environment. A similar phenomenon can be observed in the case of the contribution of education, where it is found that a large number of respondents (but slightly smaller than in the family environment) consider that education contributes little (28 respondents) or very little (14) to the training and development of the entrepreneurial spirit. Some of these results may be attributed to the age of the respondents who did not have access to modern forms of education, but, surprisingly, the same proportion of younger respondents (less than 34 years old) held similar views on the merits of education. Therefore, one can conclude that even current education does not contribute to the development of a strong entrepreneurial spirit. In fact, one of the topics frequently discussed was related to the inability of the education system to train entrepreneurs; there is a strong impression that school can train/form one to perform well, but not to initiate actions. Regarding the perception of entrepreneurs or managers on the risks of the Romanian business environment, the results of the survey show that a significant part of them consider it risky (30 respondents) and very risky (16), these numbers being higher than those of the respondents considering it as not risky at all (11) or very low risk (6). At the same time, there are a significant number of respondents (22) who value the Romanian business environment as neither risky nor very low risk.

A more distinct picture of the perception of entrepreneurs and managers regarding risk can be deduced from the analysis of the elements that may constitute risk factors for business in Romania. In this sense, the following problems that could be considered risk factors for business were identified and brought to attention: (1) rather volatile fiscal environment, (2) unpredictable legislative framework, (3) bureaucracy, (4) volatile human resources, (5) poorly prepared human resources, (6) unfair competition, and (7) difficult access to development money/capital/financial resources. Respondents were asked to express their agreement or disagreement regarding the risk potential of these factors, and the summary of responses is presented in Fig. 9.1.

To a significant extent, the respondents express their agreement regarding the fiscal and legislative environment as factors that can increase the risk of the Romanian business environment, thus supporting the hypothesis that the fiscal and legislative stability of the business environment represent a safe way to change the perception of entrepreneurs regarding the risks of an economy. In the same note, bureaucracy is perceived by a large number of respondents as a risk factor for the business environment. During formal and informal talks one observed the somewhat hostile attitude of the entrepreneurs regarding the large number of fiscal rules and financial documents that must be completed in order to fulfill the fiscal and legislative obligations. This attitude is also confirmed by the results of the survey that reveal these problems as significant risk factors

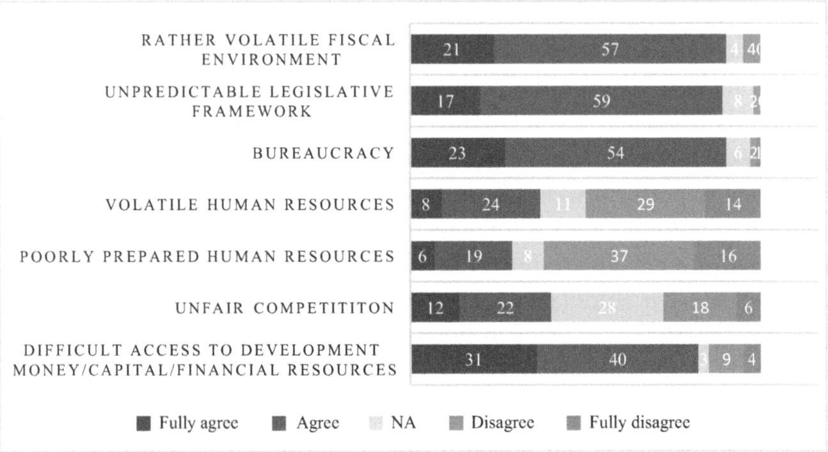

Fig. 9.1 Risk factors for business in Romania. (Source: own data processing based on the answers obtained from respondents)

for the Romanian business environment. On the other hand, a rather negative perception related to the volatility and the professionalism of the human resource is not confirmed by the empirical study. Respondents disagree with the hypothesis that volatility and human resource professionalism are risk factors for the business environment. In this context, it can be assessed that, in principle, volatility and professionalism of the human resource can be risk factors, but, in practice, the Romanian business environment is not confronted yet with these risk factors, at least for the moment.

An interesting result is obtained from the processing of the data regarding the respondents' agreement/disagreement regarding the hypothesis of unfair competition as a risk factor of the business environment. Most respondents do not express their agreement or disagreement in this regard, which may show the connection between risk perception and ethical behavior in the business environment. The lack of a clear-cut answer to this problem may reveal that a large part of the Romanian entrepreneurs and managers have a problem in positioning themselves regarding unfair competition which can thus be a practice rejected at theoretical level, but allowed at practical level. The last item (see Fig. 9.1) highlights the intrinsic connection between attitude toward risk, entrepreneurial spirit, and business financing. The answers show that 31 respondents express their total agreement, and 40 respondents agree with the hypothesis that difficult access to development capital is a risk factor for the business environment. These data show that the lack of access to easy and secure financing resources increases the risk of the business environment, thus reducing the investment appetite and entrepreneurial spirit of individuals. Most of the time, the entrepreneurial spirit of individuals is revealed by their appetite for starting new businesses. In this context, an interesting hypothesis brought to attention during the study was the correlation between the perception regarding one's own entrepreneurial spirit and the appraisals regarding the difficulties of starting one's own business. A low entrepreneurial spirit can lead to the perception that starting a business is a difficult task. In this regard, one of the items analyzed was how respondents perceive the difficulties when starting a business.

The resulting data confirm the existence of a rather strong correlation between the assessment of the entrepreneurial spirit and the perception of the difficulties of starting a business. A significant percentage of those who judged having a mediocre or even low entrepreneurial spirit pointed out that starting a business is difficult or very difficult in today's business environment. The correlation was maintained, but it was weaker, and in the case of those who considered that they had a developed entrepreneurial spirit, they stated that the difficulties in starting a business are medium to small.

On a different note, the majority of respondents consider that the Romanian business environment raises difficulties in starting a business. Thus, the main barriers to starting a business tested within the study were the following: (1) bureaucracy, (2) lack of information, (3) lack of trust in the business environment, (4) lack of an entrepreneurial mindset, (5) lack of an entrepreneurial education, (6) lack of financial education, and (7) lack of a significant number of successful role models to inspire.

These hypotheses were tested via survey, with respondents being asked to express their agreement or disagreement. A summary of the answers is presented in Fig. 9.2.

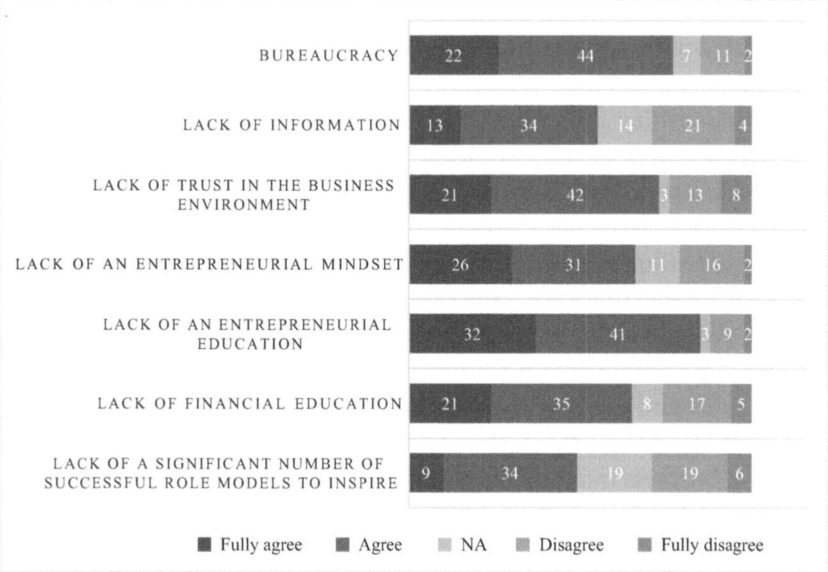

Fig. 9.2 Main barriers to starting a business in Romania. (Source: own data processing based on the answers obtained from respondents)

As revealed when processing the answers to a previous item, bureaucracy is not only seen as a risk factor but also as an important barrier to starting a business, a significant number of respondents being totally in agreement or in partial agreement. Therefore, the institutional environment is considered by many respondents as a cause for the reduced entrepreneurial appetite in Romania. On the other hand, the lack of information of individuals is perceived as a barrier to starting a business, but not as strong as bureaucracy. The hypothesis of lack of confidence in the business environment as a barrier to starting a business is confirmed by the results of the study to the same extent as bureaucracy (63 respondents totally agree or at least agree with this fact). Moreover, answers to this item seem to provide an argument for the perception of a high degree of risk regarding the business environment; risk aversion and lack of concern are, in fact, two very closely related psychological components of the entrepreneur. Also, a significant number of respondents (57 completely agree or at least agree with this) consider that the lack of a mentality favorable to the business spirit for venturing represents a clear barrier to starting a business. Closely correlated with the lack of entrepreneurial mentality, we find the lack of financial education (P coeff = 0.557, $p < 0.001$) and entrepreneurial education (P coeff = 0.698, $p < 0.001$) as barriers for entering the business environment. However, it is found that the respondents accuse much more the lack of entrepreneurial education as compared to the lack of financial education as an obstacle to starting a business, and the explanation is clear: entrepreneurial education, rather than financial education, has the main role in manifesting entrepreneurial behavior. Hence the hypothesis of the lack of financial and entrepreneurial education as factors accounting for the reduced entrepreneurial appetite is confirmed. Finally, an interesting hypothesis drawn from specialized literature and various case studies on the topic was that of the absence of a significant number of successful role models that would inspire entrepreneurial behavior. Testing via survey confirmed only partially this hypothesis (43 respondents completely agree or at least agree with this fact) because a large number of participants did not assess the item (19 respondents did not know what to answer). This phenomenon can be attributed to the fact that many of the respondents considered that there are successful role models, but that most of them are foreign and not domestic. Even under these circumstances, some respondents feel that foreign/imported successful models can be an inspiration for adopting and displaying entrepreneurial behavior.

Next, respondents were asked about the most suitable reasons/arguments for starting a business. The following hypotheses were empirically tested via survey: (1) the need for money, (2) the need for independence, (3) confidence in personal success, (4) the desire/aspiration for personal development, (5) the desire/aspiration for professional/career development, and (6) the desire to show others the skills I possess. The synthesis of the answers is presented in Fig. 9.3.

As data in the table shows, the need to make money represents a more significant argument in the decision to start a business (47 respondents totally agree or at least agree) than the need for independence (40 respondents totally agree or at least agree). This phenomenon reveals that Romanian entrepreneurs do not necessarily associate owning a business with a strong sense of independence. This result is somewhat contrary to

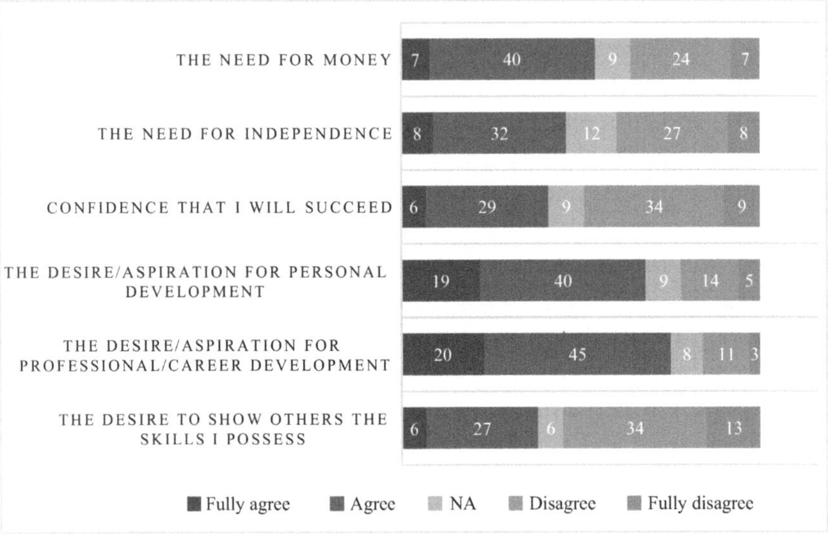

Fig. 9.3 Reasons/arguments for starting a business in Romania. (Source: own data processing based on the answers obtained from respondents)

similar studies conducted in developed market economies (especially the USA) where the need for self-management is one of the primary arguments in deciding to start a business. It can be seen that Romanian entrepreneurs have a cautious attitude in this regard, since not even confidence in their success represents a strong argument in starting a business (only 35 from 86 respondents completely agree or at least agree that "trust that I will succeed" is an argument in favor of starting a business). Moreover, the data obtained from this inquiry are strongly correlated with those regarding the perception of risk in the business environment: those who perceive the business environment as risky tend to disagree with the assumption that success is an argument for starting a business. Confidence in success is not an argument and shows a certain degree of skepticism in the case of the Romanian entrepreneurs; professionalism, or rather, the experience accumulated in a certain field, tends to represent a major argument in the decision to start a business (65 respondents totally agree or at least agree). Consequently, we may notice that the entrepreneurial enthusiasm specific to certain developed market economies is replaced in the Romanian business environment with a certain degree of pragmatism in which experience is stronger than aspiration/desire. However, upon analysis of answers to the following items, Romanian entrepreneurs are still stimulated by certain aspirations, such as personal development (59 respondents totally agree or at least agree with this fact) and professional development (65 respondents totally agree or at least agree with this fact). Therefore, starting a business is perceived by many of the respondents as a potential route to personal and professional development. Finally, Romanian entrepreneurs and managers seem not to be too influenced by the opinion of those around them, as 33 respondents express their complete or partial disagreement with the hypothesis that the desire to demonstrate to others the skills/abilities they have might constitute a valid argument in favor of starting a business.

Another significant topic undergoing empirical testing is related to ways of approaching ethical behavior in the Romanian business environment. In this respect, the respondents were asked to evaluate their own behavior, as well as that of the other actors in the business environment from an ethical perspective (see Fig. 9.4).

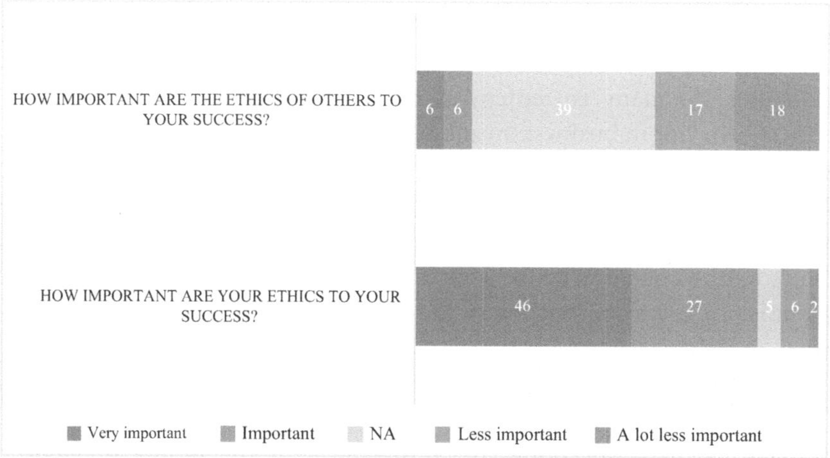

Fig. 9.4 The importance of ethics. (Source: own data processing based on the answers obtained from respondents)

Analyzed in parallel, the answers to the two items highlight at least one interesting phenomenon: the vast majority of respondents (73) consider that they attach a very high value to their own ethical behavior while they consider that the rest of the actors in the business environment are either indifferent or attach little or very little value to this problematic. There appears hence an apparent paradox: if each actor in the business environment evaluates oneself as displaying an ethical behavior, then the general image formed regarding the business environment is unlikely to show any slight concern for ethical behavior, or issues. In reality, however, the explanation of the paradox is fairly straightforward: respondents tend to judge with different units of measure their own behavior against the behavior of others. The consequence of this phenomenon can have adverse effects on an honest competitive environment: while an entrepreneur is positively evaluating a certain behavior, it is very possible for other economic agents with which one interacts to have a contrary evaluation, which can cause divergence.

To delve deeper into the topic of business ethics, a number of business ethics statements have been empirically tested. In this respect, the agreement/disagreement was tested in relation to the following hypotheses: (1) in Romania, business ethics is not a concern; (2) unethical behaviors are common in the Romanian business environment; (3) the Romanian mentality leaves room for improvement regarding business ethics; (4) business ethics is a concern only in theory and at a declarative level in Romania; (5) many entrepreneurs have difficulty recognizing what an ethical behavior in business means; (6) there is no 100% honest entrepreneur; and (7) the pursuit of profit often eliminates ethical behavior. The results are summarized in the Fig. 9.5 below.

From the data obtained it can be observed that, in general, respondents tend to agree with the fact that the Romanian business environment is not very concerned with the ethical issue (54 respondents totally agree or at least agree with this fact), as well as with the hypothesis that unethical behaviors are common in the Romanian business environment (57 respondents completely agree or at least agree with this fact). The answers to these questions are consistent with the results previously reported (Fig. 9.4). At the same time, the question remains: if the majority of respondents consider their own behavior to be ethical, then who are

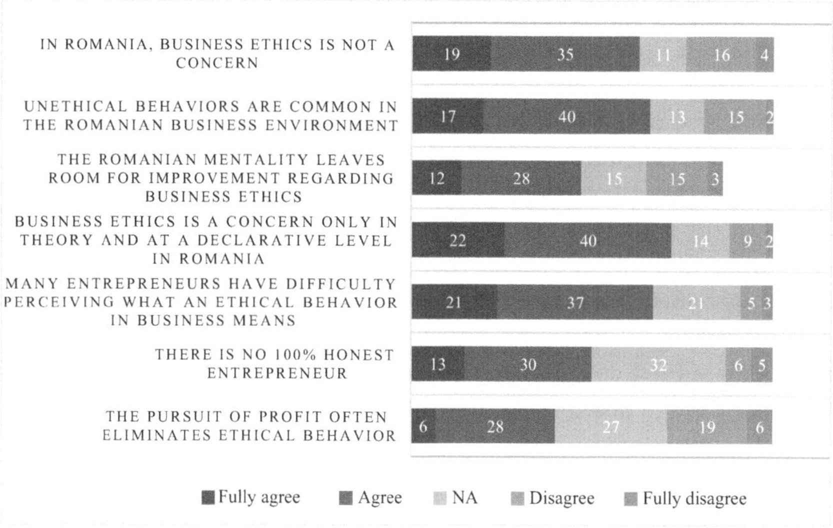

Fig. 9.5 Perception on business ethics in Romania. (Source: own data processing based on the answers obtained from respondents)

those who do not behave ethically? Another possible answer to the one formulated above could be a methodological sampling error: all those who did not behave ethically were not included in the sample. Although possible, this response is unlikely; rather assessments are highly subjective when evaluating behaviors from a business ethics perspective. This answer is similarly confirmed by the fact that the respondents consider that there is a subjective and, therefore, different interpretation of what ethics and morality mean in business (58 respondents express their full or partial agreement regarding the hypothesis that "Many entrepreneurs have difficulties in grasping the meaning of ethical behavior in business"). However, it is noted in the respondents' answers that the ethical issue is not necessarily appropriated by the Romanian mentality exclusively (only 40 respondents express their full or partial agreement regarding the hypothesis that "the Romanian mentality leaves to be desired regarding business ethics"), but, rather, points to the fact that the topic of ethics is still at theoretical, declarative, and less practical level (62 respondents express their full or partial agreement regarding the hypothesis that

"Business ethics is only a concern in theory and at the declarative level in Romania"). It is worth noting that "any means to an end" and obtaining profit regardless does not seem to be considered a strong argument justifying any type of behavior (only 34 respondents express their full or partial agreement regarding the hypothesis that "The pursuit of profit often eliminates ethical behavior," while 27 say they do not know); when it comes to the issue of business fairness of economic agents the two sides seem to be in a sort of balance (half of respondents express their full or partial agreement regarding the hypothesis that "There is no 100% honest entrepreneur," while the rest disagree or declare that they do not know). As a brief conclusion, the answers in this section reveal, on the one hand, a high dose of relativity in the assessment of ethics and morality and confirm, on the other, the hypothesis of a certain degree of immaturity with respect to ethical behavior in the Romanian business environment.

To further test the perception of ethics in business and to assess the attitude toward social responsibility, the survey applied a partial PRESOR scale comprising six items of the total ten of the original scale (Singhapakdi et al. 1996). Given that PRESOR scale practices a 7-point rating, we used it to render findings more reliable, as an alternative assessment method to the 5-point Likert scale applied in this survey.

Results show that respondents consider that business ethics and social responsibility are important and must not be neglected for the sake of profit or other competitive gains (in this case the mean is 2.583 with 1.174 standard deviation) (Table 9.1). In general, answers display a certain awareness of the respondents in the direction of social responsibility and business ethics and further sanction answers to previous items. In addition, a great majority of respondents confirmed the highest degree of compatibility between social responsibility and profitability (mean, 4.523; standard deviation, 0.204).

Table 9.1 PRESOR scale

	Obs	Range	Min	Max	Mean	Std. dev	Var.
Being ethical and socially responsible is the most important thing a firm can do	85	3	4	7	4.764	1.485	2.205
The ethics and social responsibility of a firm is essential to its long-term profitability	77	6	1	7	4.324	1.901	3.616
Overall effectiveness of a business can be determined, to a great extent, by the degree to which it is ethical and socially responsible	80	6	1	7	4.081	1.982	3.928
To remain competitive in a global environment, business firm will have to disregard ethics and social responsibility	84	3	1	4	2.583	1.174	1.378
Social responsibility and profitability can be compatible	84	5	2	7	4.523	0.204	3.529
Business ethics and social responsibility are critical to the survival of a business enterprise	82	5	2	7	4.487	1.779	3.166

Source: own data processing based on the answers obtained from respondents

9.3 Conclusions and Further Research

The original contribution of the research consisted in carrying out the empirical study which involved the administration of a survey of 17 items arising from the analysis of specialized literature and other case studies. The survey was administered to 86 respondents, entrepreneurs, and managers in Romania. The items in the survey were grouped according to the areas of interest related to the perceptions regarding the risk of the Romanian business environment, the entrepreneurial spirit, as well as assessments regarding the ethical behavior in business.

The selected sample consists of respondents who interact with the Romanian business environment as entrepreneurs or managers and thus have the experience and expertise necessary to provide relevant answers to the items asked.

The entrepreneurial spirit displayed by those who filled-in the survey and the most important contributions to the formation of this spirit were analyzed via a series of items that tried to highlight the contribution of the family environment and education to the development and manifestation of an entrepreneurial spirit.

Regarding the propensity for entrepreneurship, it is found that the proportion of those who judge themselves as individuals with a developed entrepreneurial spirit is approximately equal to those who are not convinced of their entrepreneurial spirit. This occurrence reveals that, in the Romanian business environment, there is still a lot of reduced confidence in the inner development of an entrepreneurial spirit that might be attributed, to a small degree, to family and education. A significant majority of respondents consider the contribution of the family environment to the development of their entrepreneurial spirit as small and very small. Part of the explanation for these results emphasizes the lack of entrepreneurial behaviors among family members and the lack of such role models can be understood from the perspective of the Eastern European, specifically Romanian, pre- and post-transition socio-economic environment. A similar phenomenon could be observed in the contribution of education, where it is found that a large number of respondents (but slightly smaller than in the family environment) consider that education contributes little or very little to the formation and development of the entrepreneurial spirit. Some of these results may be attributed to the age of the respondents who did not allow them the access to the modern forms of education, but, surprisingly, it is found that the same proportion is kept among the respondents of younger age, younger than 34. Therefore, one can conclude that current education still fails to contribute to the development of a strong entrepreneurial spirit. Additionally, this statement is supported by the results of the survey and by formal and informal discussions, where one of the frequently discussed topics was related to the inability of the education system to train entrepreneurs, with a strong impression that school can train one as a good performer on the job, but not as an initiator of actions. During the research the somewhat hostile attitude of the entrepreneurs regarding the large number of tax rules and financial documents that must be drawn in order to fulfill the fiscal and legislative obligations was observed. This attitude is confirmed by the results of the survey that reveal these matters as significant risk factors for the Romanian business environment. On the other hand, a somewhat negative perception expressed, connected with the volatility and the preparation of the human resource, is not confirmed by the empirical study. The resulting data confirm the existence of a rather strong relationship between the assessment of the entrepreneurial spirit and the perception of the difficulties of starting a business. A significant percentage of those who thought of themselves as having a mediocre or even low entrepreneurial spirit pointed out that starting a business is difficult or very difficult in today's business environment. The relationship was maintained, but it was weaker, and in the case of those who considered that they possessed a developed entrepreneurial spirit, they stated that the difficulties in starting a business are medium to small.

Regarding risk factors in starting and maintaining a business, bureaucracy is not only seen as a risk factor but also as an important barrier to starting a business, with a significant percentage of respondents fully agreeing or at least agreeing. To be also noted, the institutional environment is considered by many respondents as a cause for the reduced entrepreneurial appetite in Romania. On the other hand, the lack of information of individuals is perceived as a barrier to starting a business, but not as strong as bureaucracy. The hypothesis of lack of confidence in the business environment as a barrier to starting a business is confirmed by the results of the study to the same extent as bureaucracy. Moreover, the answers to this question seem to provide an argument for the perception of a high degree of risk of the business environment; furthermore, risk aversion and lack of trust are two very closely related psychological components of the entrepreneur's mindset. A significant number of respondents consider that the lack of a business mindset is a clear barrier to starting a business. Closely correlated with the lack of mentality, the lack of financial and entrepreneurial education can be identified as barriers to entering the business environment. However, it is to be noticed that the respondents focus much more on the lack of an entrepreneurial education than the lack of a financial education as a barrier to starting a business. The explanation might be that entrepreneurial education is considered much more important than financial education in manifesting entrepreneurial behavior. The hypothesis of the lack of financial and entrepreneurial education as sources of reduced entrepreneurial appetite is also confirmed.

From the data presented, the need to make money is a more significant argument in the decision to start a business than the need for independence. This phenomenon reveals that Romanian entrepreneurs do not necessarily associate owning a business with a strong sense of independence. Trust in personal success is not an argument and presents a high degree of skepticism among Romanian entrepreneurs. Instead, professionalism, expertise, or, more precisely, the experience accumulated in a certain field tends to represent the primary arguments in the decision to start a business. Accordingly, entrepreneurial enthusiasm specific to certain developed market economies is replaced in the Romanian business environment with pragmatism and the idea that experience is more important than desire. Starting a business is perceived by many of the respondents as a potential route for personal and professional development.

Regarding the ethical component, the survey indicates an interesting phenomenon: the vast majority of respondents consider that they attach great and very high value to their own ethical behavior, while about the same percentage consider that the rest of the actors in the business environment are either indifferent or give little or very little value to this problem. There is thus an apparent paradox: if each actor in the business environment sees oneself as displaying ethical behavior, then the general image of the business environment is unlikely to show any slight concern for ethical behavior. In reality, however, the explanation of the paradox is fairly straightforward: respondents tend to judge with different units of measure their own behavior relative to the behavior of others.

The consequence of this phenomenon may cause adversity in an honest competitive environment: while an entrepreneur is positively evaluating a certain behavior, it is very possible that the economic agents with whom he/she interacts have a contrary evaluation, which can cause divergence between the respective actors. As a brief conclusion, the answers to these items reveal, on the one hand, a high dose of relativity in the assessment of ethics and morality and confirm, on the other, the hypothesis of a certain degree of immaturity when it comes to ethical behavior in the Romanian business context. On the other hand, answers present a certain awareness of respondents regarding social responsibility and business ethics and further validate previous answers. Additionally, respondents confirmed the highest degree of compatibility between social responsibility and profitability (mean, 4.523; standard deviation, 0.204).

Even if representative for the objectives initially formulated in the study, a noticeable limitation is that the survey was conducted on a statistically non-representative sample. Given the relatively small number of observations, for a correct statistical treatment to be applied, the econometric highlighting of the correlations would not be relevant. Despite these methodological deficiencies, the results obtained during the analysis proved to be a good incentive for a more in-depth investigation of the subject addressed. A possible future trajectory for the continuation of the study is to increase the number of respondents to the survey, so that a valid econometric treatment, with an increased degree of confidence, might be applied. Its results would add to the reliability of the observations and conclusions highlighted so far.

References

Autio, Erkko, Robert H. Keeley, Magnus Klofsten, and Thomas Ulfstedt. 1997. "Entrepreneurial Intent among Students: Testing an Intent Model in Asia, Scandinavia and USA." In: *Frontiers of Entrepreneurship Research: Proceedings of the seventeenth annual Entrepreneurship Research Conference*, edited by Paul D. Reynolds, 133–147. Wellesley, Mass.: Babson College.

Bates, Timothy. 1995. "Self-Employment Entry across Industry Groups." *Journal of Business Venturing* 10 (2): 143–156.

Bhide, Amar. 1996. "The Questions Every Entrepreneur Must Answer." *Harvard Business Review* 74 (6): 120.

Brandstätter, Hermann. 1997. "Becoming an Entrepreneur—A Question of Personality Structure?" *Journal of Economic Psychology* 18 (2–3): 157–177.

Brenkert, George G. 2009. "Innovation, Rule Breaking and the Ethics of Entrepreneurship." *Journal of Business Venturing* 24 (5): 448–464.

Brockhaus Sr., Robert H. 1980. "Risk Taking Propensity of Entrepreneurs." *Academy of Management Journal* 23 (3): 509–520.

Bryant, Peter. 2009. "Self-Regulation and Moral Awareness among Entrepreneurs." *Journal of Business Venturing* 24 (5): 505–518.

Bucar, Branko, and Robert D. Hisrich. 2001. "Ethics of Business Managers vs. Entrepreneurs." *Journal of Developmental Entrepreneurship* 6 (1): 59.

Buchholz, Rogene A., and Sandra B. Rosenthal. 2005. "The Spirit of Entrepreneurship and the Qualities of Moral Decision Making: Toward a Unifying Framework." *Journal of Business Ethics* 60 (3): 307–315.

Carland, James W., Frank Hoy, William R. Boulton, and Jo Ann C. Carland. 2007. "Differentiating Entrepreneurs from Small Business Owners: A Conceptualization*." In *Entrepreneurship: Concepts, Theory and Perspective*, edited by Álvaro Cuervo, Domingo Ribeiro, and Salvador Roig, 73–81. Berlin, Heidelberg: Springer. https://doi.org/10.1007/978-3-540-48543-8_3.

Chau, Lewis Long-fung, and Wai-sum Siu. 2000. "Ethical Decision-Making in Corporate Entrepreneurial Organizations." *Journal of Business Ethics* 23 (4): 365–375.

Collins, Christopher J., Paul J. Hanges, and Edwin A. Locke. 2004. "The Relationship of Achievement Motivation to Entrepreneurial Behavior: A Meta-Analysis." *Human Performance* 17 (1): 95–117. https://doi.org/10.1207/S15327043HUP1701_5.

Cooper, Arnold, F. Javier Gimeno-Gascón and Carolyn Y. Woo. 1997. "Initial Human and Financial Capital as Predictors of New Venture Performance." *The Journal of Private Equity* 1 (2): 13–30

Cromie, Stanley. 2000. "Assessing Entrepreneurial Inclinations: Some Approaches and Empirical Evidence." *European Journal of Work and Organizational Psychology* 9 (1): 7–30.

Dainow, Robert. 1986. "Training and Education of Entrepreneurs: The Current State of the Literature." *Journal of Small Business & Entrepreneurship* 3 (4): 10–23.

De Clercq, Dirk, and Mourad Dakhli. 2009. "Personal Strain and Ethical Standards of the Self-Employed." *Journal of Business Venturing* 24 (5): 477–490.

Deakins, David, Mark S. Freel, and Kate Mason. 1999. *Entrepreneurship and Small Firms*. McGraw-Hill.

Donckels, Rik. 1991. "Education and Entrepreneurship Experiences from Secondary and University Education in Belgium." *Journal of Small Business & Entrepreneurship* 9 (1): 35–42.

Dunham, Laura C. 2010. "From Rational to Wise Action: Recasting Our Theories of Entrepreneurship." *Journal of Business Ethics* 92 (4): 513–530.

Dunn, Thomas, and Douglas Holtz-Eakin. 2000. "Financial Capital, Human Capital, and the Transition to Self-Employment: Evidence from Intergenerational Links." *Journal of Labor Economics* 18 (2): 282–305. https://doi.org/10.1086/209959.

Engle, Robert L., Nikolay Dimitriadi, Jose V. Gavidia, Christopher Schlaegel, Servane Delanoe, Irene Alvarado, Xiaohong He, Samuel Buame, and Birgitta Wolff. 2010. "Entrepreneurial Intent." *International Journal of Entrepreneurial Behavior & Research* 16 (1): 35–57. https://doi.org/10.1108/13552551011020063.

Gorman, Gary, Dennis Hanlon, and Wayne King. 1997. "Some Research Perspectives on Entrepreneurship Education, Enterprise Education and Education for Small Business Management: A Ten-Year Literature Review." *International Small Business Journal* 15 (3): 56–77.

Harris, Jared D., Harry J. Sapienza, and Norman E. Bowie. 2009. "Ethics and Entrepreneurship." *Journal of Business Venturing* 24 (5): 407–418.

Harris, Jared D., Harry J. Sapienza, and Norman E. Bowie. 2011. "Ethics and Entrepreneurship." *Journal of Ethics and Entrepreneurship* 1 (1): 7–26.

Hemingway, Christine A., and Patrick W. Maclagan. 2004. "Managers' Personal Values as Drivers of Corporate Social Responsibility." *Journal of Business Ethics* 50 (1): 33–44.

Honig, Benson, and Per Davidsson. 2000. "The Role of Social and Human Capital among Nascent Entrepreneurs." In *Academy of Management Proceedings*, B1–B6. Academy of Management Briarcliff Manor, New York.

Jacobowitz, Alan, and Derek C. Vidler. 1982. "Characteristics of Entrepreneurs: Implications for Vocational Guidance." *Vocational Guidance Quarterly*, 30, 252–257.

Kilby, Peter. 1971. *Entrepreneurship and Economic Development*. Free Press.

Krueger Jr., Norris F., and Deborah V. Brazeal. 1994. "Entrepreneurial Potential and Potential Entrepreneurs." *Entrepreneurship Theory and Practice* 18 (3): 91–104.

Krueger, Norris F., Michael D. Reilly, and Alan L. Carsrud. 2000. "Competing Models of Entrepreneurial Intentions." *Journal of Business Venturing* 15 (5): 411–432. https://doi.org/10.1016/S0883-9026(98)00033-0.

Longenecker, Justin G., Joseph A. McKinney, and Carlos W. Moore. 1988. "The Ethical Issue of International Bribery: A Study of Attitudes among US Business Professionals." *Journal of Business Ethics* 7 (5): 341–346.

Longenecker, Justin G., Joseph A., Mckinney, and Carlos W. Moore. 1989. "Ethics in small business." *Journal of Small Business Management* 27 (1): 27–31.

McMullan, W. Ed, James J. Chrisman, and Karl H. Vesper. 2002. "Lessons from Successful Innovations in Entrepreneurial Support Programming." In: *Innovation and Entrepreneurship in Western Canada: From Family Businesses to Multinationals*, edited by James J Chrisman, L. Adam D. Holbrook, Jess H. Chua, 207–223. University of Calgary Press.

Pajarinen, M., P. Rouvinen, and P. Ylä-Anttila. 2006. "Uusyrittäjien kasvuhakuisuus." KTM julkaisuja 29, Ministry of Employment and the Economy, Helsinki.

Payne, Dinah, and Brenda E. Joyner. 2006. "Successful US Entrepreneurs: Identifying Ethical Decision-Making and Social Responsibility Behaviors." *Journal of Business Ethics* 65 (3): 203–217.

Reitan, Bjornar. 1996. "Entrepreneurial intentions: A combined models approach." 9th Nordic Small Business Research Conference, Lillehammer, Norway.

Robinson, Peter B., and Edwin A. Sexton. 1994. "The Effect of Education and Experience on Self-Employment Success." *Journal of Business Venturing* 9 (2): 141–156.

Rokeach, Milton. 1973. *The Nature of Human Values*. New York, NY: Free Press.

Ronald K. Mitchell, Lowell Busenitz, Theresa Lant, Patricia P. McDougall, Eric A. Morse, and J. Brock Smith. 2017. Toward a Theory of Entrepreneurial Cognition: Rethinking the People Side of Entrepreneurship Research. *Entrepreneurship Theory and Practice* 27 (2): 93–104.

Scherer, Robert F., Janet S. Adams, Susan S. Carley, and Frank A. Wiebe. 1989. "Role Model Performance Effects on Development of Entrepreneurial Career Preference." *Entrepreneurship Theory and Practice* 13 (3): 53–72.

Schumpeter, Joseph A. 1934. The creative response in economic history. Essays on Entrepreneurs, Innovations, Business Cycles, and the Evolution of Capitalism. RV Clemence: New Brunswick.

Schwartz, Shalom H. 1992. "Universals in the Content and Structure of Values: Theoretical Advances and Empirical Tests in 20 Countries." In *Advances in Experimental Social Psychology*, edited by Mark P. Zanna, 25: 1–65. Academic Press. https://doi.org/10.1016/S0065-2601(08)60281-6.

Schwartz, Shalom H. 1994. "Are There Universal Aspects in the Structure and Contents of Human Values?" *Journal of Social Issues* 50 (4): 19–45. https://doi.org/10.1111/j.1540-4560.1994.tb01196.x.

Shafer, William E., and Richard S. Simmons. 2007. "Social Responsibility, Machiavellianism and Tax Avoidance: A Study of Hong Kong Tax Professionals." *Monash U. Department of Business Law & Taxation Research Paper* 6. https://doi.org/10.2139/ssrn.1028143

Shetty, Pramod. 2004. "Attitude Towards Entrepreneurship in Organisations." *The Journal of Entrepreneurship* 13 (1): 53–68.

Singhapakdi, Anusorn, Scott J. Vitell, Kumar C. Rallapalli, and Kenneth L. Kraft. 1996. "The Perceived Role of Ethics and Social Responsibility: A Scale Development." *Journal of Business Ethics* 15 (11): 1131–1140.

Stewart Jr., Wayne H., and Philip L. Roth. 2001. "Risk Propensity Differences between Entrepreneurs and Managers: A Meta-Analytic Review." *Journal of Applied Psychology* 86 (1): 145–153. https://doi.org/10.1037/0021-9010.86.1.145.

Şerban-Oprescu, A.-T., and Curea, Ş. C. 2015. "The Impact of Cultural and Educational Accumulations on Entrepreneurial Behaviour. Main Issues Encountered in Theoretical Approaches." *Theoretical and Applied Economics* 1 (602): 265–272. http://store.ectap.ro/articole/1074.pdf

Teal, Elisabeth J., and Archie B. Carroll. 1999. "Moral Reasoning Skills: Are Entrepreneurs Different?" *Journal of Business Ethics* 19 (3): 229–240.

Truls Erikson. 2002. Goal-Setting and Entrepreneurial Self-Efficacy. *The International Journal of Entrepreneurship and Innovation* 3 (3): 183–189.

Vesa P. Taatila. 2010. Learning entrepreneurship in higher education. *Education + Training* 52 (1): 48–61.

10

Managers' Perceptions of Corporate Social Responsibility Reporting and Practices: Legitimacy in the Developing Country's Banking Industry

Mohammad Tazul Islam and Katsuhiko Kokubu

10.1 Introduction

Companies irrespective of size and nature recognize the significance of the Sustainable Development Goals (SDGs) by integrating it into their organizational strategy. They might want to cherry-pick SDGs that are of direct relevance, for example, Goals 8, 9, 14, and 15, for aligning their business interests to their organizational processes and use the CSR route

M. T. Islam (✉)
Dhaka School of Bank Management, Bangladesh Institute of Bank Management, Dhaka, Bangladesh
e-mail: tazul@bibm.org.bd

K. Kokubu
Graduate School of Business Administration, Kobe University, Kobe, Japan
e-mail: kokubu@kobe-u.ac.jp

F. Farache et al. (eds.), *Values and Corporate Responsibility*, Palgrave Studies in Governance, Leadership and Responsibility,
https://doi.org/10.1007/978-3-030-52466-1_10

for addressing the other SDGs. This chapter is aligned with the theme of the book—'Values and Corporate Responsibility: CSR and the SDGs'.

Do corporates disclose corporate social responsibility (CSR) information to legitimate their actions and behaviors to the society's expectation? To get an explanation of this momentous issue, academics and researchers are inclined to explore managerial perception and motivation for making CSR disclosure in the context of developed countries considering the manufacturing sector, in particular (Cacioppe et al. 2008; Islam and Deegan 2008; Momin and Parker 2013; Ismail et al. 2014; Bhattacharyya 2014). Besides, several studies explore the perception of social reporting with perspectives from sustainability reporting theories such as stakeholder theory (Belal and Roberts 2010), legitimacy theory (Campbell et al. 2003; Bhattacharyya 2014), and institutional theory (Hossain et al. 2013). The above-anchored studies, however, provide a general explanation of managerial and non-managerial perception of CSR reporting leaving enough room for investigating CSR reporting for the emerging economies, the banking sector, in particular.

To this tune, KPMG (2017) explained that the Asia-Pacific region is the leading region for the CSR reporting globally and the growth has become predominant in the emerging economies. A recent literature survey by Zaini et al. (2018) also explicated that the majority of the studies in the emerging economies are confined to voluntary disclosure practices using content analysis, which explores the perception of such voluntary disclosure in the emerging economies. More importantly, research focused on the reporting practices of the banking industry is scanty (Botshabelo et al. 2017) even though the operational behavior of banks around the globe is broadly similar because of international operational standard (Islam and Kokubu 2018; Islam et al. 2020). Arguably, the recent catalytic role of banks in changing the corporate behavior of other industries in terms of sustainability management and disclosure has led to a change in the research perception (Sharif and Rashid 2014; Ullah and Rahman 2015), demanding new and continual research on the CSR reporting by the banking system in emerging economies.

As an emerging economy, the banking industry in Bangladesh deserves particular attention from researchers on CSR reporting. The movement of CSR reporting by the banks was endorsed by the central bank, the

Ministry of Finance (MOF), depositors, NGOs, international communities, the media, and civil society's increasing expectations of business responsibility (Jabed and Rahman 2003). These movements provide ample incentives to research on CSR reporting in the banking system of Bangladesh. However, to our knowledge, there is hardly any study conducted so far to examine the perceptions of CSR reporting in the banking system both in the developed and developing economies especially from the perspective of legitimacy theory (LT).

The current study aims to fill this gap considering Bangladesh as a case. In this study, we conducted 28 in-depth interviews with the bank officials who are involved in corporate policymaking, CSR reporting, and practices to figure out the managerial motivation for CSR reporting from the perspective of legitimacy theory (LT). The study extends prior research directly by contributing to the existing LT literature by narrating managerial perceptions in CSR reporting in the banking industry.

The study reveals that the concept of CSR reporting is opaque in the banking system in Bangladesh and the reporting is mostly bank-centric. Besides, several legitimate factors such as banking regulations, praise/award based on CSR reporting, influence from the central bank, political leaders, bank directors, top bank officials, and community pressure help influence the CSR reporting practices for the banking system in Bangladesh. Moreover, banks that are new in operation are interested to disclose more social information than the older banks to gain market legitimacy.

10.2 Literature Review

The literature on the perception in CSR reporting can be clustered in two broad categories—managerial and non-managerial (such as society, community, and NGOs). Managerial perception studies are confined to the generic explanation of corporate social reporting in the developed countries (e.g., Cacioppe et al. 2008) with the exception of O'Dwyer (2002). O'Dwyer (2002) interpreted managerial perceptions of corporate social disclosure presence and absence through the lens of organizational legitimacy theory. He found that disclosure may occasionally be part of a legitimacy process, although ultimately this is misguided, as disclosure is widely perceived as being incapable of supporting the achievement of a legitimate state.

From the non-managerial perspective of studying corporate social reporting in the developed world, Campbell et al. (2003) used legitimacy theory to explain society's perception in social and environmental reporting in three (tobacco, brewing, and retailing) of the UK's FTSE sectors and found that legitimacy theory may be an explanation of disclosure in some cases, but not in others. Further, O'Dwyer et al. (2005) presented an in-depth investigation of non-governmental organizations' (NGOs) perceptions of CSRD (corporate social responsibility disclosure) in Ireland. They found a demand for the development of stand-alone, mandated, externally verified CSRD mechanisms that predominate the perspectives.

Similarly to the developed countries, the studies in managerial perception are confined to generic explanation of corporate social reporting in the developing countries (i.e., Ismail et al. 2014; Costa and Menichini 2013; Abugre 2014) with the exception of Bhattacharyya (2014) that described from the lens of organizational legitimacy. Bhattacharyya (2014) examined the Australian and Indian managerial attitudes toward social responsibility to assess their support for factors shaping their belief and attitudes and compared differing attitudes among respondents in the counties. They revealed that to legitimize existence, Indian respondents are concerned more with social issues than their Australian counterparts.

Likewise, several studies were found in the context of Bangladesh that examined CSR practices from managerial perspectives. For instance, from an engagement-based study, Belal and Owen (2007) found that parent companies' instructions and international buyers drive the corporate social reporting practice in Bangladesh. Belal and Cooper (2011) explained that the non-disclosure of the Bangladeshi corporate managers includes lack of resources, the profit imperative, lack of legal requirements, lack of knowledge/awareness, poor performance, and the fear of bad publicity. Again, Islam and Deegan (2008) showed that the expectation of the global community drives the industry's social policies and is related to disclosure practices. Moreover, Moyeen and West (2014) explored the attitude and perception of senior managers in Bangladesh focusing on the impact of CSR promotional programs in fostering an affirmative view to the sustainable development. In contrast, studies from the non-managerial perspectives revealed a lower level of CSR reporting and practices in Bangladesh. Factors such as institutional forces (Islam and Dellaportas 2011), pressures from international markets (Belal and Roberts 2010), and some structural constraints such as high level of poverty, weak governmental structures, dependence on foreign aid, and a small group of local business people, lack of awareness in disclosure, and underdeveloped stakeholder relationship (Momin 2013) shape CSR reporting practices in Bangladesh.

Notably, all of the above studies explore perceptions of CSR reporting either in the developed or in the developing countries focusing on either the manufacturing sector or NGOs. A few studies investigate the concept of legitimacy theory in explaining managerial perception in CSR reporting, particularly in the banking industry. Although O'Dwyer (2002) and Campbell et al. (2003) used legitimacy theory, their studies were limited to developed countries' manufacturing industry, hence insufficient to conclude the perception in corporate social reporting and practices from LT aspect in the developing countries. Similarly, studies conducted by Belal and Owen (2007) and Rashid and Ibrahim (2002) were limited to explain LT to describe stakeholder perceptions in corporate social reporting. Although Khan et al. (2009), Khan and Ali (2010), and Dusuki and Dar (2007) conducted perception study in the banking industry, their studies were limited in explaining LT in their research results. Bhattacharyya's (2014) conclusion is also limited to a comparison between Australia and India, and his findings cannot be generalized for developing economies because of differences in socio-economic norms, culture, and political CSR between India and Australia. The current study addresses this LT literature gap in exploring LT contemplation to explain bank managers' perception in CSR reporting in emerging economies considering Bangladesh as a case.

10.3 Theoretical Underpinning

Three theories—stakeholder, institutional, and legitimacy theory—have been used to examine the perceived motivation for the voluntary disclosure on the corporate social and environmental issues (Deegan and Unerman 2014). Gray et al. (2010) explained that legitimacy, stakeholder, and institutional theory are all derived from political economy theory. Political economy perceives accounting reports as social, political, and economic documents (Guthrie and Parker 1990; Gray et al. 1996).

Stakeholder theory is effectively an umbrella term representing a number of alternative theories that address issues associated with an organization's relationship with its stakeholders (Deegan and Unerman 2014). Stakeholder theory can be explained from two perspectives—ethical and managerial—while the ethical branch provides perceptions in terms of how organizations should treat their stakeholders, the managerial branch emphasizes the need to 'manage' particular stakeholder groups (Deegan 2002).

On the other hand, the core concept of 'institutions', central to the 'institutional theory', is a key construct within sociology (DiMaggio and Powell 1991) providing very diverse meanings and applications. Institutional theory considers the forms organizations take and provides explanations for why organizations within a particular 'organizational field' tend to take on similar characteristics of CSR and forms (Deegan and Unerman 2014). The pillars of institution theory include regulative, normative, and cultural-cognitive dimensions, feature, and behaviors. DiMaggio and Powell (1983) explained that these pillars constrain and empower social behavior through coercive, mimetic, and normative mechanisms.

Legitimacy theory explains that organizations need to operate within the bounds and norms of their respective societies and compliance with the societal norms and expectation is assigned the status of 'legitimacy' (Deegan and Unerman 2014). Social contract' is the central premise of legitimacy theory and any kind of disparity will be considered as breach of such contract (Lindblom 1995) which generates a legitimacy gap (Islam and Kokubu 2018). To reduce this legitimacy gap legitimization strategy—gain, maintain, and regain—might be used (Suchman 1995; O'Donovan 2002).

This study adopts legitimacy theory for a number of reasons. First, as with legitimacy theory, 'legitimacy' is the core concept of 'institutional theory' (Suchman 1995) that provides a linkage between organizations and their social environment (DiMaggio and Powell 1983). Second, legitimacy theory discusses particular disclosure strategies that might be undertaken to gain, maintain, or regain legitimacy. On the other hand, institutional theory explores how—at a broader level—particular organizational forms might be adopted in order to bring legitimacy to an organization. Third, stakeholder theory is a very confusing term (Deegan and Unerman 2014) and is a somewhat troublesome label because it is used to refer to both an empirical theory of management and a normative theory of business ethics, often without clearly distinguishing between the two (Hasnas 1998, p. 26). Moreover, these two wings of stakeholder theory are contradictory and can generate vague assumptions (Islam and Kokubu 2018). Further, Omran and Ramdhony (2015) stated that legitimacy theory seems to be more suitable for organizations working in developing countries.

10.4 Methodology

The objective of this study is to examine bank managers' perceptions on CSR reporting from the lens of LT. Researchers around the globe have moved to examine managerial and other stakeholders' perceptions of CSR reporting more directly by using methods such as in-depth interviews (Belal and Owen 2007; Owen 2008). Belal and Momin (2009) have also conducted a literature review using desk-based research method and found that most CSR studies in the emerging economies are descriptive in nature using content analysis methods and measured the extent and volume of disclosures contained within the annual reports. However, there have been few studies, of late, to probe managerial motivations behind CSR reporting and practices directly through in-depth interviews.

This study conducted 28 interviews to gather evidence from 24 Dhaka Stock Exchange (DSE) listed banks (currently 30 of 56, 2016). There were 47 scheduled banks under Bangladesh Bank (BB, the central bank of Bangladesh) in 2013. Out of these 47 banks, 30 banks are listed in DSE until the year 2013. In late 2013, a total of nine new banks appeared as the scheduled banks under Bangladesh Bank. They are yet to be listed in DSE.

The interviewees ranged from operational CSR managers to Managing Directors (MDs)/Chief Executive Officers (CEOs) of the banks. The interviews were taken at the interviewee's place of business. Interviews were conducted with 7 MDs/CEOs, 17 heads of the operational wings (CSR/or GB), 1 board secretariat, and 3 CSR operational managers (Tables 10.1 and 10.2). The key reason to ask people from different levels is to explain the perception of CSR reporting from top- to lower-level employees. The interviews were conducted in 2016.

To select interviewees, arrangements were made by telephone to know the availability of the top officials and their consent to have an interview on the topic. Then an e-mail containing an abstract of the research with objectives of the research was sent. This was followed by a letter guaranteeing confidentiality and assuring that the interview record will be used anonymously. Hence, the interviewees are referred to using a reference number (See Appendix). All interviews were conducted in person. Except two, all interviews were tape-recorded with the consent of the interviewees and were subsequently translated. In the cases where interviews were not tape-recorded, detailed notes have been taken. Furthermore, the interview records have been forwarded to the concerned organizations, upon their request.

Before initiating the interview, introductions were made between the interviewee and interviewer followed by the notation of corporate social

Table 10.1 Distribution of sample interviewee

Sl. no.	Categories of banks	Listed in DSE	Sample covered	% covered (approx.)
1	Private commercial banks	22	17	77
2	Islamic banks	7	6	86
3	Government bank	1	1	100
	Total	30	24	80

Table 10.2 Interviewee status and position

Status of the interviewee	Operating position	Number of interviewees
MD/CEO, Deputy Managing Director (DMD)	Chief of the organization	7
General Manager (GM), Deputy General Manager (DGM), Executive Vice President (EVP), Senior Vice President (SVP), Senior Assistant Vice President (SAVP), Vice President (VP), Assistant Vice President (AVP), First Assistant Vice President (FAVP)	Head of the Operational Wing (CSR)/Green Banking (GB)	17
Board Secretary	Report to board	1
Senior Officer, Executive Officer	Operational manager (CSR)	3
Total		28

responsibility issues. The main topics of the interviews were CSR concept and CSR reporting, influences in CSR reporting and practices, and reporting practices by newer versus older organizations. After the interviews, data were analyzed using a process suggested by O'Dwyer (2004).

10.5 Findings

10.5.1 Corporate Social Responsibility (CSR) and CSR Reporting

Bangladesh Bank (BB) initiates CSR activities as a part of their mainstream function[1] where CSR activities and reporting were somewhat voluntarily (Circular-2, Department of Off-Site Supervision, DOS, June 2008). The concept of CSR is new in the field of sustainability activities in Bangladesh. However, the earlier shape of CSR was 'social welfare' where employee welfare activities were addressed mostly in the annual report. Again, the area and meaning of CSR are not clear to the practitioners also.

[1] Mainstream function means the core activities of a bank such as deposit mobilization and credit disbursement.

The meaning of CSR is not clear to us; some say it is a donation, some say Kairati,[2] *some say do something for poor people, and I mean CSR is what I would like to give a message for the welfare of the society.* (Interviewee-22)

Moreover, this study finds that the CSR concept is perceived to explain community involvement and investment mostly from the philanthropic aspects of CSR.

By CSR we mean helping in bolstering basic needs such as food, education, health, shelter to the poor people, helping autistic babies, ..., and philanthropic to flood-affected people. (Interviewee-11)

CSR, we mean to stand behind the people who are underprivileged, ... and natural disaster. (Interviewee-14)

Again, CSR activities of the banking industry include providing support for immediate needs due to flood, cyclone, fire accident, and so on. While CSR activities in banks include (a) CSR philanthropy (such as scholarship to students from primary to high school to graduate level, set-up educational institution, etc.) and (b) sustainable banking (such as financing to effluent treatment plant [ETP], biogas, etc.). Thus, the banks in the developing countries including Bangladeshi banks also started the sustainable and philanthropic aspects of CSR.

We do CSR by business, by taking tiny deposits and disburse Micro/SME to corporate clients and since the birth of our bank (35 years ago) we did not finance any tobacco company. (Interviewee-26)

CSR philanthropy should be sustainable not piecemeal (say giving $ 10–12 or some foods etc.) to make them beggars; it is better to give them a Rickshaw (a popular mode of transport for short distance used in Bangladesh) and make them independent to earn. (Interviewee-19)

[2] Kairati is a Bengali term which means giving money/donation to beggars or poor people or underprivileged people. It is also termed as helping people. A few corporates explain that CSR means to do "Kairati."

This study also finds that rarely a banking company follows any structure for CSR reporting. The banking sector of Bangladesh reports CSR information to regulators which is mandatory (Circular-3, Green Banking and Corporate Social Responsibility, GB/CSR, department, BB; June 13, 2013) while CSR reporting to annual report, company's website, bulletin board, published booklet, and other media is voluntarily. BB quarterly reporting has some incentives such as impact on the bank's CAMELS[3] rating, BB yearly publication indicating the CSR positions of the banks, and so on.

> *We have CSR reporting structure for BB reporting which is done internally and mandatorily, while CSR reporting in the annual report is done voluntarily without any formatted structure which varies yearly to our bank.* (Interviewee-10)

> *Now we report CSR based on BB format and there is no practice of Global Reporting Initiative (GRI), International Standard Organization (ISO) 26000 or Global Compact (GC) based reporting.* (Interviewee-15)

However, international standard practice in CSR reporting for annual reports started in 2013 voluntarily by some banks. Moreover, the interviewees recognize the essence of international standards in CSR reporting.

> *The GRI based CSR reporting to annual report is the reflection of getting training of our CSR team from abroad and I do believe BB will ask all banks to submit CSR reporting based on international standard.* (Interviewee-13)

10.5.2 Legitimacy in CSR Reporting and Practices

The voluntary disclosure perception of CSR information on the annual report has been anchored in Bangladeshi corporations (Momin 2013; Sobhani et al. 2009) for organizational legitimacy. Further, the reporting of corporate governance issues to annual report is on 'comply' basis as

---

[3] CAMELS means Capital adequacy, Asset quality, Management capability, Earnings, Liquidity, and Sensitivity.

required by the Bangladesh Securities and Exchange Commission (SEC/CMRRCD/2006-158/admin/02-08 and SEC/CMRRCD/2006-158/134/admin/44). Companies legitimate their behavior voluntarily as 'social contract' the central premise of legitimacy theory (Deegan 2002, 2007) and regulatory compliance as a threat to organizational legitimacy.

> *We do corporate social reporting one for voluntarily and second for regulatory reason where the later part is common for all banks … also to know our stakeholders as they have a right to know about CSR and to maintain the international standard.* (Interviewee-1)

> *CSR reporting is done to ensure transparency to the shareholders, know people, build trust on us, … and give the message that we are not away from the society.* (Interviewee-4)

Moreover, banks are facing some influences for practicing and reporting CSR information from regulators, employees, local community, NGOs, political leaders, and civil society. Earlier studies (Belal and Owen 2007; Islam and Deegan 2008) found that the Bangladeshi corporate legitimate their actions and behaviors by CSR reporting as they have influences from powerful stakeholder groups.

> *I rather say CSR reporting and practice is a regulatory driven approach which was initiated by BB voluntarily, … and as regulator took the initiatives the banking industry has to follow.* (Interviewee-3)

> *Four basic reasons for CSR reporting are—BB impact on the evaluation of the bank's CAMELS rating, … praise/award based on CSR reporting, extending brand image of the bank, and to show my competitors that we are superior in doing social welfare.* (Interviewee-8)

However, influences from different political party people and top officials of the bank and relationship with the top officials became powerful means in practicing and reporting CSR initiatives where the practitioners have to follow them to ensure their business existence—legitimization.

> *All CSR activities performed by our banks are due to influences, ... either from political or governmental or BB references ... recently we gave tube well and sanitary toilet to the people living in the Enclaves, we went there because BB told us to do.* (Interviewee-12)

Moreover, this study added that those in the banking industry are not able to do their CSR reporting and practices according to their choice, but rather they legitimate the influences from the powerful stakeholders which is supportive of the findings of the earlier study (see Belal and Owen 2007).

> *What I like to do in CSR area I cannot do because of influences from BB, Board of Director (BoD), political parties and the desires of the top officials ... and we do accordingly nothing more.* (Interviewee-20)

> *To help political party member sometimes, we give funds to 'Prime Minister's Relief Fund' due to political influences .... Sometimes Minister of Parliament (MP) asked for philanthropic donation directly from us, we just report this fund as CSR to BB only.* (Interviewee-27)

Nevertheless, the banking industry is now designing products and processes based on community desires and expectations, without which operational existence is impossible—the core of legitimacy theory 'social contract' (Lindblom 1995; Deegan 2002; Deegan and Unerman 2014).

10.5.3 Legitimacy in CSR Reporting by Newer Versus Older Organizations

The general adage of legitimacy theory is that as firms grow the involvement of stakeholders increases, which requires disclosing more social information (Deegan 2002). This study finds that newer firms disclose more social information than the older firms to gain market legitimacy and to ensure their organizational legitimacy. Further, this study supports the broader thrust of legitimacy theory for gaining, repairing, or maintaining legitimacy (Suchman 1995).

Newer banks have deposit crisis, and they want to become familiar in the market by doing more CSR reporting in the press, media, annual report, website, billboard, etc. (Interviewee-4)

Further, CSR is now moved as an advertising tool of the banks. Earlier, banking companies counted substantial advertisement expenses to different electronic and print media for ensuring their market presence, that is, maintaining legitimacy (O'Donovan 2002; Suchman 1995). Banks spend philanthropic donation believing that it will elevate their market image.

Newer banks are not familiar to people, and have lower deposit, fewer customers, no bank branch … they expose themselves by using CSR reporting as their promotional campaign. (Interviewee-11)

We have a good image in the market, and we do not care about deposit because we have sufficient deposit while the newer banks … have opposite situation. (Interviewee-27)

Furthermore, the legitimate underlying factors of lower CSR reporting by the older banks are older banks' structural barriers, red-tapism in implementing policy, the absence of cutting-edge technology know-how, older employees, the absence of congenial subordinate and superior relationship, and mental inertia of the Board of Directors (BoD) in disclosing CSR information to the public.

While older banks have a traditional approach to management, structural barriers, … slower in knowledge adoption and they reports lower; newer banks are very familiar and orientated with CSR approach … higher tech-know-how, free from structural barriers and they reports more. (Interviewee-10)

As an older bank we are away from publicity by doing CSR because of the philosophy of our management, … while newer banks used CSR reporting as a media strategy to expand their business. (Interviewee-22, 23)

Moreover, as a part of 'social contract' the core of legitimacy theory (Lindblom 1995), the banking company continuously explores the new market. The newer banks do more CSR reporting compared to the older banks to diversify the risk of loan disbursement.

> *The recent experiences of corporate clients are not good because of loan default, the newer banks explored the market to Micro & SME finance, green banking, financial inclusion ... etc. for their own sustainability terming as CSR.* (Interviewee-3)

Thus, based on the above discussion, this study supports the broader thrust of legitimacy theory by explaining that newer companies disclose more social information than the older ones to gain/build market legitimacy, and/or to increase market image/brand, and/or to gain/build customer trust. The study finding is supportive to the earlier study findings (i.e., Suchman 1995; Deegan 2002).

10.6 Conclusion and Policy Remarks

This study aims to extend and interrogate the use of legitimacy theory to infer managers' perceptions in corporate social reporting in the developing country's banking industry—Bangladesh as a case. This study conducted 28 interviews with 24 DSE listed commercial banks (30 of 56; 2016), where the interviewees were ranged from operational CSR manager to MD/CEO of the bank. This study extends prior research directly by contributing to the existing LT literature by narrating managerial perceptions in the banking industry where there is no published paper.

This study finds that the corporate social responsibility concept is not clear to the practitioners and regulators (Interviewee-22); it is mostly confined to the philanthropic aspects of CSR. The practice of CSR practices in Bangladesh includes supporting the immediate needs of the citizens as well as CSR philanthropy by sustainable support and sustainable banking. Sustainable supports indicate support to enhance the livelihood of the poor citizens. Further, the sustainable banking as CSR by business includes sustainable financing projects which are socially and environmentally friendly (Interviewee-11; 26). Again, this study finds that there is no structured format for CSR reporting; instead the reporting format is bank-centric (Interviewee-10; 15).

From legitimacy theory aspects, this study finds that the legitimate reasons for CSR reporting in the banking industry of Bangladesh are influences from the stakeholders (i.e., regulators, employees, local community, NGOs, political leaders, and civil society). This study identified regulatory-driven approach (Interviewee-3); BB impact on CAMELS rating and praise/award based on CSR reporting (Interviewee-8); BB direct influences (Interviewee-3; 12); influences from political leaders (Interviewee-20; 22; 27); BoD and top officials' desire (Interviewee-20); and community (Interviewee-8; 13) are the legitimate factors of CSR reporting. This finding is supportive to earlier studies (Belal and Owen 2007; Islam and Deegan 2008) that Bangladeshi corporations legitimate their actions and behaviors by CSR reporting as they have influences from powerful stakeholder groups.

According to legitimacy theory contemplation, newer organizations are required to gain market legitimacy (O'Donovan 2002) due to the legitimate market crisis; they are required to disclose more CSR information compared to the older ones. This study explains that newer banks disclose more CSR information than the older banks for a number of reasons: to address the scarcity of deposits (Interviewee-4); to counter a market image crisis (Interviewee-4); to build a market position in the industry, to gain awareness and market reputation, to increase the number of customers, because there are no bank branches in the rural area (Interviewee-11); or to diversify the loan recovery risk (Interviewee-3). On the other hand, older banks disclose less social information than the newer banks because of the prevailing market reputation (Interviewee-27); absence of product selling crisis (Interviewee-27); traditional approach to management, red-tapism in implementing policies, organization's structural barrier, and legitimization problems in adoption (Interviewee-10; 22; 23) as key.

The practical implications of this study are multifold. The findings, first, facilitate regulators to adopt an appropriate balance of legislation, reform, and their enforcement to make improvements in the CSR reporting practices and enhancement of organizational legitimacy. Second, for ensuring international standard and structured reporting, the commercial banks can start practicing CSR reporting based on international guidelines (e.g., ISO 26000; GRI). Third, necessary steps should be taken in widening CSR conception and removing the misconception of CSR by formulating policies and training to the regulators and practitioners.

Acknowledgement This study was supported by JSPS KAKENHI Grant number JP 19H01547 and the Environmental Research and Technology Development Funds (S-16 JPMEERF16S11600) of the Environment Restoration and Conservation Agency, Japan.

Appendix: Interviewee Reference Number

Interviewee reference number	Operating position of the interviewee
1	Head of Agriculture Support and Green Banking
2	Head of CSR and Green Banking (GB), SME, and agriculture
3	Head of SME, agriculture, and GB
4	Head of CSR and GB
5	Head of GB
6	Head of GB
7	Head of Green Finance and Internal Credit
8	Head of CSR
9	Head of CSR
10	Head of comm. and Brand; Head of CSR
11	Former chairman, Bangladesh Krishi Bank (BKB)
12	Head of CSR
13	Head of CSR and GB
14	Head of CSR
15	Shariah Secretariat, Head of CSR
16	Head of SME and Head of CSR & GB
17	Operating officer, brand marketing and corporate affairs
18	Head of CSR
19	Head of CSR
20	Head of CSR & Administration
21	Head of comm. and Branding; Head of CSR
22	Chief Executive Officer (CEO)
23	CEO

(continued)

(continued)

Interviewee reference number	Operating position of the interviewee
24	CEO
25	CEO
26	CEO
27	Head of CRM-1, CSR
28	Head of CSR

References

Abugre, James. "Managerial role in organizational CSR: Empirical lessons from Ghana." *Corporate Governance* 14, no. 1 (2014): 104–119.

Belal, Ataur and Stuart Cooper. "The absence of corporate social responsibility reporting in Bangladesh." *Critical Perspectives on Accounting* 22, no. 7 (2011): 654–667.

Belal, Ataur and Mohammad Momin. "Corporate social reporting (CSR) in emerging economies: A review and future direction." *Research in Accounting in Emerging Economies* 9 (2009): 119–143.

Belal, Ataur and David Owen. "The views of corporate managers on the current state of, and future prospects for, social reporting in Bangladesh: An engagement based study." *Accounting Auditing and Accountability* 20, no. 3 (2007): 472–494.

Belal, Ataur and Robin Roberts. "Stakeholders' perceptions of corporate social reporting in Bangladesh." *Journal of Business Ethics* 97 (2010): 311–324.

Bhattacharyya, Asit. "Managerial attitude and support for social responsibility through the lens of legitimacy theory—A cross country comparison." *Social Responsibility Journal* 10, no. 4 (2014): 716–736.

Botshabelo, Ishmael, Christian Mbekomize and Percy Phatshwane. "Corporate Social Responsibility Reporting in banking industry: An analysis of disclosure levels in Botswana." *International Journal of Business and Management* 12, no. 12 (2017): 224–241.

Cacioppe, Ron, Nick Forster and Michel Fox. "A survey of managers' perceptions of corporate ethics and social responsibility and actions that may affect companies' success." *Journal of Business Ethics* 82 (2008): 681–700.

Campbell, David, Barrie Craven and Philip Shrives. "Voluntary social reporting in three FTSE sectors: A comment on perception and legitimacy." *Accounting Auditing and Accountability* 16, no. 4 (2003): 558–581.

Costa, Roberta and Tamara Menichini. "A multidimensional approach for CSR assessment: The importance of the stakeholder perception." *Expert System with Application* 40 (2013): 150–161.

Deegan, Craig. "Organizational legitimacy as a motive for sustainability reporting." In: J. Unerman, J. Bebbington and B. O'Dwyer (eds.), *Sustainability accounting and accountability*. Abingdon: Routledge, 127–149, 2007.

Deegan, Craig. "The legitimizing effect of social and environmental disclosures—A theoretical foundation." *Accounting Auditing and Accountability* 15, no. 3 (2002): 282–311.

Deegan, Craig and Jeffry Unerman. *Financial accounting theory*. McGraw-Hill, 2014.

DiMaggio, Paul and Walter Powell. "Introduction." In: P.J. DiMaggio and W.W. Powell (eds.), *The new institutionalism in organizational analysis*. Chicago, IL: University of Chicago Press, 1–38, 1991.

DiMaggio, Paul and Walter Powell. "The iron cage revisited: Institutional isomorphism and collective rationality in organizational fields." *American Sociological Review* 48 (1983): 146–160.

Dusuki, Asyruf and H. Dar. "Stakeholders' perceptions of corporate social responsibility of Islamic banks: Evidence from Malaysian economy." *Advances in Islamic Economic and Finance* 1 (2007): 249–278.

Gray Rob, Owen David. and Adams Carol. Accounting & accountability: Changes and challenges in corporate social and environmental reporting (1996), London: Prentice Hall.

Gray, Robert, David Owen and Carol Adams. "Some theories for social accounting: A review essay and a tentative pedagogic categorization of theorizations around social accounting." *Advances in Environmental Accounting & Management* 4 (2010): 1–54.

Guthrie, James and David Parker. "Corporate social disclosure practice: A comparative international analysis." *Advances in Public Interest Accounting* 3 (1990): 159–175.

Hasnas, John. "The normative theories of business ethics: A guide for the perplexed." *Business Ethics Quarterly* 8, no. 1 (1998): 19–42.

Hossain, Md., Rebecca Rowe and Mohammad Quaddus. "A managerial perspective of corporate social and environmental responsibility (CSER) reporting: Evidence from a developing country." In *the 7th Asia Pacific*

Interdisciplinary Research in Accounting (APIRA) Conference, 26–28 July, Japan, 2013.

Islam, Mohammad and Craig Deegan. "Motivations for an organization within a developing country to report social responsibility information: Evidence from Bangladesh." *Accounting Auditing and Accountability* 21, no. 6 (2008): 850–874.

Islam, Mohammad and Steven Dellaportas. "Perceptions of corporate social and environmental accounting and reporting practices from accountants in Bangladesh." *Social Responsibility Journal* 7, no. 4 (2011): 649–664.

Islam, Mohammad and Kokubu Katsuhiko. "Corporate social reporting and legitimacy in banking: A longitudinal study in the developing country." *Social Responsibility Journal* 14, no. 1 (2018): 159–179.

Islam Mohammad, Kokubu Katsuhiko and Nishitani Kimitaka . "Corporate social reporting in the banking industry of Bangladesh: a test of legitimacy theory." *Social Responsibility Journal* (2020): https://doi.org/10.1108/SRJ-05-2019-0185.

Ismail, Mimunah, Mohd Rozi, Mohd Roziah and Mohd Rasdi. "Orientation, attitude, and competency as predictors of manager's role of CSR-implementing companies in Malaysia." *European Journal of Training and Development* 38, no. 5 (2014): 415–435.

Jabed, Md. and Kazi Rahman. "Corporate responsibility in Bangladesh; where do we stand?" CPD Report no. 54 (2003): accessed 24 November 2019. https://www.cpd.org.bd/pub_attach/DR-54.pdf

Khan, Md. and Md. Ali. "An empirical investigation and users' perceptions on intellectual capital reporting in banks: Evidence from Bangladesh." *Journal of Human Resource Costing and Accounting* 14, no. (2010): 48–69.

KPMG. "The KPMG survey of corporate responsibility reporting 2017". KPMG the road Ahead (2017); accessed 26 November 2019.https://assets.kpmg/content/dam/kpmg/xx/pdf/2017/10/kpmg-survey-of-corporate-responsibility-reporting-2017.pdf.

Khan, Md., Abdel Halabi and Martin Samy. "Corporate social responsibility (CSR) reporting: A study of selected banking companies in Bangladesh." *Social Responsibility Journal* 5, no. 3 (2009): 344–357.

Lindblom, Charles. "The implication of organizational legitimacy for corporate social performance and disclosure." In *Critical Perspectives on Accounting Conference*, New York, 1995.

Momin, Mahmood. "Social and environmental NGOs' perceptions of corporate social disclosures: The case of Bangladesh." *Accounting Forum* 37 (2013): 150–161.

Momin, Mahmood and David Parker. "Motivations for corporate social responsibility reporting by MNC subsidiaries in an emerging country: The case of Bangladesh." *The British Accounting Review* 45, no. 3 (2013): 215–228.

Moyeen, Abdul and Brain West. "Promoting CSR to foster sustainable development: Attitude and perceptions of managers in a developing country." *Asia-Pacific Journal of Business Administration* 6, no. 2 (2014): 97–115.

O'Donovan, Gray. "Environmental disclosures in the annual report: Extending the applicability and predictive power of legitimacy theory." *Accounting Auditing and Accountability* 15, no. 3 (2002): 344–371.

O'Dwyer, Brendan. "Managerial perceptions of corporate social disclosure: An Irish story." *Accounting Auditing and Accountability* 15, no. 3 (2002): 406–436.

O'Dwyer, B. "Quantitative data analysis: Illuminating a process for transforming a 'Messy' but 'Attractive' 'Nuisance'." In: C. Humphrey and B. Lee (eds.), *The real life guide to accounting research*. Oxford: Elsevier, 391–407, 2004.

O'Dwyer, Brendan, Jeffry Unerman and Bradley Jay. "Perceptions on the emergence and future development of corporate social disclosure in Ireland: Engaging the voices of non-governmental organizations." *Accounting Audit and Accountability* 18, no. 1 (2005): 14–43.

Omran, Mohammed and Dinesh Ramdhony. "Theoretical perspectives on corporate social responsibility disclosure: A critical review." *International Journal of Accounting and Financial Reporting* 5, no. 2 (2015): 38–55.

Owen, David. "Chronicles of wasted time? A personal reflection on the current state of, and future prospects for, social and environmental accounting research." *Accounting Auditing and Accountability* 21, no. 2 (2008): 240–267.

Rashid, Md. and Saadiatul Ibrahim. "Executive and management attitudes towards corporate social responsibility in Malaysia." *Corporate Governance: The International Journal of Business in Society* 2, no. 4 (2002): 10–16.

Sharif, Mehmoona and Kashif Rashid. "Corporate governance and corporate social reporting: An empirical evidence from the commercial banks of Pakistan." *Quality and Quantity* 5, no. 48 (2014): 2501–2521.

Sobhani, Farid, Azlan Arman and Yuserrie Ziauddin. "Revisiting the practices of corporate social and environmental disclosure in Bangladesh." *Corporate Social Responsibility and Environmental Management* 16, no. 3 (2009): 167–183.

Suchman, Mark. "Managing legitimacy: Strategic and institutional approaches." *Academy of Management Review* 20, no. 2 (1995): 571–610.

Ullah, Md. and Mohammad Rahman. "Corporate social responsibility reporting practices in banking companies in Bangladesh: Impact of regulatory change." *Journal of Financial Reporting and Accounting*, 13, no. 2 (2015): 200–225.

Zaini, Syeliya, Grant Samkin, Umesh Sharma and Howard Davey. "Voluntary disclosure in emerging countries: A literature review." *Journal of Accounting in Emerging Economies* 8, no. 1 (2018): 29–65.

11

Implementation of Corporate Social Responsibility Initiatives for Tanzania Corporations and Not-for-Profit Organizations

Omary Swallehe

11.1 Introduction

Studies, for example Du et al. (2008) and Sen et al. (2006) show that many people/customers tend to favor companies that act in favor of community initiatives than those which do not. Recently, the concept of corporate social responsibility (CSR) in creating competitive advantage to the business firms has been attracting the attention of many researchers (McWilliams et al. 2006; Baumgartner and Winter 2014; Galbreath 2009; Lamberti and Noci 2012). Studies further reveal that through participation in community projects, firms can draw positive attitudes and support from the public and other stakeholders. According to Baumgartner and Winter (2014), the benefits include, but are not limited to, the company's reputation, credibility and ultimately competitive advantage. In

O. Swallehe (✉)
Mzumbe University, Morogoro, Tanzania
e-mail: oswalehe@mzumbe.ac.tz

F. Farache et al. (eds.), *Values and Corporate Responsibility*, Palgrave Studies in Governance, Leadership and Responsibility,
https://doi.org/10.1007/978-3-030-52466-1_11

most cases, both business leaders and stakeholders have regarded CSR as an impetus towards achieving organizational objectives and social well-being (McWilliams et al. 2006).

The modern business environment does not allow companies to be inward looking and working only with the view of making profit as the sole responsibility. Companies should be looking forward to making efforts to solve community problems as part of their daily routine. The success of modern companies, both public and private, hinge on and are heavily correlated with achieving consumer loyalty, employees' retention and productivity and overall organizational image and reputation. According to Arli and Lasmono (2009), CSR is linked to the criterion consumers use to purchase products and services.

This is to say, when the company is perceived to have been doing things in line with expectations of the community, then, it will be regarded positively and will be favored ahead of competitors and the opposite is also true. So, CSR initiatives affect stakeholder's perception of quality and a company's reputation.

According to Yoon and Gurhan-Canli (2004), in a situation where consumers perceive CSR initiatives in a positive way, the organization's offerings from this particular firm will be regarded as of superior quality. In the same view, if the customer is having negative perception of the CSR activities performed by the organization, automatically the products/services will be regarded as of poor quality. The behavior of many corporations are under close scrutiny by many constituencies such as customers, suppliers, shareholders, employees, banks, communities at large, media and competitors, to mention but a few (Baumgartner and Winter 2014) urges that, through supporting those companies which act responsibly towards community projects, consumers feel that they can make a lot of difference and ultimately change the behavior of the corporations which do not support community affairs.

Other researchers such as Sen et al., Baumgartner and Winter (2014) and Yoon and Gurhan-Canli (2004) contend that customers normally use CSR initiatives of the organizations to make evaluations. One of the core external-behavioral outcomes of CSR activities is purchase behavior, which presupposes that several contingent conditions are satisfied. The other outcomes of evaluations include: customer retention, the ability and willingness of the customers to convey word-of-mouth marketing about the organization and willingness to pay premium prices for the products and services offered (Bhattacharya and Sen 2004).

According to Freeman (1984), the ability of the firm to manage and ultimately satisfy the interests of the various and diverse stakeholders leads to significant improvements of the organizational performance at the marketplace.

The driving force for many organizations to invest significantly in CSR initiatives lies in its ability to manage stakeholders. In fact, many companies have conducted CSR programmes as a way to promote socially responsible actions and effectively respond to their stakeholder demands (Maignan and Ferrell 2004). Business stakeholders are often defined as any group or individual who would affect or be affected by the achievement of the organization's objectives (Clarkson 1995). The stakeholders of the organizations can be categorized into primary and secondary stakeholders as well as internal and external stakeholders. Stakeholders may include shareholders, employers, investors, managers, employees, customers, banks, suppliers, governments, to mention few of them. The CSR initiatives of the organizations have impacts on the natural environment, communities, individuals and organization.

Studies like McWilliams et al. (2006), Baumgartner and Winter (2014), Galbreath (2009) and Lamberti and Noci (2012) show that both private and public organizations have been implementing CSR initiatives for many years with differing objectives. While many business organizations are likely to use CSR among their marketing strategy in presenting their products or service to a market, it is not clear how the public organizations can reap frogging the value of CSR initiatives. Moreover, while the literature for the CSR's benefits in private and business-oriented organization is abundant, the same is scanty, at least in developing countries like Tanzania (Lamberti and Noci 2012).

The literature concerning CSR for Buinsess organizations is plenty , similarly, studies show how not for profit organizations can benefit from CSR initiatives in terms of increased donations for example charities and non-governmental organizations (Lichtenstein et al. 2004; Bhattacharya and Sen 2004). Moreover, scholars such as Lichtenstein et al. (2004) argue that more studies about the impact the CSR has on not-for-profit organizations. This is because the CSR has been measured and viewed as of great benefit to the profit-oriented or rather corporations supporting the not-for-profit institutions. Benefits accrued to the corporations like competitive advantage, positive word of mouth from the community, donations and existence of volunteer programs cannot be seen from not-for-profit organizations.

Researchers, for example Waagstein, Patricia Rinwigati (2011) and N. Andrews (2016) have studied the challenges for mandatory CSR in Indonesia and Ghana respectively. The two studies have highlighted the challenges for mandatory CSR in Indonesia and Ghana. Among the challenges frequently mentioned by the two studies are: companies are not willing to spend, for example, 2% of their net profits on community issues and urge that they can spend even more should the concept comes from their own initiatives. A majority of the companies are not supporting mandatory CSR and believe that successful CSR initiatives should be voluntary and not mandatory (Waagstein 2011; Andrews 2016). The idea that a certain percentage of corporate profitability needs to be spend for CSR initiative for organizations contradicts the implementation of CSR by not-for-profit organizations.

The way CSR is implemented differs significantly between countries as some countries like Tanzania are considered to be at the rudimentary stage while other countries might be at an advanced stage in implementing the initiatives. This study attempted to find an answer to the research question ***how CSR initiative is implemented by Tanzania corporations and not for profit organizations?*** The findings of this will add significantly to the already available literature on the best ways of making corporations and public organizations realize the usefulness of CSR in value creation.

11.2 Literature Review

As there is no universally acceptable definition of Corporate Social Responsibility, different scholars have defined CSR in different ways. According to Chandler and Werther (2014) and Coombs and Holladay (2012), corporate social responsibility is the voluntary action a company or organization implements to pursue goals, with a responsibility to its stakeholders. In the same line, European Commission (2014) defines corporate social responsibility as "the responsibility of enterprises for their impacts on society".

Kim and Reber (2008) suggest that corporate social responsibility is a "central relationship-building activity within organizations". In this case therefore, there are so many benefits accrued to the organizations engaging in CSR initiatives, which include but are not limited to increased level of voluntary spirit among individuals, a good working environment for the employees, cost efficiency, media coverage in a positive manner and good public image. Others may include long-lasting impact, especially on corporate reputation, organizational value and loyalty amongst stakeholders.

Research suggests that a company's CSR efforts can bring about so many benefits for the organization, such as a positive image of the company (Lichtenstein et al. 2004), positive reputation of an organization (Jo 2011; Kim and Lee 2011), legitimacy and enduring customers support (Bortree 2009), a higher purchase intention among consumers (David et al. 2005), and an increased level of stakeholder loyalty (Gomez and Chalmeta 2011).

Hong and Rim (2010) studied the link between CSR initiatives and perceptions of the stakeholders and found out that, CSR has indirect impact on the word of mouth marketing in terms of creating reputation, company value and stakeholders' goodwill.

The benefits mentioned above are all relating to the private and profit-oriented firms while the public and not-for-profit organizations are side-lined to a great extent. Furthermore, it is not clear on whether the communities do benefit the same way as the corporations are benefiting from CSR initiatives. The study therefore looks at stakeholders' theory, Legitimacy and Social Contract Theory to inform the study.

11.2.1 Legitimacy Theory

Deegan (2000) defines Legitimacy as "a generalized perception or assumption that the actions of an entity are desirable, proper, or appropriate within some socially constructed system of norms, values, beliefs and definitions". To this end, organizations attempt to establish congruence between "the social values associated with or implied by their activities and the norms of acceptable behavior in the larger social system of which they are part" (Dowling and Pfeffer 1975).

Organizational legitimacy is not a steady state, but variable. This variability is not only temporal but also spatial or across stakeholders and cultural groups. Therefore, depending on an organization's perception of its state or level of legitimacy, an organization may employ 'legitimation' strategies (Lindblom 1993). According to legitimacy theory, the participation of an organization with a community will enhance the corporate image, through the action that an organization will take. Thus, building a relationship between the organization and community will improve the company image, resulting in better performance of the product or service of the company.

11.2.2 Stakeholder Theory

Instead of starting with a business and looking out into the world to see what ethical obligations are there, stakeholder theory starts in the world (Freeman 1984). It lists and describes those individuals and groups who will be affected by (or affect) the company's actions and asks, "What are their legitimate claims on the business?" "What rights do they have with respect to the company's actions?" and "What kind of responsibilities and obligations can they justifiably impose on a particular business?" In a single sentence, stakeholder theory affirms that those who are alive or are touched by a corporation hold a right and obligation to participate in directing it. Donaldson and Preston (1995, p. 67) held that the stakeholder theory has a normative core based on two major ideas. (1) stakeholders are persons or groups with legitimate interests in procedural and/or substantive aspects of corporate activity (stakeholders are identified by their interests in the corporation, whether or not the corporation has any corresponding functional interest in them) and (2) the interests of all stakeholders are of intrinsic value (that is, each group of stakeholders merits consideration for its own sake and not merely because of its ability to further the interests of some other group.

11.2.3 Social Contract Theory

Society as described by Gray and Adams (1996) is a social contract between the members of the community and the society itself. The context of corporate social responsibility companies is not implementing CSR activities just because it is part of the business day to day operations, but rather because the community expects the business to operate in that way. The social contract theory was developed by Donaldson and Dunfee (1999) with the view of letting managers make decisions in light of the ethical context. They went on differentiating the social contract into macro and micro social contracts. Macro social contract is when the organizations provide support to the community and that could be regarded as micro social contract. This might be regarded as part of the commercial benefit of enhanced reputation, but also links to gaining and maintaining legitimacy (Suchman 1995). Moreover, the theory of social contract is in line with the current study in the sense that organizations have developed to become more integrated with the community by providing support to its local community and the entire involvement of community development in order to meet the desires of community and to enhance corporate image. The analysis of the literature and the theories above in particular amplifies the fact that Corporate Social Responsibility is a tool mostly used by commercial organizations. For public organizations and not-for-profit establishments, CSR is limited in its applications and the benefits accrued by these organizations are not that much compared with commercial establishments. While the corporations can draw financial benefits from CSR initiatives in terms of creating competitive advantage over competition, the public and not-for-profit organizations only obtain social and legitimacy benefits although they implement CSR initiatives. The current study tried to find answers to the two basic questions as follows:

(a) How is CSR defined in the context of public and not-for-profit organizations (in Tanzania?)?

We tried to figure out whether practitioners in business and public organizations regard CSR in the same way. CSR has been debated over for many years and it is believed that serious discussion begun back in 1950s. Secchi (2007) and Lee (2008) contended that the definition of CSR has evolved from time to time in terms of its meaning and scope.

In the early twentieth century, social performance was tied with market performance. The pioneer of this view, Oliver Sheldon (1923, cited in Bichta 2003), however, encouraged management to take the initiative in raising both ethical standards and justice in society through the ethic of economizing, that is, economize the use of resources under the name of efficient resource mobilization and usage. By doing so, business creates wealth in society and provides better standards of living. CSR is considered by many as an obligation of the organizations to comply voluntarily with activities aimed at improving the standard of the people within and outside the organizations such as employees, customers and general public. Others consider CSR in the ethical side by looking at the way organizations perform their duties in line with the community benefits.

It involves activities such as working hand-in-hand with the communities to solve the problems, establishing socially responsive projects, relationship with workers, customers, families and involving them in environmentally friendly initiatives and sustainability.

(b) What are the benefits of CSR accrued to public and not-for-profit organizations?

The studies show that CSR initiatives take a different outlook in public and profit-oriented organizations. There are very few findings of the benefits of CSR initiatives to the public and nonprofit organizations.

Despite the scarce research studies which investigated the benefits of CSR to the public and not-for-profit organizations, there are however, many positive outcomes of CSR such as increased identification and more favorable perceptions among the public.

Accountability is one of the benefits the public and nonprofit can enjoy the same way corporations are enjoying. Things like transparency, recycling, working in environmentally friendly initiatives, good governance, and ethical communications are all the benefits enjoyed by both public organizations and corporations. Again, both public bodies and corporations face the ethical issues such compensation of the employees, financial integrity, conflict of interest, investment policies, accountability and long-term thinking of the organization. The CSR initiatives could therefore benefit these organizations equally, in terms of building trust and credibility, accountability and transparency in their daily operations (McElhaney 2009).

The survey conducted most recently shows that few of the public and nonprofit organizations employees believed that their workplaces had ethics and compliancy programs designed and implemented like corporations (Chandler and Werther 2014; Coombs and Holladay 2012). The problem can be addressed through developing proper institutional mechanisms, greater programmes to educate the public, and bringing more transparency and inclusive performance metrics. While the CSR definitions and perceptions can differ slightly between public and corporations, the benefits of the initiatives are broadly similar because each has stakeholders. So, from stakeholders' point of view, both the public and corporations need to design the CSR initiatives that will be aimed at solving community problems and participate fully in communities' development initiatives. The literature on the benefits of the public and corporations towards CSR initiatives are plenty. However, few studies have reported how CSR initiatives can work to benefit both organizations and society. There should be a proper means of implementing the CSR initiatives from both the corporations and the society.

Both theoretical and empirical literature review analyzed above show that CSR initiatives are more evident in corporations than in public organizations. Corporations do benefit from using CSR as a competitive tool while public corporations cannot draw financial benefits of the CSR initiatives.

11.3 Methodology

In this study, we have used focus group discussion of forty-five (45) participants from corporations, public and nonprofit organizations. In essence, the study comprises of thirty people from corporations, eight participants who are people dealing with community engagement from public institutions and seven participants from NGOs. The corporations were drawn from banking industry (12), Mobile telecommunication Industry (3), Manufacturing Industry (10) and Retailing (5). The study used convenience sampling to draw participants. We wrote to these corporations and public organizations inviting them to take the focus group discussion for the study. In total, we sent 85 invitation letters and 45 confirmed to participate.

Hughes and DuMont (1993) defined focus groups as generally understood to be a group of 6–15 participants, with an interviewer, or moderator, asking questions about a particular topic. Focus groups are in-depth group interviews employing relatively homogeneous groups to provide information around topics specified by the researchers. It was a carefully planned interview to make sure that the two topics, definitions of CSR and benefits of CSR to the corporations and not-for-profit organizations, are explored in great detail. The two topics of the study were then organized into five themes: strategic CSR, organization ownership of CSR initiatives, origin of CSR ideas and types of support, beneficiaries of CSR supports and legal enforcement available.

In the first place, the researchers explained the meaning and essence of conducting this particular study. In the second instance, we tried to see how the subject matter of the discussion is potentially understood by different participants. After satisfying all the processes and requirements for the focus group discussion, data and information were collected from the participants. Then, we prepared and distributed 10 questions to the participants regarding the roles of organizations' CSR activities in relation to community development.

Collected data were then organized and analyzed using content analysis under five themes based on the questions developed for this study and then summarized using content analysis method.

Despite the ten questions given to the participants, the author was able to categorize the findings into five themes: strategic CSR, organization ownership of CSR initiatives, origin of CSR ideas and types of support, beneficiaries of CSR supports and legal enforcement available. The subsequent section will present and discuss the findings of the study summarized into the above themes and followed by the discussion.

11.4 Findings

The main objective of this study was to investigate how the CSR initiatives can work for both organizations and communities. In the first place we put forward a probing question to the participants asking them to show their understanding of CSR concept and whether it is practiced at their organizations. As was expected, the overwhelming majority of the participants showed great understanding of the concept and this was not a surprise as all the people are actively involved in CSR and community affairs from these organizations. However, we had two different views of the participants on whether CSR should be recognized by law or it has the initiatives from individual organizations. One of the participants said

> *when CSR is left to be the discretion of the organizations then the moral responsibility differs significantly between people. As the result, we may end up having corporations which do not contributing significantly to the community well-beings.*

The participant went on pinpointing the corporations which destroy the environment and are not actively participating in the process of solving the problems brought by the organizations. The participant further said,

> *If it is not going to be properly captured into out legislatures, then community problems will be recurring and no one can afford to solve them in the future.*

The participant was supported by the other participants and who went ahead even to propose the percentage of the income from the corporations to be set as for community affairs. Another participant thought that it has to be an initiative performed by organizations themselves. In this discussion on whether CSR initiatives need to be recognized by law or not, we found that participants from public and nonprofit organizations tend to support the view that CSR needs to be recognized by laws and legislations while the overwhelming majority of the participants from the corporations were of the view that there should be some initiatives from the corporations themselves. Their views are in line with that of the social contract theory which was developed by Donaldson and Dunfee (1999) who think that managers should be left to make decisions in light of the ethical context.

Then, we wanted the participants to discuss the view that both corporations and public organizations can benefit in the same way from CSR initiatives. Differing opinions were given with majority of the participants from public organizations and NGOs believing that they are not benefiting at all on participating in the community development initiatives.

After probing deeper and expanding the horizons of the CSR initiatives, the participants were in agreement that they do benefit, but not financially. It was agreed that corporations do benefit from financial and non-financial outcomes, while the public organizations benefit from only non-financial outcomes. This is in line with Legitimacy Theory, which according to Deegan (2000), can be considered as "a generalized perception or assumption that the actions of an entity are desirable, proper, or appropriate within some socially constructed system of norms, values, beliefs and definitions". To this end, organizations attempt to establish congruence between "the social values associated with or implied by their activities and the norms of acceptable behavior in the larger social system of which they are part". Then we wanted the participants to discuss how the CSR activities are performed in their organizations and tried to compare with the best practice. We put forward the question on whether they have proper and well-documented CSR plans. The researcher was caught by surprise to find out that only five participants had said "YES, they do" while the remaining said "NO"; it implies they are working without CSR. This is contrary to the best practice of CSR initiatives which require firms to plan these initiatives and regards it as the source of competitive advantage (Lubin and Esty 2010; McElhaney 2009). Other organizations have officers who deal with community affairs and the majority of the initiatives were reported to originate from within the corporations and not from the communities. We then embarked on the roles played by corporations and public organizations for the well-being of societies/communities. We prepared 10 items (listed below) and asked the participants to discuss how effectively they have participated in these roles:

- To share the negative consequences as a result of industrialization
- Closer ties between corporations and community
- Helping to get talent
- Role in Transfer of Technology (ToT)
- CSR helps to protect environment
- CSR is for human right corporate sustainability
- Interdependency between a corporation and community
- A CSR program can be seen as an aid to alleviate poverty
- A CSR program helps in gathering data for other public organization functions
- For corporate sustainability goals

Majority of the corporations and public organizations seemed to be participating in almost all of the above initiatives. However, their roles in environmental protection and a tool for poverty alleviation were ranked highly by participants. It was agreed by all participants that both the organizations and communities do benefit from the CSR activities, though the magnitude of benefits differ significantly because different organizations have different approaches on CSR initiatives.

11.5 Discussion of the Findings

The findings of the current study contradict the works of other researchers such as Branco and Rodrigues (2006), Ullmann (1985), Vogel (2005), Porter and Kramer (2006) that CSR is not the source of competitive advantage but rather moral obligation of the contributing organizations to the community well-being. Researchers, for example, Branco and Rodrigues (2006) and Orlitzky and Swanson (2008) have shown strong correlation between CSR initiatives of the organizations and competitive advantage. Other researchers have investigated the nature of relationship between CSR and Corporate financial performance with contradicting and inconclusive findings (Ullmann 1985; Vogel 2005; Brammer et al. 2005; Porter and Kramer 2006; Cardan and Darragh 2004; Barnett 2007).

Furthermore, advocates of CSR have outlined the benefits of corporate social responsibility to include, but not restricted to, the increased engagement and retention, stronger partnership with the community, increased corporate reputation and brand image, competitive advantage and stronger financial performance (Porter and Kramer 2006; Werther and Chandler 2004; Kramer and Porter 2011). Ideally, CSR benefits of an organization can be divided into those benefits which are tangible and those which cannot be seen by bare eyes. Tangible benefits to the contributing firms are those that can be quantified in financial and physical terms, whereas intangible benefits are harder to quantify and are non-physical in nature (Ullmann 1985; Vogel 2005; Porter and Kramer 2006).

Corporate reputation, reducing business risks, boosting sales revenue, brand image, customer loyalty and customers value have been identified conceptually by researchers to be external benefits of the CSR initiatives (Logsdon and Wood 2002; Orlitsky et al. 2003; Orlitzky and Benjamin 2001; Auger et al. 2003). On the other hand, internally, the benefits include learning organization, ability to attract better workforce, employee motivation, employee commitment and employee morale (Backhaus et al. 2002; Fulmer et al. 2003; Ballou et al. 2003; Branco and Rodrigues 2006; Orlitzky and Swanson 2008; Maxfield 2008; Frank 1996).

The contradiction of the current study with currently available literature with regard to CSR as competitive tool could have been contributed significantly with the nature of the corporations interviewed and general understanding of the CSR by practitioners. In addition, this concept is still new in Tanzania and many studies have not been conducted in the area as yet. CSR implementation is still at the rudimentary stage and much has to be learnt by corporations and public organizations with regard to CSR implementation and how firms can leverage the benefits of CSR.

The findings in the current study suggest that, implementation of CSR initiatiaves is discreational and not mandatory as it can be seen from other countries experience. this is contrary to the works of Waagstein and Patricia Rinwigati (2011) and N. Andrews (2016), who investigated the challenges of mandatory CSR in Indonesia and Ghan respectively.

11.6 Conclusion and Research Implications

Generally, CSR, as it can be seen from the study is a very important concept and a tool for competitive advantage in modern business settings.

The analysis of the theories and the understanding of the concept as per the discussion in the focus group require organizations to look at CSR in a multidisciplinary manner in the way people regard it and how it is practiced. In this study, we have seen that different people regard CSR differently and the practice is different from one organization to the other. Moreover, theories reviewed for the study largely explain the meaning and application of the concept, but they consider contextual issues. This is to say different organizations in different countries can practice CSR differently. The challenges for implementing CSR initiatives differ significantly from one country to the others.

It can be concluded that there is differing opinions among the study participants from public organizations and NGOs. Participants from public organizations believed that they are not benefiting at all (financially) on participating in the community development initiatives. It was agreed that corporations do benefit from financial and non-financial outcomes, while the public organizations benefit from only non-financial outcomes.

CSR planning is not undertaken by majority of the organizations despite the benefits of the CSR to both corporations and public organizations. In many of the interviewed corporations, there is no congruence between their business strategy and CSR initiatives. Others do not have even specific officers to deal with community initiatives and fail to benefit from competitive advantage brought by CSR activities.

In this study, we have seen so many roles played by the CSR activities to bring about community and society well-being. However, the significant roles can be enhanced when the organizations are focusing on looking at CSR as the source of competitive advantage and not just the moral obligation of the corporations to the community. There should be congruence between the overall business strategy of an organization and the CSR initiatives. Making CSR successful for corporations and public organizations implies the concept needs to be clearly understood by practicing firms. There should be proper planning and policies guiding CSR operations in these organizations. The value of CSR initiatives needs to be shared across the organizational departments.

Although CSR implementation in Tanzania is still at rudimentary stage, corporations and public organizations have much to learn from organizations that are benefiting from CSR implementation. With regard to whether CSR implementation should be mandatory or voluntary, it is not in the scope of this study, but future research in developing world can take this as an area for further studies.

References

Andrews, Nathan. "Challenges of corporate social responsibility (CSR) in domestic settings: An exploration of mining regulation vis-à-vis CSR in Ghana." *Resources Policy* 47 (2016): 9–17.

Arli, D. I., & Lasmono, H. K. Consumers' perception of corporate social responsibility in a developing country. *International Journal of Consumer Studies* 34 no. 1 (2010): 46–51. https://doi.org/10.1111/j.1470-6431.2009.00824.x

Auger, P., Burke, P., Devinney, T. M. & Louviere, J. J. "What will consumers pay for social product features?" *Journal of Business Ethics* 42, no. 3 (2003): 281–304.

Backhaus, K. B., Stone, B. A. & Heiner, K. "Exploring the relationship between corporate social performance and employer attractiveness." *Business & Society* 41 (2002): 292–318.

Ballou, B., Godwin, N. H. & Shortridge, R. T. "Firm value and employee attitudes on workplace quality." *Accounting Horizons* 17, no. 4 (2003): 329–341.

Barnett, M. L. "Stakeholder influence capacity and the variability of financial returns to corporate social responsibility." *Academy of Management Review* 37, no. 3 (2007): 794–816.

Baumgartner, R. J. & Winter, T. "The sustainability manager: A tool for education and training on sustainability management." *Corporate Social Responsibility and Environmental Management* 21 (2014). 167–174.

Bhattacharya, C. B. & Sen, S. "Doing better at doing good: When, why, and how consumers respond to corporate social initiatives." *California Management Review* 47, no. 1 (2004): 9–24.

Bichta, C. "Corporate socially responsible industry (CSR) practices in the context of Greek." *Social Responsibility and Environmental Management* 10 (2003): 12–24.

Bortree, D. S. "The impact of green initiatives on environmental legitimacy and admiration of the organization." *Public Relations Review* 35, no. 2 (2009): 133–135. https://doi.org/10.1016/j.pubrev.2009.01.002

Brammer, S., Brooks, C. & Pavelin, S. "The stock performance of America's 100 best corporate citizens." SSRN (2005).

Branco, M. C. & Rodrigues, L. L. "Corporate Social Responsibility and resource-based perspectives." *Journal of Business Ethics* 69 (2006): 111–132.

Cardan, S. D. & Darragh, O. "A halo for angel investors." *The McKinsey Quarterly* 1 (2004): 6–8.

Chandler, D. & Werther Jr., W. *Strategic corporate responsibility: Stakeholders, globalization, and sustainable value creation*. Los Angeles, CA: SAGE Publications, Inc., 2014.

Clarkson M. E. A Stakeholder Framework for Analyzing and Evaluating Corporate Social Performance. *Academy of Management Review* 20 no. 1 (1995): 92–117.

Coombs, W. T. & Holladay, S. J. *Managing corporate social responsibility: A Communication approach*. Chichester, UK: Wiley-Blackwell, 2012.

David, P., Kline, S. & Dai, Y. "Corporate social responsibility practices, corporate Identity, and purchase intention: A dual-process model." *Journal of Public Relations Research* 17, no. 3 (2005): 291–313.

Deegan, C. *Financial accounting theory*. Sydney: McGraw-Hill Book Company, 2000.

Donaldson, T. & Dunfee, T. W. *Ties that bind: A social contracts approach to business ethics*. Harvard Business School Press, 1999.

Donaldson, T. & Preston, L. E. "The Stakeholder Theory of the Corporation: Concepts, Evidence, and Implications." *Academy of Management Review* 20, no. 1 (1995): 65–91.

Du, Shuili, Bhattacharya, C. B. & Sen, Sankar. "Reaping relational rewards from Corporate Social Responsibility: The role of competitive positioning." *International Journal of Research in Marketing* 24, no. 3 (2008): 224–241.

European Commission. "Corporate social responsibility." (2014). Retrieved August 31, 2018, from http://ec.europa.eu/enterprise/policies/sustainable-business/corporate-social responsibility/index_en.htm

Ferris, G. R., Arthur, M. M., Berkson, H. M., Kaplan, D. M., Harrell-Cook, G. & Frink, D. D. "Toward a social context theory of the human resource management-organization effectiveness relationship." *Human Resource Management Review* 8, no. 3 (1998): 235–264.

Frank, R. H. "Can socially responsible firms survive in a competitive environment?" In D. M. Messick & A. E. Tenbrunsel (Eds.), *Codes of conduct: Behavioral research into business ethics*. New York: Russell Sage Foundation, 1996, pp. 86–103.

Freeman, R. E. *Strategic management: A stakeholder approach*. Boston, MA: Pitman, 1984.

Fulmer, I., Gerhart, B. & Scott, K. "Are the 100 best better? An empirical investigation of the relationship between being a 'Great place to work' and firm performance." *Personnel Psychology* 56 (2003): 965–993.

Galbreath, J. "Building corporate social responsibility into strategy." *European Business Review* 21 (2009): 109–127.

Gomez, L. M. & Chalmeta, R. "Corporate responsibility in US corporate websites: A pilot study." *Public Relations Review* 37, no. 1 (2011): 93–95. https://doi.org/10.1016/j.pubrev.2010.12.005

Gray, R., Owen, D., & Adams, C. *Accounting & accountability: changes and challenges in corporate social and environmental reporting*. Prentice Hall, 1996.

Hong, S. Y. & Rim, H. "The influence of customer use of corporate websites: Corporate Social responsibility, trust, and word-of-mouth communication." *Public Relations Review* 36, no. 4 (2010): 389–391. https://doi.org/10.1016/j.pubrev.2010.08.002

Hughes, D. and DuMont, K. "Using focus groups to facilitate culturally anchored research." *American Journal of Community Psychology* 21, no. 6 (1993): 775–806.

Jo, S. "Factors shaping activists' perceptions of corporate organizations: An empirical case from South Korea." *Public Relations Review* 37, no. 2 (2011): 178–180. https://doi.org/10.1016/j.pubrev.2011.01.002

John Dowling, Jeffrey Pfeffer. "Organizational legitimacy: Social values and organizational behavior." *The Pacific Sociological Review* 18, no. 6 (1975): 122–136.

Kim, S. & Lee, Y. J. "The complex attribution process of corporate social responsibility motives." *Public Relations Review* 38 (2011): 168–170. https://doi.org/10.1016/j.pubrev.2011.09.024

Kim, S. & Reber, B. H. "Public relations' place in corporate social responsibility: Practitioners define their role." *Public Relations Review* 34, no. 4 (2008): 337–342. https://doi.org/10.1016/j.pubrev.2008.07.003

Kramer, Mark R. & Michael Porter. "Creating shared value." *Harvard Business Review* 89, no. 1/2 (2011): 62–77.

Lamberti, Lucio & Noci, Giuliano. "The relationship between CSR and corporate strategy in medium-sized companies: evidence from Italy." *Business Ethics: A European Review* 21, no. 4 (2012): 402–416.

Lee, M. P. "Review of the theories of corporate social responsibility: Its evolutionary path and the road ahead." *International Journal of Management Reviews* 10, no. 1 (2008): 53–73.

Lichtenstein, D. R., Drumwright, M. E. & Braig, B. M. "The effect of corporate social responsibility on customer donations to corporate-supported nonprofits." *Journal of Marketing* 68, no. 4 (2004): 16–32. http://www.jstor.org/stable/30162013

Lindblom, C. K. "The implications of organisational legitimacy for corporate social performance and disclosure", paper presented at the Critical Perspectives on Accounting Conference, New York, NY, 1993.

Logsdon, J. M. & Wood, D. J. "Business Citizenship: From Domestic to Global Level of Analysis." *Business Ethics Quarterly* 12, no. 6 (2002): 155–187

Lubin, D. & Esty, D. "The sustainability imperative." *Harvard Business Review*, May (2010): p. 43.

Maignan, I. & Ferrell, O. "Corporate social responsibility and marketing: An integrative framework." *The Journal of the Academy of Marketing Science* 32, no. 1 (2004): 3–19.

Maxfield, S. "Reconciling corporate citizenship and competitive strategy: Insights from economic theory." *Journal of Business Ethics* 80 (2008): 367–377.

McElhaney, K. "A strategic approach to corporate social responsibility." *Leader to Leader* 52, no. 1 (2009): 30–36.

McWilliams, A., Siegel, D. S. & Wright P. M. "Corporate social responsibility: Strategic implications." *Journal of Management Studies* 43 (2006): 1–18.

Orlitzky, M. & Benjamin, J. D. Corporate social performance and firm risk: A meta-analytic review. *Business & Society* 2001 Dec 40(4) pp. 369–396.

Orlitzky, M. & Swanson, D. Toward integrative corporate citizenship: Research advances in corporate social performance. Springer 2008 Oct 24.

Porter, M. E. & Kramer, M. R. "The link between competitive advantage and Corporate Social Responsibility." *Harvard Business Review* 84, no. 12 (2006): 78–92.

Secchi, D. "Utilitarian, managerial and relational theories of corporate social responsibility." *International Journal of Management Reviews* 9, no. 4 (2007): 347–373.

Sen, Sankar, Bhattacharya, C. B. & Korschun, Daniel. "The role of Corporate Social Responsibility in strengthening multiple stakeholder relationships: A field experiment." *Journal of the Academy of Marketing Science* 34, no. 2 (2006): 158–166.

Suchman, M. C. "Managing Legitimacy: Strategic and Institutional Approaches." *Academy of Management Review* 20 no. 3: 571–610.

Ullmann, A. "Data in search of a theory: A critical examination of the relationship among social performance, social disclosure, and economic performance." *Academy of Management Review* 10 (1985): 540–577.

Vogel, D. J. "Is there a market for virtue?" *California Management Review* 47, no. 4 (2005): 19–45.

Waagstein, Patricia Rinwigati. "The mandatory corporate social responsibility in Indonesia: Problems and implications." *Journal of Business Ethics* 98, no. 3 (2011): 455–466.

Werther, W. B. & Chandler, D. "Strategic corporate social responsibility as global brand insurance." Business Horizons no. 4 (2005): 317–324.

Yoon, Y. & Gürhan-Canli, Z. The effects of corporate social responsibility (CSR) on Product Quality Evaluations. Advances in Consumer Research 31 (2004).

12

A Revaluation of All Values: Nietzschean Populism and Covid-19

David McQueen, Francisca Farache, and Georgiana Grigore

The weak and the misfits shall perish: first tenet of our love of man. And we should even help them to do so. What is more harmful than any vice? Active sympathy for all the misfits and the weak—Christianity. (Friedrich Nietzsche 1888, The Antichrist, translated Wayne 2004)

spending £350 billion to prolong the lives of a few hundred thousand mostly elderly people is an irresponsible use of taxpayers' money. (Toby Young 2020, The Critic)

D. McQueen (✉)
Bournemouth University, Bournemouth, UK
e-mail: dmcqueen@bournemouth.ac.uk

F. Farache
Brighton Business School, University of Brighton, Brighton, UK
e-mail: f.farache@brighton.ac.uk

G. Grigore
School of Business, University of Leicester, Leicester, UK

F. Farache et al. (eds.), *Values and Corporate Responsibility*, Palgrave Studies in Governance, Leadership and Responsibility,
https://doi.org/10.1007/978-3-030-52466-1_12

In *Ecce Homo*, first written in 1888, a year before he lost his sanity, Friedrich Nietzsche announced with characteristic bombast: 'I am no man, I am dynamite'. Nietzsche's destructive power lay in systematically reducing the values of his age to rubble through all-out philosophical and rhetorical war. These were Christian values, the cornerstone of Western civilisation, which Nietzsche rails against and literally curses, like a demented Archangel in *The Antichrist*, also written in 1888. For Nietzsche, the crisis of 'the death of God', which science and rationalism ushered in, enabled the overturning of bedrock assumptions and values on which society stood. Nietzsche, the son of a pastor, recognised and preached the need to embrace the full implications of this crisis in faith and was thereby instrumental in dynamiting the bedrock values of the nineteenth century, if not the preceding two millennia. His destruction of all that was sacred, his 'revaluation of all values' or 'reversing of perspectives' was, and remains, a shocking act of philosophical violence against not only the pious moralising of churchgoers, but the broader ethical values of the Enlightenment. Nietzsche's scorched-earth approach to morality was supposed to liberate man to create his own values—free from what he considered 'pitiful' Christian-inspired empathy and hypocritical selflessness, the 'slave morality' of the herd. Nietzsche proclaimed that in killing God and rejecting an afterlife, man can finally define his own future—become the Superman (*Übermensch*)—living fully, creatively, instinctually, *ruthlessly* and in the present. Nietzsche wrote of a vast difference between these superior individuals and 'the rabble' or unthinking and engulfing herd who he regarded with anti-egalitarian disdain and suspicion, especially in his latter works (see Hargis 2010).

Nietzsche died, insane, in August 1900 in Weimar in the care of his sister Elisabeth Förster-Nietzsche who established an archive of his works there and supported, and was financially supported by, the Nazi Party. Hitler who, like Mussolini, was an admirer of Nietzsche, met Elisabeth and was photographed staring intently at a bust of his philosopher hero at the archive which he visited several times. Following the collapse of the Weimar Republic in 1933 and the establishment of the Third Reich, the Nazi state shredded German's rights and enacted Hitler's fanatical ideology embodied in notions of a Germanic 'Master Race'. This ultimately resulted in the murder and death of countless millions by Hitler's pitiless, politically indoctrinated Aryan *Übermensch* in SS uniforms. While most modern scholars of Nietzsche (who attacked anti-Semitism and nationalism) reject the claim that his philosophy enabled Nazism or the atrocities of the Holocaust, it is not so easy to uncouple his philosophical legacy from fascist and far-right ideology. Both scorn compassion and ideas of equality whilst celebrating strength, ruling élites, martial values and the 'will to power'. Yet Nietzsche's 'revaluation of all values' has inspired thinkers of every political persuasion and also laid the philosophical foundations for existentialism, critical theory, post-structuralism and postmodernism as well as inspiring, according to Harvard psychologist Steven Pinker, 'Nazism, Bolshevism, the Ayn Randian fringe of libertarianism, and the American alt-right and neo-Nazi movements today' (Drochon 2018).

Nietzsche's reputation was gradually rehabilitated and 'de-nazified' in the post-war era (see Whyte 2008) and he is regarded by many today as at the forefront of the canon of great thinkers, even the philosopher of values *par excellence* (Râmbu 2016). He is championed as an ardent yet benign European who believed in the value of mixed races, opposed Bismarck's militarist ambitions for Germany and detested Wagner's anti-Semitism as well as the proto-Nazi views of his sister's husband, Bernhard Förster. The biographer Sue Prideaux (2018) goes so far as to claim, with evidence from his life rather than his work, that Nietzsche was no misogynist and was prepared to accept women into university and intellectual life as equals. Georges Bataille, Thomas Mann, Albert Camus, Michel Foucault, Walter Kaufmann and many others have sought to establish the 'radical incompatibility' between Nietzsche and fascists and populist nationalists of the twentieth century who claimed allegiance to his philosophy (Wistrich and Golomb 2002, p. 162).

Nevertheless, Nietzsche wrote presciently in *Ecce Homo* that 'Some day my name will be linked to the memory of something monstrous, of a crisis as yet unprecedented on earth'.[1] So indeed, his work was seized and curated by the Nazis, published in 'field grey editions' to rouse and harden the hearts of German soldiers (Whyte 2008, p. 173) and his ruthless, anti-democratic ideals embraced and weaponised by National Socialist

[1] (Nietzsche and Large 1888/2007, p. 88).

ideologists such as Alfred Baeumler, Alfred Rosenberg and Martin Heidegger (see Whyte's 2008 excellent discussion of this). Nazi leaders, propagandists and ideologists appropriated, and selectively cited, Nietzsche's published and unpublished work[2] and elevated him as a far-sighted prophet of 'heroic realism' and racial war. They were not alone in this view as those fighting against the Third Reich condemned the 'real design' of Nazis as:

> *[…] nothing less than the Nietzschean transvaluation of values; the education of Germans in Germanity, the nihilistic revolution which would not stop at smashing countries, but would wreck the very hearts of men, utterly destroying the civilization of the west.* (Butler, cited Voegelin 1944, p. 183)

The global conflagration of 1939–1945 was the 'monstrous' crisis that cast its shadow over Nietzsche's legacy for decades to come and still leaves many readers queasy at his pronouncements on women, democracy, the 'herd-animal' or 'ruling and Caesarian spirits'.[3] Yet while aspects of Nietzsche's reactionary politics repulse many progressive critics, linking the ideas of Friedrich Nietzsche to contemporary populists in the mould of President Donald Trump, President Jair Bolsonaro or Prime Minister Boris Johnson is a problematic exercise, not least because Nietzsche explicitly rejects ideas like nation, state and homeland. Indeed, given that Nietzsche viewed the idea of a motherland as 'the parasitic force that infects and impedes the creative genius of the wandering artist' (Clemente et al. 2018, p. 44) he would most likely have sneered at Johnson's grandiose Brexit promises, Trump's boorish 'America First' dogma or Bolsonaro's

[2] Nietzsche's Nachlass which Elisabeth Förster-Nietzsche and her editors sifted through and falsified for her edition of The Will to Power.

[3] 'A question keeps coming back to us, a tempting and evil question perhaps. Would not the time have come, now that the type "herd-animal" is developing ever more in Europe, to try and begin with a clear-principled, artificial and conscious breeding of the opposite type and its virtues? And would it not even be for the demo-cratic movement itself a kind of goal, salvation and justification, if someone appeared who would put it to his service—if at last its new and sublime perfection of slavery (for that is what European democracy will be in the end) would be complemented by that higher species of ruling and Caesarian spirits who would place itself on top of it, who would take hold of it, who would elevate itself by means of it? Towards new, hitherto impossible, to their visions? To their tasks?' (from The Will to Power Aphorism 954, cited Voegelin 1944, p. 201).

vulgar, nationalist rhetoric (whilst, perhaps, loudly cheering his antediluvian views on women).

Nietzsche may have described himself as an 'anti-anti-Semite' (see Duffy and Mittelman 1988; Wistrich and Golomb 2002) in his long feud with Wagner and proclaimed his *anti-populist* attitudes at every opportunity, but it is instructive to trace the connecting threads between his work and contemporary populism. For de Vreese et al. (2018, pp. 425–426) populism is as much a style of communication as a set of ideas communicated. It is, they argue, a 'communication phenomenon' containing a characteristic set of key messages or frames that firstly appeal to the 'will of the people'; secondly denounce corrupt élites and a malfunctioning establishment; and thirdly (in 'complete populism') offer to exclude threatening 'out-groups'. Nietzsche's writing carries faint traces of this populist ideological baggage in his attack on parliamentary government and church establishments and celebrities of the age. His pseudo-aristocratic snobbery against the working class *and* the bourgeoisie fills him with bile when contemplating the 'will of the people', but he is not against the possibility of manipulating 'the herd', or of identifying outgroups when it suits him, including slaves, women and 'degenerates' (see the discussion of how Nietzsche fuelled eugenic experiments in Stone 2002).

Yet it is not an easy matter to trace *any* consistent political ideology in Nietzsche's sprawling, anecdotal and profoundly ambiguous body of work, although there have been numerous efforts (see Siemens and Roodt 2008; Donaldson 2000; Drochon 2016). By the same token it is not immediately clear what the diverse populist insurgencies around the world today actually share in terms of core ideas and goals. Nationalist, authoritarian, chauvinist perhaps and, like Nietzsche in some respects, encouraging a corrosively sceptical attitude to logic or 'truth' and dismissive of experts, scientists and journalists. Furthermore, what Abbey and Appel (1998) rightly identify as Nietzsche's repugnant attitudes to the weak and his attack on equality and haughty contempt for liberal institutions are a match for some of the more illiberal views expressed by Donald Trump, Jair Bolsonaro, Narendra Modi, Recep Tayyip Erdoğan, Viktor Orbán and other populists who have come to dominate the global political scene at the time of writing. Nietzsche's iconoclastic, polemical and shocking language does have the grandiose and menacing style of a demagogue about it, the violent tone of Mussolini and Hitler,[4] and the calculated aim to offend political enemies embodied in the outbursts of Orbán, Trump or his tropical alter ego Bolsonaro.

12.1 Nietzschean Populists and Covid-19

Nietzsche's performative, exclamatory style of address and his attack on 'herd values' resonate in further unsettling ways as we enter the third decade of the twenty-first century with populist leaders at the helm of nations as diverse as Turkey, India, Russia, Hungary, Brazil, Poland, the USA and the UK. These populist leaders and their governments came to be judged against more liberal and democratic governments in their response to an unprecedented pandemic crisis that shut down much of the world economy in 2020. In this year, the new SARS-like coronavirus, named Covid-19, swept across every national border, left healthcare systems reeling and had observers reaching for comparisons with the World War of 1939–1945 in terms of its global impact on every household and business. Of course, the destructive force of Covid-19 as measured by deaths or physical destruction was unlikely to come near that of the Second World War, or even the Spanish flu of 1918–1920 which killed an estimated 500 million people (*The Economist* 2020). Nevertheless the scale of the pandemic, the range of responses by governments around the world to it, talk of 'herd immunity', attitudes to the vulnerable and weak and a revaluation of previously unassailable precepts and dogmas force us to assess our own moral values and previously unexamined ideas of 'how to live' as never before.

In the sections that follow we explore these issues in three ways: firstly, we provide an overview of national responses to the pandemic and compare how populist (male) leaders met the challenge compared to more 'conventional', liberal (and often female) leaders. Secondly, and linked to Nietzschean ideas outlined above, we critique the notion of 'herd

[4] Hitler's oratorial style is captured perfectly by Chaplin's deranged and gibberish speech as Adenoid Hynkel in The Great Dictator (1940).

immunity' and how illiberal, if not eugenicist, discourse developed around the elderly, 'the vulnerable' and/or those with 'pre-existing conditions'. This discourse was seen to impact policy decisions and the framing of a 'choice' laid before voters between saving the economy or protecting the weakest of 'the herd', the latter framed, to a greater or lesser extent, by various populist leaders as an unaffordable or unworkable option. Finally, the debates around a post-lockdown world are briefly explored, particularly the opportunity to radically reassess current norms and values and perhaps reshape the global economy in ways that could rescue the 'revaluation of all values' from the darker Nietzschean ideas touched on above. The health crisis is still ongoing whilst we finish writing up this chapter, so we only report on events that happened until April 2020.

12.2 The Good, the Bad and the Ugly: How Nation-States Met the Challenge of Covid China

The hugely differing responses to the pandemic around the globe were a clear illustration of national preparedness, spending priorities, political attitudes and the weight given to saving human lives and shielding healthcare services against protecting businesses, the stock market and the wider economy. In China, the initial response to the outbreak was delay, denial and suppression of information about the virus for at least three weeks with doctors who first identified the threat of the novel coronavirus in Wuhan at the end of December 2019 reprimanded for discussing the illness with fellow doctors online. A local 'wet market' selling fresh meat, seafood and live, exotic wildlife was thought to be the source of Covid-19 which is a close relative of other viruses found in horseshoe bats possibly via an intermediary host, such as pangolin, although this awaits further research[5] (World Organisation for Animal Health 2020). By December

[5] A more disturbing theory is that the virus originated in a bio-lab, perhaps in Wuhan close to the wet market identified as the likely source. French Nobel Prize-winning AIDS researcher Luc Montagnier claimed in an interview on France's CNews that COVID-19 was 'not natural' and suggested that this disease may have resulted from work done by molecular biologists who were

30th, the hashtag 'Wuhan Sars' was trending on the Chinese microblog Weibo, before censors removed it (*Financial Times* 2020). Under President Xi Jinping, China's authoritarian leader, increasing political repression allegedly made officials more hesitant to report cases without authorisation from the top (*Washington Post* 2020). By January 10th, Fudan University researchers in Shanghai had sequenced data on the virus, showing it to be from the same family as the SARS coronavirus and publicised their findings via the World Health Organisation. While cases surged and millions travelled home to Wuhan for the Lunar New Year the WHO alert of January 12th was 'reassured' by the quality of ongoing investigations noting 'The government reports that there is no clear evidence that the virus passes easily from person to person' (WHO 2020). On January 18th, with 62 infected patients, Wuhan held a mass banquet for tens of thousands of people despite knowledge of the virus amongst local officials. Five million departed Wuhan in the weeks before the city was quarantined on January 22nd, which helped the virus spread all over the country and overseas. An unnamed senior advisor to China's central government was critical of Wuhan's mayor, who had, in his view:

> *[…] neither the expertise nor the willingness to follow health experts' advice. His concern is that an escalation in disease prevention may hurt the local economy and social stability.* (*Financial Times* 2020)

The mayor's response would prefigure more widespread and lethal inaction and failure of leadership to the rapidly spreading virus in numerous countries around the world.

On January 20th, President Xi made his first public comments on the virus, saying the outbreak 'must be taken seriously', while a leading Chinese epidemiologist, Dr Zhong Nanshan, announced on national television for the first time that the virus was transmissible from person to person on national television. By then, more than 3000 people had been infected during almost a week of public silence. On January 23rd, Wuhan finally came under a tight lockdown suspending all public

attempting to create an AIDS vaccine, although this claim was widely disputed by other scientists (see Snopes.com 2020).

transportation and air links out of the city of 11 million people. Other cities in the Hubei region quickly followed suit.

12.3 Taiwan, Singapore and South Korea

Taiwan has been in a state of constant readiness to combat epidemics arising from China since being hit by a SARS outbreak in 2003. The island closed off all travel from China, its biggest trading partner, even as Wuhan remained open and the WHO was advising against such a step.[6] By April 2020, Taiwan still had only a handful of fatalities while shops, restaurants, bars, schools, universities and offices stayed open (*Japan Times* 2020). The government of President Tsai Ing-wen, whose deputy Chen Chien-jen is an epidemiologist, enforced very strict testing and contact-tracing measures in the early stages of the crisis. The tracking and tracing were highly effective, and by April 2020 Taiwan was able to export millions of face masks to help the European Union and announced it was donating 10 million face masks to other countries most in need (CNN 2020a).

South Korea and Singapore also acted quickly, leveraging their IT infrastructure and capabilities to respond to the emerging pandemic. On January 23rd, densely populated Singapore reported its first case of Covid-19, but by April 21st it had reported only 11 deaths compared to New York's 14,828 Covid-related fatalities. Within 24 hours of each new infection being discovered in Singapore, more than 100 contact tracers assembled a complete contact map of the person spanning 14 days, using several digital footprints (Knowledge@Wharton 2020). Dr Clarence Tam from the National University of Singapore explained how:

> *Singapore invested heavily in developing capacity and an infrastructure to deal with these types of outbreaks over the past 10 to 15 years, including increasing capacity for intensive care and patient isolation facilities, building expertise in infectious disease.* (*CNET* 2020)

---

[6] In fact, Taiwan was not receiving WHO updates and was barred from the World Health Assembly even as an observer since Tsai's 2016 election, due to pressure from Beijing (*The Diplomat* 2020).

Some of the early success in Singapore slipped away as the virus spread in densely crowded, foreign worker dormitories, but the official number of deaths was still a remarkably low 14 towards the end of April (ECDC 2020). South Korea also orchestrated a rapid and effective response to the pandemic: installing drive-through tests for the virus, body sterilisers to spray on visitors passing through malls and thermal scanners to test visitors' body temperature in other venues. The government used drones to disinfect large public areas, distributed a self-health check mobile app to track movements of overseas visitors taken up by over 90% of those it was offered to and mobile apps which tracked and monitored those under quarantine (Knowledge@Wharton 2020). The number of deaths by the end of April was around 244 (ECDC 2020).

12.4 New Zealand and the Nordic Countries

In New Zealand, Prime Minister Jacinda Ardern took early action to shut down tourism and impose a month-long lockdown on the entire country, whilst carrying out widespread testing which helped limit coronavirus deaths to just 19 by the end of April, when the government claimed it had stopped community transmission and thereby had effectively eliminated the virus (BBC 2020a).

Early, aggressive contact-tracing and the quarantining of suspected coronavirus cases characterised the response of Iceland, while Denmark and then Norway were also quick to adopt tough measures. Finland followed Sweden's more laissez-faire response before adopting its own strict restrictions on March 17th (Euractiv 2020). The higher total number of deaths per million in Sweden reflected the country's almost unique decision to impose mostly voluntary restrictions rather than legally binding orders. Elementary schools, bars, restaurants and businesses remained open, though with social distancing and other safety measures encouraged. The strategy developed by the epidemiologist Anders Tegnell and the Swedish government was essentially to pursue herd immunity allowing the virus to spread slowly while sheltering the elderly and the vulnerable until much of the population gained immunity, or a vaccine became available (Politifact 2020). By April 29th, Sweden reported 231 cases per million against Denmark's 75, Norway's 39 and Finland's 36 per million. This was also worse than Germany which reported 76 cases per million, but still less than the UK's, Italy's or Spain's which were 326, 452 and 509 deaths per million respectively (Statistica 2020). Italy and Spain were amongst the first European countries to experience the full impact of the pandemic, so these figures remain a provisional snapshot at this time.

In April 2020, Noam Chomsky, in an interview reported by *Al Jazeera*, commented:

> *China, South Korea, Taiwan, Singapore [...] seemed to have contained at least the first surge of the crisis.*

He explained that how the West prepared for the crisis differed markedly between countries:

> *In Europe, to some extent, it's happened. Germany ... did have spare diagnostic capacity and was able to act in a highly selfish fashion, not helping others but for itself at least, to evident reasonable containment. [...] Other countries just ignored it. The worst was the United Kingdom [...].* (*Al Jazeera* 2020)

12.5 The UK's Herd Immunity Policy and the Fallacy of Balance

On March 5, 2020, the British Prime Minister Boris Johnson explained in a television interview on ITV's *This Morning* that his experts had, at that point, recommended 'slightly counterintuitively' that things like closing schools or stopping big gatherings 'don't work as well, perhaps as people think' in stopping the spread of the virus. When asked by the show's presenter Philip Schofield if the government's delay in shutting down schools and public events was part of an effort to delay the spread of the disease 'so that it doesn't all happen at once and overwhelm the NHS', Johnson replied using a striking phrase:

> *[...] one of the theories is, that perhaps you could sort of take it on the chin, take it all in one go and allow the disease, as it were, to move through the popula-*

> *tion, without taking as many draconian measures. I think we need to strike a balance. I think it is very important—we've got a fantastic NHS, we'll give them all the support that they need. We'll make sure they have all the preparations, all the kit that they need for us to get through it, but I think it would be better if we take all the measures that we can now just to stop the peak of the disease being as difficult for the NHS as it might be.* (*This Morning* 2020)

This reply is interesting for two reasons. Firstly, Johnson's promise to have 'all the kit' the NHS needed—a promise comprehensively demolished by investigative reporters (see *Panorama* 2020) which revealed 'no gowns, visors, swabs or body bags in the government's pandemic stockpile when Covid-19 reached the UK' and which led to some NHS workers 'wearing bin bags' (BBC 2020b). Secondly, the strategy Johnson reveals of 'striking a balance' between, on the one hand, letting the virus spread almost unchecked through the public (a variation of the voluntary distancing and isolation approach taken by Sweden) and, on the other, gradually applying a brake through recommendations, such as hand washing and social distancing before introducing more draconian and mandatory measures. The 'balance fallacy' of this position, it might be argued, was between allowing the pandemic to take its 'natural' course, thereby accepting 'on the chin' the (potentially avoidable) deaths of hundreds of thousands of people, and *slowing* these avoidable deaths, thereby preventing a collapse of the NHS. The third option of *avoiding* deaths, wherever possible, by aggressively contact-tracing and quarantining suspected cases whilst closing down public events and travel from countries in the grip of the pandemic (as Taiwan, South Korea and New Zealand had done) was not considered.

A similar use of 'balance' rhetoric is often seen in CSR studies, where profitability is 'balanced' against doing good in society. The problem lies in the rhetoric of balance, or the false dilemma it invites and the ways in which such paradoxical situations are resolved. Entertaining the notion of 'herd immunity' and allowing people to die so that the economy grows, while those who survive have more money, is ethically problematic, but not inconsistent with how some corporations view morality and how they 'manage' false paradox. For example, in their study of the Volkswagen emissions scandal, Gaim et al. (2019) reveal that paradoxical promises were embraced at a 'discursive' level in responses to the scandal but lacked substance when implemented 'on the ground'. The authors then argue that such rhetoric can trigger dysfunctional organisational behaviours, and they caution organisations and their staff from being 'overconfident' in attempting to resolve false paradoxes. Promises embraced at a 'discursive' level but lacking substance when implemented 'on the ground' would come to characterise the government's many promises around the protective 'kit' or PPE mentioned above.

However, the herd immunity strategy came under renewed scrutiny when on March 16, 2020, the Imperial College Covid-19 Response Team released a report presenting the modelling which informed government policies in the UK and other countries. In this report two potential strategies for dealing with the crisis were explored: *mitigating*, which focused on the slowing down of the pandemic, and *suppression*, aimed at reversing epidemic growth. The study showed that mitigation—or a combination of isolation, quarantine of suspected cases and social distancing for the vulnerable groups only—'might reduce peak healthcare demand by 2/3 and deaths by half', but suppression was actually the preferred option. Suppression—and related practices such as social distancing for all, isolation and quarantine of the cases and family members, school and university closures—was indicated as the most effective way to reduce transmission. The report concluded that a herd immunity strategy could lead to 250,000 deaths with 'mitigation' and 510,000 without (Imperial College 2020, p. 16). Media reports indicated that this revelation stopped further public discussion of a herd immunity scenario, and the government shifted towards more cautious public health policy, acknowledging the implications of the latest scientific findings in the 'hope' that excess death could be limited to 20,000 (*The Telegraph* 2020).

The government's belated move from the illusion of 'herd immunity', towards the instruction to 'stay at home, protect the NHS, save lives', came, arguably, at least a week too late. Did this move signal a significant shift in the science, or were the government effectively forced to abandon the herd immunity strategy in the face of a devastating national death toll without any guarantee, as the WHO would warn, that such 'immunity' was even possible? Across the private sector businesses, (independent) schools, sports venues, restaurants and bars were closing, unable to justify the risks to their staff and customers and putting corporate responsibility ahead of their profits, or even their ability to continue trading. Most sporting organisations including English Premier League, British football and Rugby Union were shutting down around March 13th and 14th. Some universities were also closing, although many (remarkably) remained open into the third week of March apparently unwilling to confront the deadly reality of the pandemic in their 'risk assessment' procedures. In the absence of government intervention, the four-day Cheltenham Festival in Gloucestershire went ahead from March 10th to 13th with over 60,000 attending each afternoon and a Champions League match at Anfield between Liverpool and Atlético Madrid on March 11th attended by more than 50,000 (with over 3000 Spaniards from Madrid at a time when Spain was already in partial lockdown) are thought to have contributed significantly to spreading the virus (The Guardian 2000). Welsh rock band Stereophonic defended their decision to go ahead with shows in Glasgow, Manchester and Cardiff in mid-March attended by 40,000 fans by pointing to UK government guidance that there was 'no need' for a ban on large public gatherings. The band were responding to social media criticism of the band both in Britain and beyond, including China where one bemused post asked 'The whole world is working hard [to contain the virus], but why is the UK still holding concerts?' (cited Bandwagon 2020).

The national lockdown measures finally announced at 8.30 pm on the evening of March 23rd were the most draconian in British history, allowing people to leave their home only for very limited purposes—shopping for food, travelling to and from work where working from home was not possible, for medical need, caring for a vulnerable person or for one form of exercise a day. These measures were necessary because, as Johnson explained:

> *To put it simply, if too many people become seriously unwell at one time, the NHS will be unable to handle it—meaning more people are likely to die, not just from coronavirus, but from other illnesses as well. So, it's vital to slow the spread of the disease.*

The consequence of the UK government's initial, almost Nietzschean tranquillity in February at the prospect of the population as a 'herd' that would be thinned may also help explain the apparently incomprehensible indifference of the prime minister and others indicated in *The Sunday Times* exposé of April 19th. The normally conservative supporting *Times* headlines 'Coronavirus: 38 days when Britain sleepwalked into disaster' pointed to the fact that Boris Johnson skipped five Cobra meetings on the virus, that calls to order protective gear were ignored and that 'scientists' warnings fell on deaf ears'. These failings in February, the report observed, 'may have cost thousands of lives' (*The Times* 2020).

12.6 Donald Trump: The USA's 'medic-in-chief'

If, in Chomsky's view, the UK was the worst in Europe, he nominated the USA as 'the worst of all'. The US president's chaotic leadership was partly responsible, Chomsky argued:

> *One day [US President Donald Trump] says, "There is no crisis, it's just like flu". The next day, "It's a terrible crisis and I knew it all along". The next day, "We have to go back to the business, because I have to win the election". The idea that the world is in these hands is shocking.* (*Al Jazeera* 2020)

US Covid-19 deaths which by the end of April were at 178 cases per million, compared to New Zealand's 4 or South Korea's 5 per million (Statistica 2020), stand as an indictment of that country's preparation for and response to the pandemic and are likely to eventually exceed the UK's dire record of 326 per million deaths. There is no space to rehearse the rambling absurdities of Donald Trump's numerous press briefings that include describing the crisis as a 'hoax', that the virus would disappear 'like a miracle', to suggesting that his scientists explore injecting light or disinfectant as a cure. However, his mendacious attacks on the WHO and decision to halt US funding of that body were a low in a catalogue of dangerous quackery and 'ridiculous behaviour' that baffled the watching world (see *The Intercept* 2020a). More worryingly the

Centers for Disease Control and Prevention (CDC) was sidelined by a newly formed Coronavirus Task Force, led by the science-denying Vice-President Mike Pence. This excluded everyone from the CDC except CDC's director, Dr Robert Redfield. According to Charles Duhigg writing in *The New Yorker* (2020):

> *"The C.D.C. was ordered into lockdown", a former senior official at the agency told me. "They can't speak to the media. These are people who have trained their entire lives for epidemics—the finest public-health army in history—and they've been told to shut up!"*

Since then, as Duhigg notes, the primary spokesperson was not a scientist but President Donald Trump—'a politician notoriously hostile to science'. Political analyst Marwan Bishara noted how the rhetoric of 'war' was mobilised around the world during the pandemic, nowhere more so than in the USA where President Trump used the war as a pretext for further deregulation, restrictions on immigration and political point scoring that appealed to his base of supporters:

> *Unnecessary, preventable mortalities become "casualties of war". Thus, when Trump and his supporters demand the "liberation" of certain states from their reluctant governors and demand an early "return to normal" by reopening the economy, they merely see the potential rise in mortalities as the inescapable "collateral damage" of war.* (*Al Jazeera* 2020)

Celebrity talk show host Dr Mehmet Oz, who has advised President Trump, told *Fox News'* Sean Hannity that the idea of reopening schools 'may only cost us 2 to 3 percent in terms of total mortality', a trade-off 'some folks' would consider:

> *We need our mojo back, [...] Let's start with things that are really critical to the nation where we think we might be able to open without getting into a lot of trouble. I tell you, schools are a very appetizing opportunity.* (cited *The New York Times* 2020a)

The discourse around virility was typical of some of the language of the far right used to defend sacrifices necessary to win the 'wider war'. On March 22nd, President Trump famously tweeted that 'we cannot let the cure be worse than the problem itself' laying the groundwork to ease the measures put in place to deal with the coronavirus. Trump began to distance himself from his lead expert Dr Anthony Fauci, the immunologist who heads the National Institute of Allergy and Infectious Diseases (NIAID), saying he disagreed with him on things like whether malaria drugs could be effective against coronavirus and showed impatience with the lockdown, tweeting repeatedly that 'people want to return to work'.

Through his impatience, erratic messaging and claims around the nation's supposed 'tremendous testing capacity', Trump soon found himself at odds with many state leaders, including New York's Governor Andrew Cuomo who urged him not to act in a 'dictatorial' style (*New York Times* 2020b). Yet Cuomo and New York's Mayor Bill de Blasio also came in for criticism for micro-managing health supervisors and 'dithering' over how to react to the pandemic compared, for instance, to Seattle where scientists took the lead in tracking, tracing and locking down Washington State. This happened with the assistance of corporates like Microsoft who told their employees to stay at home on March 4th, when there were only 12 known Covid cases across the nation. This resulted in a hundred thousand people suddenly staying home and shifting attitudes in other companies so that by the time of the lockdown in mid-March, many bars, restaurants and places of business were already empty (*The New Yorker* 2020).

The swift corporate responsibility shown by Microsoft and other tech firms and the leadership shown in Seattle and other cities across America lies in stark contrast to the blustering ineffectiveness of the American president. Yet if Donald Trump made UK Prime Minister Boris Johnson appear a model of responsibility, Brazilian President Jair Bolsonaro's response to the global pandemic made Trump appear relatively measured and informed.

12.7 The Trump of the Tropics

Jair Bolsonaro, the right-wing Brazilian president, is well known for his outrageous statements and crude actions: from claiming Leonardo DiCaprio gave cash 'to set the Amazon on fire' (BBC 2019) to tweeting a pornographic video (Phillips 2019). However, his Covid-19 dealings were astonishing, even by his own standards. He adopted infantile 'macho' discourse calling for Brazilians to face Covid-19 as 'males', in his own words: 'We need to face it like a man, dammit' (Harris and Schipani, *FT* 2020). The president was vehemently opposed to social distancing measures and urged Brazilians to return to work, calling Covid-19 a fantasy and 'a media trick'.

From the start of the Covid-19 pandemic, Bolsonaro made statements downplaying the gravity of the situation and claiming the measures taken around the globe and by Brazilian governors were unnecessary, echoing Trump's early assertion that the crisis was a 'hoax'. At the beginning of March 2020, Bolsonaro stated that 'it is a lot of fantasy, the coronavirus issue, it is not all of this the media is portraying' and that 'other flus killed more than this one' (Arcanjo 2020a).

During his televised address to the nation, on March 24th, the Brazilian president criticised the closures of school and commerce, attacked Brazilian governors who were supporting the new measures to tackle Covid-19 and blamed the press for what he called a 'hysterical climate' within the country. Bolsonaro claimed that:

> *From my track record as an athlete, if I was infected with the virus, I wouldn't have to worry. I would feel nothing and won't be affected, at most, I would have the symptoms of a little cold or little flu.* (Della Coletta 2020)

He suggested this 'immunity' was also shared by Brazilians at large, as the right-wing president asserted that Brazilians are immune to diseases and should be investigated, as:

> *They never catch anything. You see some bloke jumping into the sewage, he gets out, has a dive, right? And nothing happens to him.* (cited Phillips 2020)

Needless to say, there was no scientific evidence produced to support his arguments. An institutional publicity video from the Presidency of the Republic summarised and officially communicated the government's proposals for the pandemic. The video showed self-employed people and health professionals willing to return to their normal work routine. The campaign 'Brazil cannot stop' encouraged the population to return to work, even the ones infected by and self-isolating due to Covid-19 (Arcanjo 2020c). However, on March 28th the Federal Court of Justice in Rio de Janeiro prevented the campaign from being broadcast as it publicised information which was 'not corroborated by scientific evidence'. The Court concluded that a publicly founded campaign cannot spread false information (Oliveira 2020).

It is not only the Brazilian president's words that are alarming but also his actions. On March 15th, the president took the streets of Brasilia, Brazil's capital, to join protesters against the social distancing measures adopted by the country, thus protesting against the Brazilian Congress. He then decided to shake hands and said, during a radio interview:

> *If I decided to shake people's hands, I am sorry, but I did not ask the people to come to the streets, this is my right. After all, I came from the people. I came from the Brazilian people.* (Arcanjo 2020a)

The president was out and about in various instances visiting supermarkets, pharmacies and shops shaking people's hands and taking selfies with his supporters. When questioned by journalists about where he was going, the president replied 'I have the constitutional right to come and go. No one will hinder my freedom to come and go' (Carvalho 2020a). The president appeared to show understanding of the need for social distancing when he mentioned in a radio interview that he will have a 'traditional small birthday party' for his wife and himself (Mariani et al. 2020). However, he then went to the construction site of a new hospital in Goias State on April 11th. Again, this behaviour was against the recommendations from doctors and experts as his visits often result in large public gatherings (Carvalho 2020b).

During the ongoing epidemic, the president took part in another protest, on April 19th, even more controversial than the one in March, as he was supporting the coup d'état that took place in Brazil in 1964. This coup marked the end of democracy in Brazil and the establishment of military dictatorship that lasted until 1985. It was the darkest time of Brazil's most recent history, yet during his speech Bolsonaro boasted that:

> *People can rely on their president to do everything necessary to maintain our democracy and to guarantee what is most sacred among us, that is our freedom.* (Arcanjo 2020b)

Bolsonaro argued against social distancing claiming that only people in high-risk groups should follow such guidelines and advocated that people should be free to do what they wish (not respecting the guidelines from WHO and the Brazilian government). The Brazilian president also engaged in a crusade against governors who enforced social distancing, claiming the governors' actions would have a catastrophic impact on the economy. He criticised the Rio de Janeiro governor because he closed the beaches, although Bolsonaro alleged that after the closure there were, in fact, more people on the beaches. He even suggested that the number of deaths in Sao Paulo had been altered, saying that:

> *It is really high for Sao Paulo. … Without wanting to dispute with anyone, there is a state there, that guided by decree, that, ultimately, if there is not concrete cause of death, coronavirus should be added.* (Arcanjo 2020a)

However, like Trump, Jair Bolsonaro is capable of many handbrake turns in his views that can have a disorientating effect, laying waste to any norms of behaviour in public office. On April 1st, the president suddenly changed his tone and acknowledged that the country was facing the major threat. The president switched to a religious discourse as he claimed that:

> *we, together with pastors and religious leaders, will ask the Brazilian people for a day of fasting in order for the country to be free from this evil as soon as possible.* (Arcanjo 2020a)

The president had changed his narrative again by mid-April to claim that the country was already almost free from the virus, but that unemployment was its main issue. The focus on employment and the economy is recognised by some as a reminder that the Brazilian president has his eyes on the municipal polls this year and the 2022 presidential election.

Three former health ministers denounced the president to the UN High Commissioner for Human Rights. They accused Bolsonaro of violating the human right to health and life and of potential genocide for failing to follow the recommendations of health authorities and the World Health Organization for the Covid-19 pandemic (Bergamo 2020).

By the end of April, the Brazilian health system was collapsing as Rio de Janeiro and four other major cities warned that their hospitals could not take any more patients. The country is expected to become one of the world's pandemic hot spots. Experts claim that the number of infections and deaths will be much higher than has been reported because of the lack of testing. Despite this calamity the president continues with his discourse that Covid-19 is only a *gripezinha* (small flu), a minor disease, and that social distancing is not needed (Phillips 2020). More than 200 people with Covid-19 symptoms or confirmation of contamination by the virus were waiting for a bed on the intensive care unit in Rio de Janeiro on April 24, 2020 (in the municipal, state or federal health service network). All but one hospital, located in the state's countryside, had reached full capacity on Covid-19 wards (Albuquerque and Barbon 2020). To make matters worse, towards the end of April Bolsonaro fired his popular Health Minister Luiz Henrique Mandetta who had openly contradicted him. Bolsonaro seemed to prefer the risk of overwhelming hospitals if it meant 'saving' the economy and many of his followers supported this approach. As Andrew Fishman writing in *The Intercept* noted:

> *It is as if there is a group focused on people and health and another on the market, companies and money, but this divided, antagonistic and perhaps radical approach is not the one that will most help society to get through this problem.* (*The Intercept* 2020b)

Here we see the underlying similarity between the apparent binary choice faced by populist and democratic leaders alike. Sacrifice the elderly and vulnerable minority (and minorities), those with 'underlying conditions', the weakest of the 'herd', or sacrifice the economy and livelihoods of the nation's healthy majority. This false dichotomy offered between a Nietzschean 'masculine' elite coldly prepared to accept deep sacrifices in 'the herd' for the greater wellbeing of the nation and weak, 'feminine' leaders who put the health of all their nation's citizens first in an efficient, rapid but caring response indicated an existential choice between painful sacrifices. Yet the example of numerous countries (not always led by women—but many which are) including Taiwan and New Zealand, in particular, suggests that socially responsible leadership pays off in economic terms (with far less economic disruption) *as well as* lower Covid-19 mortality rates. Nietzschean populists have done nothing to save their economies—quite the opposite, they appear to have created far deeper long-term harm.

How are these apparently stark political choices being seen by the citizens they impact? While in the UK, there is a round of applause for the NHS at 8:00 pm on Thursdays, in Brazil, there is the *panelaços*—a protest involving banging pans (*panelas* in Portuguese) to demonstrate peoples' anger at Bolsonaro's handling of the crisis. The *panelaços* take place every time the president makes a televised statement. Moreover, in some places around the country, this has become a daily exercise, at 8:30 pm, to show widespread discontentment.

As the leader of the Chamber of Deputies in the Brazilian Congress stated:

> *The whole world is united against the coronavirus. In Brazil, we have to fight against the corona and the virus of authoritarianism.* (Uribe 2020)

While there is much more to learn about the virus, the evidence currently suggests that male death rates are higher than females, although the reasons for this are still not clear (Statista 2020). There has also been some media commentary around the fact that countries led by women have been more successful at managing the corona crisis so far at least (CNN 2020b; Wittenberg-Cox 2020). From Germany to Taiwan and from New Zealand to the Nordic countries (Finland, Norway and Denmark—Sweden being an exception and having a male as prime minister), these countries are, at the time of writing, doing relatively well and have been able to start to ease their lockdown measures well before other countries. Obviously, this does not mean that countries that have male leaders are not doing well, e.g. South Korea, Greece and Australia. However, when compared with male politicians such as Donald Trump and Jair Bolsonaro that are disregarding science and appealing to strong emotions, one can start to consider that maybe a 'macho' narrative or 'masculine' ruthlessness (in the Nietzschean sense) does not bode well in the current crisis.

12.8 The Debates Around a Post-Lockdown World

While many commentators are gripped with anxiety about the huge economic damage the Covid-19 pandemic may cause and the opportunity for authoritarian governments to widen and deepen the intrusive powers of the modern surveillance state (see Harari 2020), others are suggesting the possibility of more positive change, that nothing can be the same after this pandemic and that it is time for a radical rethink of the way we organise our economy around a neoliberal, globalised market system (see Politico 2020). For some commentators, putting the world on an extended lockdown gave everyone the chance to reassess their priorities; to re-evaluate the way we care for the sick and vulnerable; to reflect on our hectic, consumeristic lifestyles; and to consider if other more sustainable, democratic and caring ways of conducting our affairs were possible. The fact that countries were forced, in most cases, to respond urgently to the Covid crisis focused attention on the need for more urgent action on the climate emergency that may have helped spawned the virus. Journalist Paul Mason, writing in the *New Statesman* (2020), argued that the threat of financial and economic collapse could not be met by the usual government-backed soft loans and low-interest bank capital, but required a huge 'bazooka' aimed at the existing system:

> *After this is over, it will be impossible for capitalism to return to normal. Because this is not some "exogenous shock"—like an asteroid hitting an otherwise blameless planet. Wave after wave of zoonotic viruses have been produced*

during the breakneck and poverty-stricken urbanisation of the Global South, and by the deforestation and destruction of habitats. The fact that these viruses then hit societies with poor public health systems, insanitary and crowded housing, elites that do not care, and populations suffering massively from "co-morbidities" such as asthma, heart disease and Type 2 diabetes is, likewise, not an accident. It is a product of a social system called capitalism.

Commentators remain very worried about increased corporate control and surveillance over an atomised citizenry working from home, while an underclass continues to work (delivering, farming, working in factories) and exposing itself to contagion. However, they also pointed to progressive transformations that had already taken place around healthcare funding, debt freezing and state aid to unemployed workers. As sociologist Jana Tsoneva (2020) wrote:

Socialist solutions are unceremoniously imposing themselves. Britain effectively nationalised the rail. New York City put an abrupt end to years of helpless hand-wringing that not much can be done about homelessness by housing thousands of homeless people suffering from COVID-19 in hotels. Portugal suspended the byzantine asylum categorisation regime and afforded its refugee population residency benefits. California set up a disaster relief fund for undocumented migrants. US cities are restoring water access to households falling behind on their bills. And who would have expected that Donald Trump, of all people, would roll out a variant of universal basic income for a few months?

These surprising policy moves indicated that ideas dismissed as radical and utopian just a few months earlier were being adopted by right-wing leaders whose values were being challenged by the harsh realities of a deadly global pandemic that did not recognise borders or bend to their bombastic and empty rhetoric. So, while the devastating medical and economic impacts of Covid-19 make themselves felt, including the potential loss of jobs for 1.6 billion workers in the informal economy (ILO 2020), there are signs of resilience, hope and opportunities for positive change. A report by the German news site DW indicated that many African countries had responded quickly, decisively and based on scientifically sound solutions in preparation for the virus based on their experience with other pandemics. This 'rational' response, like that of several countries explored above, stood in contrast to the emotional histrionics and attention seeking of many populist leaders. It also prompted calls by African cultural leaders such as Wole Soyinka for a transformation of Africa's healthcare system and a move towards economic independence and a more diversified economy (DW 2020).

The pandemic has led to some authoritarian leaders, such as Hungarian Prime Minister Viktor Orbán, assuming sweeping new powers and in others cracking down on political opponents and religious and racial minorities (see, for instance, developments in Turkey, India and the Philippines), but it has also shown that empathetic democratic leaders that respect scientific advice and act quickly and compassionately are in a stronger position to ease their countries out of the current crisis. The sheer statistics around the Covid-19 pandemic indicate that macho bluster and disregard for the need to protect the vulnerable and sick and not just the healthy members of 'the herd' fails on economic as well as moral grounds. This presents an opportunity for a 'revaluation of all values' in ways that Nietzsche's fascist, eugenicist and authoritarian disciples would certainly reject, but that his more progressive champions might celebrate.

12.9 Conclusion

Our survey of Nietzsche's troubling notions of the 'herd', 'masculine', warrior values and attitudes to empathy for the weakest members of society have been shown to resonate in disturbing ways across the twentieth and twenty-first centuries. They take a dark and deadly turn under Hitler and Mussolini in the 1930s and 1940s and appear to throw a deeply troubling light on the response of several right-wing populist leaders (notably Boris Johnson, Donald Trump and Jair Bolsonaro, but also others) to the coronavirus pandemic sweeping the globe in 2020. What seemed, at worse, shocking unpreparedness and a casual disregard for the wellbeing of vulnerable groups, or the wider safety of the nation, indicated a lack of social responsibility that was thrown into dramatic relief by the quick, decisive action of other leaders, organisations and businesses. The pandemic also brought concerns around the growing power of some authoritarian governments to crack down on criticism, suppress opposition and monitor and control the activities of its citizens.

However, in the aftermath of the pandemic and the massive changes it has brought about there are signs of hope for what Nietzsche might have described as a 'transvaluation of all values'. Crises often bring about such a radical rethinking of long-held values. Heraclitus observed that 'War is the Father of All Things', but as Claudia von Werlhof added 'Nature is the Mother of Life' (cited Mies 2006). Nature, like war, can bring death and destruction on a terrifying scale as review of natural disasters and pandemics shows only too clearly, but it also brings about radical and necessary change. In this respect the current pandemic gripping the world at the time of writing may be regarded as the 'dynamite' of our age.

References

Abbey, Ruth and Fredrick Appel. 1998. Nietzsche and the will to politics. *The Review of Politics* 60 (1): 83.

Al Jazeera. 2020. Noam Chomsky: 'Coronavirus pandemic could have been prevented' 3rd April. *Al Jazeera*. Available at: https://www.aljazeera.com/news/2020/04/noam-chomsky-coronavirus-pandemic-prevented-200403113823259.html Accessed 23/04/2020.

Albuquerque, A.L. and J. Barbon. 2020. Mais de 200 pessoas com sintomas ou confirmação de coronavírus estão na fila para UTI no Rio. *Folha de Sao Paulo*. 24 April 2020. Available at: https://www1.folha.uol.com.br/cotidiano/2020/04/mais-de-200-pessoas-com-sintomas-ou-confirmacao-de-coronavirus-estao-na-fila-para-uti-no-rio.shtml Accessed 25/04/2020.

Arcanjo, D. 2020a. O que Bolsonaro ja disse sobre coronavirus de histeria e gripezinha ao 'e daí?'; assista a video. *Folha de Sao Paulo*. 13 April 2020. Available at: https://www1.folha.uol.com.br/poder/2020/03/veja-o-que-bolsonaro-ja-disse-sobre-coronavirus-de-certa-histeria-a-fantasia-e-nerouse.shtml Accessed 26/04/2020.

Arcanjo, D. 2020b. Veja possíveis crimes cometidos por Bolsonaro em ato pró-golpe. *Folha de Sao Paulo*. 20 April 2020. Available at: https://www1.folha.uol.com.br/poder/2020/04/veja-possiveis-crimes-cometidos-por-bolsonaro-em-ato-pro-golpe-leia-discurso-comentado.shtml Accessed 25/04/2020.

Arcanjo, D. 2020c. Veja o que Bolsonaro já fez para confrontar medidas de combate ao coronavirus. *Folha de Sao Paulo*. 30 March 2020. Available at: https://www1.folha.uol.com.br/poder/2020/03/veja-o-que-bolsonaro-ja-fez-para-confrontar-medidas-de-combate-ao-coronavirus.shtml Accessed 25/04/2020.

Bandwagon. 2020. Stereophonics receive backlash for holding massive arena shows in time of COVID-19. *Bandwagon*. 19 March. Accessed at: https://www.bandwagon.asia/articles/china-stereophonics-uk-arena-live-concerts-covid-19-coronavirus-quarantine-2020

BBC. 2019. Brazil's Bolsonaro says DiCaprio gave cash 'to set Amazon on fire'. *BBS News*. 30 November 2019. Available at: https://www.bbc.co.uk/news/world-latin-america-50613054 Accessed 19/04/2020.

BBC. 2020a. Coronavirus: New Zealand claims no community cases as lockdown eases. *BBC News*. Available at: https://www.bbc.co.uk/news/world-asia-52436658 Accessed 27/04/2020.

BBC. 2020b. Coronavirus: UK failed to stockpile crucial PPE. *BBC News*. 28 April 2020. Available at: https://www.bbc.co.uk/news/newsbeat-52440641

Bergamo, M. 2020. Ex-ministros da Saúde denunciam Bolsonaro à ONU por potencial genocídio em pandemia. *Folha de Sao Paulo*. 25 April 2020. Available at: https://www1.folha.uol.com.br/colunas/monicabergamo/2020/04/ex-ministros-da-saude-denunciam-bolsonaro-a-onu-por-potencial-genocidio-em-pandemia.shtml Accessed 26/04/2020.

Carvalho, D. 2020a Bolsonaro é alvo de gritos de apoio e panelaço e, sem cuidado, cumprimenta apoiadores em Brasília. *Folha de Sao Paulo*. 10 April 2020. Available at: https://www1.folha.uol.com.br/poder/2020/04/bolsonaro-e-alvo-de-gritos-de-apoio-e-panelaco-em-novo-passeio-por-brasilia.shtml Accessed 17/04/2020.

Carvalho, D. 2020b. Bolsonaro visita obra de hospital, provoca novas aglomerações e é criticado por Mandetta e Caiado. *Folha de Sao Paulo*. 11 April 2020. Available at: https://www1.folha.uol.com.br/poder/2020/04/bolsonaro-visita-obra-de-hospital-provoca-novas-aglomeracoes-e-e-criticado-por-mandetta-e-caiado.shtml Accessed 17/04/2020.

Clemente, Matthew, Bryan J. Cocchiara, John Panteleimon Manoussakis and William J. Hendel. 2018. *MisReading Nietzsche*. Eugene, OR: Pickwick Publications.

CNET. 2020. Singapore's coronavirus playbook: How it fought back against the COVID-19 pandemic. *CNET*. 22 March. Available at: https://www.cnet.

com/news/singapores-coronavirus-playbook-how-one-country-fought-back-against-covid19-epidemic/ Accessed 23/04/2020.

CNN. 2020a. Taiwan will spend up to $35 billion on virus stimulus plan and is donating 10 million masks. *CNN*. 1 April 2020. Available at: https://edition.cnn.com/world/live-news/coronavirus-pandemic-04-01-20-intl/h_577cb658e3c628bdcd503fff1e00222a Accessed 23/04/2020.

CNN. 2020b. Women leaders are doing a disproportionately great job at handling the pandemic. So why aren't there more of them? *CNN*. 16 April 2020. Available at: https://edition.cnn.com/2020/04/14/asia/women-government-leaders-coronavirus-hnk-intl/index.html Accessed 19/04/2020.

de Vreese, Claes H., Frank Esser, Toril Aalberg, Carsten Reinemann and James Stanyer. 2018. Populism as an expression of political communication content and style: A new perspective. *International Journal of Press/Politics* 23 (4): 423–438.

Della Coletta, R. 2020. Em pronunciamento, Bolsonaro critica fechamento de escolas, ataca governadores e culpa mídia. *Folha de Ṣao Paulo*. 24 March 2020. Available at: https://www1.folha.uol.com.br/poder/2020/03/em-pronunciamento-bolsonaro-critica-fechamento-de-escolas-ataca-governadores-e-culpa-midia.shtml Accessed 24/05/2020.

The Diplomat. 2020. Taiwan, shut out from WHO, confronts deadly Wuhan Coronavirus. *The Diplomat*. 24 January 2020. Available at: https://thediplomat.com/2020/01/taiwan-shut-out-from-who-confronts-deadly-wuhan-coronavirus/ Accessed 22/04/2020.

Donaldson, Ian Linton. 2000. The Role of Philosophy and Hierarchy in Friedrich Nietzsche's Political Thought. Available at: https://search-ebscohost-com.libezproxy.bournemouth.ac.uk/login.aspx?direct=true&db=edsble&AN=edsble.326233&site=eds-live&scope=site

Drochon, Hugo. 2016. *Nietzsche's great politics*. Princeton: Princeton University Press.

Drochon, Hugo. 2018. Why Nietzsche has once again become an inspiration to the far-right. *New Statesman*. 29 August. Available at: https://www.newstatesman.com/2018/08/why-nietzsche-has-once-again-become-inspiration-far-right

Duffy, Michael F. and Willard Mittelman. 1988. Nietzsche's Attitudes Toward the Jews. *Journal of the History of Ideas* 49 (2): 301.

DW. 2020. Coronavirus: How Africa is bracing for pandemic's impact. *DW*. 27 April. Available at: https://p.dw.com/p/3bT6u

ECDC. 2020. Situation update worldwide, as of 28 April 2020. *European Centre for Disease Prevention and Control.* Available at: https://www.ecdc.europa.eu/en/geographical-distribution-2019-ncov-cases Accessed 28/04/2020.

The Economist. 2020. How the Spanish flu of 1918–20 was largely forgotten. *The Economist.* 18 April 2020. Available at: https://www.economist.com/international/2020/04/18/how-the-spanish-flu-of-1918-20-was-largely-forgotten Accessed: 20/04/2020.

Euractiv. 2020. Nordic family showing cracks in COVID-19 response. *Euractiv.* 18 March. Available at: https://www.euractiv.com/section/all/short_news/nordic-family-showing-cracks-in-covid-19-response/

Financial Times. 2020. Coronavirus: The cost of China's public health cover-up. *The Financial Times.* 6 February 2020. Available at: https://www.ft.com/content/fa83463a-4737-11ea-aeb3-955839e06441 Accessed 23/04/2020.

Gaim, M., S. Clegg and M.P.E. Cunha. 2019. Managing impressions rather than emissions: Volkswagen and the false mastery of paradox. *Organization Studies.* 0170840619891199.

The Guardian. 2000. Officials to investigate potential Covid-19 link with Liverpool match. *The Guardian.* 24 April. Available at: https://www.theguardian.com/world/2020/apr/24/officials-to-investigate-potential-covid-19-link-with-liverpool-match

Harari, Yuval Noah. 2020. The world after coronavirus. *Financial Times.* 20 March 2020. Available at: https://www.ft.com/content/19d90308-6858-11ea-a3c9-1fe6fedcca75 Accessed 20/4/2020.

Hargis, Jill. 2010. (Dis)Embracing the herd: A look at Nietzsche's shifting views of the people and the individual. *History of Political Thought* 31 (3): 475.

Harris, B. and A. Schipani. 2020. Bolsonaro doubles down on denialism. *Financial Times.* 1 April. Available at: https://www.ft.com/content/36020f3c-cf50-427b-a83a-bda122bec593

ILO. 2020. ILO monitor: COVID-19 and the world of work. Third edition. *International Labour Organisation.* 29 April. Accessed at: https://www.ilo.org/wcmsp5/groups/public/%2D%2D-dgreports/%2D%2D-dcomm/documents/briefingnote/wcms_743146.pdf

Imperial College. 2020. Report 9: Impact of non-pharmaceutical interventions (NPs) to reduce Covid-19 mortality and healthcare demand. *Imperial College Covid-19 Response Team.* Available at: https://www.imperial.ac.uk/media/imperial-college/medicine/sph/ide/gida-fellowships/Imperial-College-COVID19-NPI-modelling-16-03-2020.pdf

The Intercept. 2020a. Trump's ridiculous behavior at pandemic briefings baffles a watching world. *The Intercept*. 11 April 2020. Available at: https://theintercept.com/2020/04/10/trumps-ridiculously-political-briefings-pandemic-unique-democratic-world/

The Intercept. 2020b. Brazil's Jair Bolsonaro, the world's most powerful coronavirus denier, just fired the health minister who disagreed with him. *The Intercept*. 16 April. Available at: https://theintercept.com/2020/04/16/bolsonaro-fires-health-minister-brazil-coronavirus/

Japan Times. 2020. Hong Kong, Taiwan and South Korea buck global lockdown trend. *The Japan Times*. 8 April. https://www.japantimes.co.jp/news/2020/04/08/asia-pacific/hong-kong-taiwan-south-korea-buck-global-lockdown-trend/

Knowledge@Wharton. 2020. Combating COVID-19: Lessons from Singapore, South Korea and Taiwan. Wharton University of Pennsylvania. Available at: https://knowledge.wharton.upenn.edu/article/singapore-south_korea-taiwan-used-technology-combat-covid-19/ Accessed 23/04/2020.

Mariani, D., F. Takahashi and D. Yukari. 2020. Bolsonaro é antepenúltimo em ranking de tuítes de presidentes sobre coronavirus. *Folha de Sao Paulo*. 18 March 2020. Available at: https://www1.folha.uol.com.br/poder/2020/03/bolsonaro-e-antepenultimo-em-ranking-de-tuites-de-presidentes-sobre-coronavirus.shtml Accessed 24/05/2020.

Mason, Paul. 2020. The coronavirus crisis shows we need an entirely new economic system. *New Statesman*. 18 March 2020. Available at: https://www.newstatesman.com/politics/economy/2020/03/coronavirus-crisis-economic-collapse-capitalism Accessed 20/04/2020.

Mies, Maria. 2006. "War Is the Father of All Things" (Heraclitus) "But Nature Is the Mother of Life" (Claudia von Werlhof). This paper is adapted from the keynote address given at "Ecology, Imperialism and the Contradictions of Capitalism", a Capitalism Nature Socialism Anniversary Conference held at York University in Toronto, July 22–24, 2005. *Capitalism Nature Socialism* 17 (1): 18–31.

New York Times. 2020a. Dr. Oz Faces Backlash after saying schools could reopen. *New York Times*. 17 April. Available at: https://www.nytimes.com/2020/04/17/business/media/dr-oz-apology-coronavirus.html

New York Times. 2020b. Cuomo urges Trump not to act in a 'dictatorial' style. *New York Times*. 14 April 2020. Available at: https://www.nytimes.com/2020/04/14/nyregion/coronavirus-new-york-update.html

New Yorker. 2020. Seattle's leaders let scientists take the lead. New York's did not. *The New Yorker*. 26 April 2020. Available at: https://www.newyorker.com/magazine/2020/05/04/seattles-leaders-let-scientists-take-the-lead-new-yorks-did-not

Nietzsche, Friedrich Wilhelm, and Duncan Large. 1888/2007. *Ecce Homo: How to become what you are*. Oxford World's Classics. Oxford: OUP Oxford.

Nietzsche, Friedrich Wilhelm, and Thomas Wayne. 1888/2004. *Ecce Homo: How one becomes what one is; & the antichrist: A curse on Christianity*. Classics Series. New York: Algora Publishing.

Oliveira, M. 2020. Coronavírus: MPF move ação contra campanha de Bolsonaro contra isolamento. 27 March 2020 [in Portuguese]. Available at: https://noticias.uol.com.br/saude/ultimas-noticias/redacao/2020/03/27/mpf-move-acao-contra-campanha-de-bolsonaro-contra-isolamento.htm Accessed 23/04/2020.

Panorama. 2020. Has the government failed the NHS? BBC Panorama. Available at: https://www.bbc.co.uk/iplayer/episode/m000hr3y/panorama-has-the-government-failed-the-nhs

Phillips, T. 2019. Brazil's Bolsonaro ridiculed after tweeting explicit carnival video. *The Guardian*. 6 March 2019. Available at: https://www.theguardian.com/world/2019/mar/06/bolsonaro-carnival-pornographic-tweet-ridiculed Accessed 25/04/2020.

Phillips, T. 2020. Jair Bolsonaro claims Brazilians never catch anything as Covid-19 cases rise. *The Guardian*. 27 March 2020. Available at: https://www.theguardian.com/global-development/2020/mar/27/jair-bolsonaro-claims-brazilians-never-catch-anything-as-covid-19-cases-rise Accessed 17/04/2020.

Politico. 2020. Coronavirus will change the world permanently. Here's how. *Politico*. 19 March 2020. Available at: https://www.politico.com/news/magazine/2020/03/19/coronavirus-effect-economy-life-society-analysis-covid-135579 Accessed 20/04/2020.

Politifact. 2020. Sweden, mostly open, has higher COVID-19 death rate than Denmark. *The Poynter Institute*. Available at: https://www.politifact.com/factchecks/2020/apr/28/facebook-posts/sweden-mostly-open-has-higher-covid-19-death-rate-/

Prideaux, Sue. 2018. Far right, misogynist, humourless? Why Nietzsche is misunderstood. *The Guardian*. 6 October 2020. Available at: https://www.theguardian.com/books/2018/oct/06/exploding-nietzsche-myths-need-dynamiting Accessed 21/4/2020.

Râmbu, Nicolae. 2016. *The Axiology of Friedrich Nietzsche (Edition 1)*. Peter Lang International Academic Publishers.

Siemens, Herman, and Vasti Roodt. 2008. *Nietzsche, Power and Politics: Rethinking Nietzsche's Legacy for Political Thought*. Berlin: De Gruyter.

Snopes.com. 2020. Did this Nobel Prize winner say COVID-19 was created in a lab? *Snopes*. Available at: https://www.snopes.com/fact-check/luc-montagnier-covid-created-lab/

Statista. 2020. More men dying of COVID-19 than women. 3 April 2020. Available at: https://www.statista.com/chart/21345/coronavirus-deaths-by-gender/ Accessed 10/04/2020.

Statistica. 2020. Coronavirus (COVID-19) deaths worldwide per one million population as of April 29, 2020, by country. *Statistica*. Available at: https://www.statista.com/statistics/1104709/coronavirus-deaths-worldwide-per-million-inhabitants/

Stone, Dan. 2002. *Breeding superman: Nietzsche, race and eugenics in Edwardian and interwar Britain*. Liverpool University Press.

The Telegraph. 2020. UK coronavirus death toll of 20,000 'a good outcome', says chief scientific adviser. *The Telegraph*. 17 March 2020. Available at: https://www.telegraph.co.uk/news/2020/03/17/governments-hopeful-scenario-20000-people-will-die-coronavirus/

The Times. 2020. Coronavirus: 38 days when Britain sleepwalked into disaster. *Insight: The Sunday Times*. 19 April 2020. Available at: https://www.thetimes.co.uk/article/coronavirus-38-days-when-britain-sleepwalked-into-disaster-hq3b9tlgh

This Morning. 2020. Boris Johnson on Coronavirus. *This Morning*. 5 March 2020. Available at: https://www.youtube.com/watch?v=vOHiaPwtGl4&feature=youtu.be Accessed 29/04/2020.

Tsoneva, Jana. 2020. How the pandemic endorsed leftist politics. *Al Jazeera*. 30 April. Accessed at: https://www.aljazeera.com/indepth/opinion/pandemic-endorsed-leftist-politics-200429100802621.html

Uribe, G. 2020. Forças Armadas trabalham por estabilidade e obedecem à Constituição, diz Defesa. *Folha de Sao Paulo*. 20 April 2020. Available at: https://www1.folha.uol.com.br/poder/2020/04/forcas-armadas-trabalham-por-estabilidade-e-obedecem-constituicao-diz-defesa.shtml Accessed 24/04/2020.

Voegelin, Eric. 1944. Nietzsche, the crisis and the war. *The Journal of Politics* 6 (2): 177–212.

Washington Post. 2020. China didn't warn public of likely pandemic for 6 key days. *Washington Post*. 15 April 2020. Available at: https://www.washingtonpost.com/health/china-didnt-warn-public-of-likely-pandemic-for-6-key-days/2020/04/16/12325c40-7f9a-11ea-84c2-0792d8591911_story.html Accessed 23/04/2020.

WHO. 2020. Novel Coronavirus—China. Disease outbreak news: Update 12 January 2020. W.H.O. Available at: https://www.who.int/csr/don/12-january-2020-novel-coronavirus-china/en/ Accessed 23/04/2020.

Whyte, Max. 2008. The uses and abuses of Nietzsche in the Third Reich: Alfred Baeumler's "Heroic Realism". *Journal of Contemporary History* 43 (2): 171.

Wistrich, Robert S. and Jacob Golomb. 2002. *Nietzsche, godfather of fascism?: On the uses and abuses of a philosophy*. Princeton, NJ: Princeton University Press.

Wittenberg-Cox, A. 2020. What do countries with the best Coronavirus responses have in common? Women leaders. *Forbes*. 13 April 2020. Available at: https://www.forbes.com/sites/avivahwittenbergcox/2020/04/13/what-do-countries-with-the-best-coronavirus-reponses-have-in-common-women-leaders/#447886553dec Accessed 23/04/2020.

World Organisation for Animal Health. 2020. Questions and answers on the 2019 Coronavirus disease (COVID-19). World Organisation for Animal Health. Available at: https://www.oie.int/scientific-expertise/specific-information-and-recommendations/questions-and-answers-on-2019novel-coronavirus/ Accessed: 23/04/2020.

Young, Toby. 2020. Has the government overreacted to the Coronavirus crisis? *The Critic*. 31 March 2020. Available at: https://thecritic.co.uk/has-the-government-over-reacted-to-the-coronavirus-crisis/

Index[1]

[1] Note: Page numbers followed by 'n' refer to notes.

F. Farache et al. (eds.), *Values and Corporate Responsibility*, Palgrave Studies in Governance, Leadership and Responsibility,
https://doi.org/10.1007/978-3-030-52466-1

The manufacturer's authorised representative in the EU is Springer Nature Customer Service Centre GmbH, Europaplatz 3, 69115 Heidelberg, Germany. If you have any concerns regarding our products, please contact ProductSafety@springernature.com

Printed and bound by CPI Group (UK) Ltd, Croydon, CR0 4YY
30/09/2026
02225696-0003